Benchmarking for Higher Education

SRHE and Open University Press Imprint
General Editor: Heather Eggins

Benchmarking for Higher Education

Edited by
Norman Jackson
and
Helen Lund

Society for Research into Higher Education
& Open University Press

Published by SRHE and
Open University Press
Celtic Court
22 Ballmoor
Buckingham
MK18 1XW

email: enquiries@openup.co.uk
world wide web: http://www.openup.co.uk

and
325 Chestnut Street
Philadelphia, PA 19106, USA

First Published 2000

A catalogue record of this book is available from the British Library

ISBN 0335 20453 8 (pb)   0335 20454 6 (hb)

Library of Congress Cataloging-in-Publication Data
Benchmarking for higher education / edited by Norman Jackson and Helen
   Lund.
        p.   cm.
   Includes bibliographical references (p.   ) and index.
   ISBN 0–335–20453–8 (pbk.). — ISBN 0–335–20454–6 (hc.)
   1. Education, Higher—Great Britain—Administration.
   2. Education, Higher—Great Britain—Evaluation.   3. Benchmarking
   (Management)—Great Britain.   I. Jackson, Norman, 1950–
   II. Lund, Helen S. (Helen Sarah), 1959–
   LB2341.B436   2000
   378.41—dc21   99–42613
                                                                      CIP

Typeset by Graphicraft Limited, Hong Kong
Printed in Great Britain by St Edmundsbury Press,
Bury St Edmunds, Suffolk

Contents

Notes on Contributors

Authors

Vaneeta D'Andrea is Director of Educational Development, Policy and Standards at Roehampton Institute, Roehampton Lane, London, SW1J 5PJ. *v.dandrea@roehampton.ac.uk*

Michael Carr is Registrar at the University of Liverpool, Senate House, Liverpool, L69 3BX. *M.D.Carr@liverpool.ac.uk*

Richard Coleman is a member of the Institutional Planning Service, UCAS, Fulton House, Jessop Avenue, Cheltenham, Gloucestershire, GL50 3SH. *r.coleman@ucas.ac.uk*

John Fielden is Director of the Commonwealth Higher Education Management Service, 36 Gordon Square, London, WC1H 0PF. *j.fielden@acu.ac.uk*

Linda Hodgkinson is a member of the Vocational Qualifications Centre, Open University, Walton Hall, Milton Keynes, MK7 6AA. *L.Hodgkinson@open.ac.uk*

Norman Jackson is an Assistant Director at the Quality Assurance Agency for Higher Education (*n.jackson@qaa.ac.uk*) and a Senior Research Fellow in the School of Educational Studies at the University of Surrey, Guildford, Surrey, GU2 5XH. *N.Jackson@surrey.ac.uk*

Helen Lund is a Researcher at the Commonwealth Higher Education Management Service (CHEMS), 36 Gordon Square, London, WC1H 0PF. *h.lund@acu.ac.uk*

Dugald Mackie is Secretary to Council, University of Glasgow, Quality Assurance Office, Glasgow, GL1 8QQ. *d.mackie@mis.gla.ac.uk*

Rikki Morgan is Dean of Languages and Social Sciences, Anglia Polytechnic University, East Road, Cambridge, CB1 1PT. *Rikki.Morgan@anglia.ac.uk*

Ilfryn Price is Director, Facilities Management Graduate Centre, Sheffield Hallam University, Unit 7, Science Park, Sheffield, S1 1WB. *I.Price@shu.ac.uk*

James Tannock is a senior lecturer in the Department of Manufacturing Engineering and Operations Management, University of Nottingham, University Park, Nottingham NG7 2RD. *James.Tannock@nottingham.ac.uk*

Stephen Town is Director of Library and Information Services, Cranfield University, Royal Military College of Science (RMCS), Shrivenham, Swindon, Wiltshire, SN6 8LA. *stown@rmcs.cranfield.ac.uk*

Liz Viggars is a member of the Institutional Planning Service, UCAS, Fulton House, Jessop Avenue, Cheltenham, Gloucestershire GL50 3SH. *r.coleman@ucas.ac.uk*

Mantz Yorke is Director of the Centre for Higher Education Development, Liverpool John Moores University, IM Marsh Campus, Barkhill Rd, Aigburth, Liverpool L17 6BD. *m.yorke@livjm.ac.uk*

Important contributions through interview

John Rushforth is the Chief Auditor at the Higher Education Funding Council for England, Northavon House, Coldharbour Lane, Bristol, BS16 1QD.

Ben Johnson-Hill is the senior consultant at Ben Johnson-Hill Associates, 7 Gregory Boulevard, Nottingham, NG7 6LD.

John Haywood is the Managing Consultant at the Southern Universities Management Services (SUMS), University of Reading, London Road, Reading, RG1 5AQ.

List of Abbreviations

AC	Audit Commission
APQC	American Productivity Quality Center
ASP	Academic Standards Panel
AUCC	Association of Universities and Colleges of Canada
AUDE	American Universities Data Exchange
AUDE	Association of University Directors of Estates
AUE	Association of University Engineers
BACS	Bankers Automated Clearing System
BMC	Benchmarking Club of Technical Universities (Germany)
BRM	Building Repairs and Maintenance
BUFDG	British Universities Finance Directors' Group
CAUBO	Canadian Association of University Business Officers
CAUL	Council of Australian University Librarians
CBA	Computer-based assessment
CCT	Compulsory competitive tendering
CHEMS	Commonwealth Higher Education Management Service
CIPFA	Chartered Institute of Public Finance and Accountancy
CNAA	Council for National Academic Awards
COU	Council of Ontario Universities
CRE	Conference of Rectors of European Universities
CSF	Critical success factor
CUBO	Conference of University Business Officers
CVA	Comparative value added
CVCP	Committee of Vice-Chancellors and Principals
DENI	Department of Education for Northern Ireland
DES	Department of Education and Science
DETYA	Department of Education, Training and Youth Affairs (Australia)
DfEE	Department for Education and Employment

EDI	Electronic Data Interchange
EFQM	European Foundation for Quality Management
EPC	Engineering Professors' Council
EUPEN	European Physics Education Network
FDTL	Fund for the Development of Teaching and Learning
FE	Further education
FM	Facilities management
FMGC	Facilities Management Graduate Centre
FTE	Full-time equivalent
GAP	Graduate Attributes Profiling
HE	Higher education
HEFCE	Higher Education Funding Council for England
HEFCW	Higher Education Funding Council for Wales
HEI	Higher education institution
HEMS	Higher Education Management Statistics Group
HEQC	Higher Education Quality Council
HEQP	Higher Education Quality Profile
HESA	Higher Education Statistics Agency
HMI	Her Majesty's Inspectorate
HRM	Human resources management
IBC	International Benchmarking Clearinghouse
IPD	Institute of Personnel and Development
IPS	Institutional Planning Service
JPG	Joint Planning Group for Quality Assurance in HE
JPIWG	Joint Performance Indicators Working Group
MIS	Management information systems
NACUBO	National Association of College and University Business Officers (USA)
NAO	National Audit Office
NCIHE	National Committee of Enquiry into Higher Education (Dearing Committee)
NHS	National Health Service
NLE	New learning environment
NTU	Northern Territory University
NUCCAT	Northern Universities Consortium for Credit, Accumulation and Transfer
OU	Open University
PCFC	Polytechnics and Colleges Funding Council
PI	Performance indicator
PSB	Professional and statutory bodies
QA	Quality assurance
QAA	Quality Assurance Agency
QCA	Qualifications and Curriculum Authority
RAE	Research Assessment Exercise
RMCS	Royal Military College of Science
SACWG	Student Assessment and Classification Working Group

SBG	Subject Benchmarking Group
SCONUL	Standing Committee of National University Libraries
SHEFC	Scottish Higher Education Funding Council
SRB	Single Regeneration Budget
SRHE	Society for Research into Higher Education
SUMS	Southern Universities Management Service
TDLB	Training and Development Lead Body
TQM	Total Quality Management
TRIADS	Tripartite Assessment Delivery System
TVU	Thames Valley University
UCAS	Universities and Colleges Admissions Service
UCISA	Universities and Colleges Information Systems Association
UFC	Universities Funding Council
UGC	University Grants Committee
UNESCO	United Nations Educational, Scientific, and Cultural Organization
VfM	Value for Money (studies)
WWW	World Wide Web

Introduction

1
Introduction to Benchmarking

Norman Jackson and Helen Lund

Overview

This chapter introduces the idea of benchmarking as a process for improving practice, process and performance (including degree outcomes) in higher education. It provides a definition of benchmarking for higher education, describes different types of benchmarking activity and outlines a number of conceptual frameworks to help explain the ways in which the method can be applied. These frameworks provide a point of reference for the case study materials described in subsequent chapters and lay the foundation for a better overall appreciation of this method of self-evaluation and self-improvement.

Introduction

There is a Greek myth that tells how the goddess Athena sprang fully grown from the head of her father Zeus. Though some academics and administrators in universities who find themselves involved in benchmarking for the first time might feel that they are being confronted with a phenomenon almost as alien as parthenogenesis, this is not really the case. Rather, benchmarking in higher education is best seen as the latest in a long line of steps that UK higher education institutions (HEIs) have been encouraged to take in pursuit of a better understanding and measurement of their practices and performance in order to promote improvement. Indeed, it will be argued in the concluding chapter that benchmarking is integral to the notion of the 'evaluative state' (Henkel 1991) that now underpins public sector policy in the UK.

What is benchmarking?

The primary purpose of this volume is to gain a better understanding of the meaning of the concept of benchmarking as it is being used and developed in higher education. The term benchmark was originally used in survey-ing to denote a mark on a survey peg or stone that acts as a permanent reference point against which the levels of various topographic features can be measured. It has also acquired a more general meaning as a refer-ence or criterion against which something can be measured. The first use of the term in an educational sense is accorded to R.K. Melton, 'Stand-ards represent benchmarks with which students compare their ability and performance' (*Student Physician* 1957, cited in the *New Oxford English Dictionary*).

The term benchmarking was first applied to a process of organizational self-evaluation and self-improvement by Xerox. Faced with a rapidly declin-ing market share in the early 1980s, the company pioneered the method of comparing and evaluating its business processes, products and performance against competitors. The organizational learning acquired through this pro-cess led to dramatic reductions in costs and an improved share of the market (Camp 1989). The methodology was transferred and adapted to higher edu-cation in North America in the early 1990s (Alstete 1995), followed rapidly by Australia and more recently the UK and, to a lesser extent, continental Europe (Schofield 1998 and Chapter 14).

There are many definitions of benchmarking (reflecting different per-sonal interpretations of process and outcomes) but fundamentally the process involves (Alstete 1995: 20) 'analysing performance, practices, and processes within and between organizations and industries, to obtain information for self-improvement'. The process of analysing the information enables bench-marks (reference points) to be created which can be used to promote change in the direction that is most likely to lead to improvement. Learn-ing from others and adopting/adapting 'best practice' is a distinctive feature of the benchmarking process.

Why are we benchmarking?

Although universities are essentially not-for-profit public service organiza-tions they must generate sufficient income to support and reinvest in the educational enterprise. Universities are in no doubt that they operate in a series of competitive markets – local, regional, national and global. In the commercial world benchmarking is used to identify new, innovative and more effective ways of doing things to gain and maintain competitive advant-age. In the world of higher education gaining competitive advantage is an important motivating factor but institutional reputation, based on such mat-ters as research standing, the public perception of the currency of awards and the employability of graduates, is also important. In both the national and international market place there are clearly competitive advantages in establishing and maintaining a reputation for high-quality education and research. Benchmarking is being used as a way of reinforcing peer groups and helping to maintain and enhance institutional reputation.

Public confidence in the academic standards of an institution is dependent on robust mechanisms for self-regulation and external quality assurance (see Jackson 1997a for the meaning of regulation). As higher education (HE) markets become more sophisticated there is a need to provide information that will enable degree outcomes to be compared and differentiated (a degree in this subject from this HEI is similar/different to a degree in this subject from that HEI). The rapid expansion of HE in the United Kingdom (UK) and increased diversity in all aspects of delivery, the assessment of learning and outcomes have increased public demands for explicit information that will enable degree outcomes to be differentiated (HEQC 1997a). Benchmarking is being developed to improve the capacity of HE to demonstrate more transparent levels of comparability and difference between awards in different institutions and subjects.

The educational enterprise is underpinned by a range of administrative and managerial functions, technical and other support services (e.g. registry, libraries, IT infrastructure, financial services, personnel, estates, catering, student services, etc.). Creative and cost-effective management of these functions is vital if universities are to continue to deliver excellence in the face of declining per capita state funding and rapid change. Benchmarking provides a vehicle for sharing practice within functional communities, identifying smarter ways of doing things and new solutions to common problems, and identifying ways of reducing costs while optimizing the quality of service offered to students and other clients.

Definition for UK higher education

There are many definitions of benchmarking. Robert Camp, who pioneered benchmarking at Xerox, coupled the process of 'finding and implementing best practice' with the reason for doing it ('to improve work processes that will satisfy customers'; Loveday 1993: 43). Price (1994: 5) also coupled process, 'the open and collaborative evaluation of services and processes', with purpose, 'the aim of emulating or improving best available practice'.

Both definitions indicate that benchmarking is fundamentally an approach to self-evaluation through comparative analysis for the purpose of self-improvement. The two fundamental purposes of any method of self-evaluation in HE are:

- to facilitate improvement – development – change and
- to satisfy expectations and requirements for professional accountability (Kells 1992 and 1995; Jackson 1997b).

Processes for self-evaluation in UK HE satisfy, to varying degrees, both of these purposes (Jackson 1997b). It might therefore be anticipated that benchmarking processes will also be part of this continuum.

A number of contributors to this volume have adopted definitions similar to those used by Camp (1989) and Price (1994). It can however be argued

Figure 1.1 Definitions of benchmarking and their relationship to the purposes of self-evaluation

'Benchmarking is the open and collaborative evaluation of services and processes with the aim of emulating or improving best available practice' (Price 1994)

Accountability and standards

←————————————————————————————→

Development and competitive advantage

'Benchmarking is a process to facilitate the systematic comparison and evaluation of practice, process and performance to aid improvement and self-regulation' (Jackson 1998a)

that the process characteristics contained in these definitions are primarily geared to the development end of the continuum of self-evaluation activities (and to contexts where best practice can be readily identified); they do not reflect the accountability purpose of self-evaluation. Jackson (1998a) proposed a broader definition for benchmarking in UK HE which accommodates notions of accountability as well as development, e.g. 'a process to facilitate the systematic comparison and evaluation of practice, process and performance to aid improvement and regulation'. The contributions to this volume reflect both sets of definitions.

Conceptualization

Benchmarking can be conceived in a number of ways. At the simplest level it might be viewed as a strategy for enabling people to think outside the boxes (e.g. departments, service or functional units or institutions) they normally inhabit (Spendolini 1992). Benchmarking is, first and foremost, a learning process structured so as to enable those engaging in the process to compare their services/activities/products in order to identify their comparative strengths and weaknesses as a basis for self-improvement and/or self-regulation. Benchmarking offers a way of identifying 'better and smarter' ways of doing things and understanding why they are better or smarter. These insights can then be used to implement changes that will improve practice or performance.

Types of benchmarking

All schemes for classifying benchmarking activities are somewhat artificial because many exercises will contain elements of different classification schemes. Nevertheless, classification is useful in developing a conceptual understanding of processes and purposes, and in creating a vocabulary to describe and distinguish between different types of activity. Benchmarking activities can be classified according to the nature of the referencing processes that underpin the activity (Jackson 1998b) and/or whether the process is:

- implicit or explicit
- conducted as an independent or a collaborative exercise
- internal or external to an organization
- focused on the whole process (vertical benchmarking) or part of a process as it manifests itself across different functional units (horizontal benchmarking)
- focused on inputs, process or outputs (or a combination)
- based on quantitative and/or qualitative methods.

Implicit or explicit benchmarking

Schofield (1998) classified benchmarking activities according to whether the activity is *implicit* (a by-product of information-gathering exercises such as a survey undertaken by a national agency), or *explicit* (a deliberate and structured process to facilitate comparison and identify directions for change that will lead to improvement). This volume is concerned mainly with explicit benchmarking.

Independent or collaborative benchmarking

Some benchmarking practitioners would argue that one of the defining characteristics of benchmarking is that it is a collaborative process. But there are instances where a single institution or administrative unit within an institution may wish to compare its own practice and performance against information in the public domain or a customized database provided by an external agency or consultant. Examples of this type of approach can be found in some institutional approaches to departmental review (Chapter 3); in the benchmarking of educational outcomes against information provided by subject benchmarking groups (Chapter 7) or national awarding body (Chapter 8); in the use of customized databases for evaluating student recruitment (Chapter 10); and in the evaluation of institutional costs and performance against customized datasets (Appendix A). Collaborative benchmarking involves the active participation of two or more organizations or organizational units in a formal structured process that facilitates comparison of agreed practices, processes or performance (Chapters 4, 5, 6, 11, 12, 13, 14, 15 and Appendix B).

Figure 1.2   Classification of benchmarking

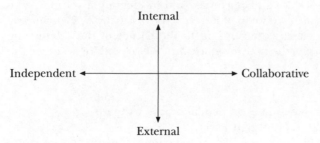

Internally or externally focused benchmarking

Camp (1989) proposed a four-fold classification of benchmarking activity based on whether the process is internally or externally focused. *Internal benchmarking* is a process used in decentralized organizations where performance in similar processes is compared between operating units. In universities this can mean comparisons between different academic departments or schools or between different administrative or service units. Three types of external benchmarking were recognized by Camp.

Competitive benchmarking focuses on measuring performance against competitor organizations. The goal is to study, analyse and understand the approaches and methods used by competitors. In universities this might take the form of comparing staff and student recruitment strategies with the institution's main competitors. Because there is the potential to gain competitive advantages over direct competitors or reduce a competitor's market advantage, this is the most sensitive of benchmarking strategies.

Functional benchmarking is a process used to compare own practice with other organizations fulfilling similar functions. This could mean, for example, a university comparing its admissions or procurement procedures with other universities. It could also mean examining regulatory procedures, staff development activities, and teaching and learning methodologies between institutions or departments in different institutions.

Generic benchmarking (also known as 'best in class') compares the processes of an organization to organizations which operate in a different context but are recognized as truly innovative and market leaders in their field. The criterion for benchmaking is *who performs this activity best?* For example, a university might compare its facilities management processes with those of an airline, manufacturing company or hospital. The difference between functional and generic benchmarking is that the latter seeks to identify and understand why the 'best of the best' is the best.

A further refinement of this typology is offered by Schofield (1998) who distinguishes between *external competitive* and *external collaborative* benchmarking. This is an important distinction to make in the HE context, because the market imperative to gain competitive advantage is counterbalanced by

Figure 1.3 Typology of externally focused benchmarking activities

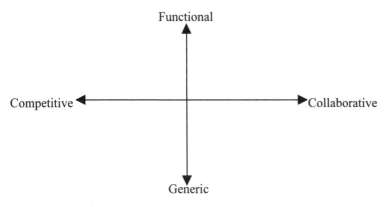

the respect for collaboration as a means of improving both the quality and reputation of the public service as a whole, i.e. it is in the collective as well as the individual interest to collaborate.

Scope of benchmarking – vertical and horizontal processes

Benchmarking can be focused on a single business or academic process (process is used to embrace the totality of practice, behaviour, value and belief systems, procedures, performance/outcomes and products) or incorporate a number of processes that collectively enable a function to be discharged. Alstete (1995) classified benchmarking processes into vertical and horizontal components. *Vertical benchmarking* aims to quantify or qualitatively understand work processes in a discrete functional area. For example, in a university environment this might be an evaluation of the teaching, learning and assessment practices within a department, or the way a registry discharges its administrative functions. In contrast, *horizontal benchmarking* examines work processes that cross-cut the functional areas and organizational units. In a university environment this might take the form of a study which examines the way different departments engage in the admissions process or the induction of students.

Figure 1.4 Nature of benchmarking activities

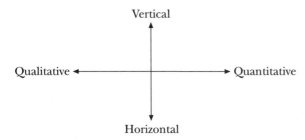

Figure 1.5   Different foci for benchmarking activities

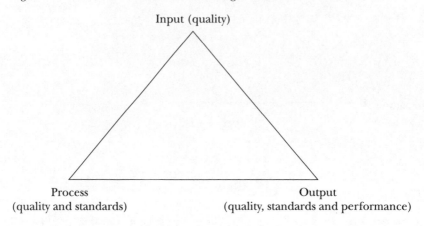

Quantitative and qualitative approaches

Quantitative and qualitative approaches

The extent to which a benchmarking process uses quantitative or qualitative methodologies provides another rationale for classification. Benchmarking requires the construction of information bases relating to work practices, processes and procedures, professional behaviours and value systems, and performance. Some aspects of HE lend themselves to a quantitative approach; others require a more qualitative/discursive type of approach. In many cases, the sheer complexity of interacting variables and the particularities of context require a mixture of quantitative and qualitative approaches.

Price's (1994) classification of benchmarking distinguished between two different types of activity. The qualitative comparison of function, service or technology typically involves an informed discussion process usually facilitated by an independent consultant, to compare what has been done and achieved. In contrast a quantitative comparison of function, service or technology involves a more rigorous and systematic approach using agreed measures of performance to compare what has been done and achieved. Price (1994) defined functional or process benchmarking as the quantitative analysis of what has been done, combined with the qualitative analysis of how it is done and the factors and conditions that influence how it is done.

Input – process – output focus

Benchmarking can be focused on the process and/or the inputs into and outputs from the process (Figure 1.5). For example, in their evaluation of benchmarking procurement practices, HEFCE (1997e) used the terms *output benchmarking* – a comparison of the outputs of specific activities between organizations, and *process benchmarking* – a comparison of the capabilities

Figure 1.6 Referencing processes used in benchmarking

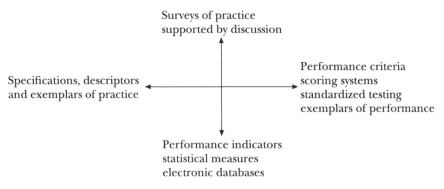

Source: Jackson 1998b

and systems used by organizations to achieve their results. Benchmarking of academic practices can also utilize this framework for specifying the focus for benchmarking activities (Chapter 7). Many benchmarking exercises will, however, seek to understand the relationship between inputs, process and outcomes.

Referencing processes

Benchmarking is fundamentally about comparing one thing with another. Activities can therefore be classified according to the referencing processes (mechanism for comparison) that is used. Jackson (1998b) described four different referencing processes (Figure 1.6). A benchmarking exercise might rely exclusively on one particular approach or it might utilize a combination of approaches.

Nature of benchmarks in HE

Benchmarking originated in the manufacturing industrial sector where the metrics relating to inputs – process – outputs enabled a quantitative approach to benchmarking to be adopted. The variations in contexts – inputs – processes which characterize public services like higher education are often less amenable to this approach. The benchmarks in HE are therefore likely to be more diverse than in a more predictable and controllable industrial environment. In most situations in HE benchmarks can be qualitative, semi-quantitative (descriptive/discursive information perhaps supported by some numerical indicators or performance criteria) or quantitative (e.g. statistical indicators or performance criteria linked to scoring devices). Current attempts to develop methodologies that are suitable for complex academic processes that involve implicit judgements operating within localized social constructs will lead to new types of qualitative or quantitative benchmarks. Similarly, some aspects of benchmarking in HE that have traditionally emphasized the quantitative approach are now incorporating more qualitative discursive dimensions into the process.

The types of benchmarks described in this volume include: numerical and other indicators of performance and costs (e.g. Chapters 9 to 13); 'process-related criteria' such as those used in the assessment for the Malcolm Baldridge or European Quality Award (Loveday 1993; Seymour 1996) and adapted by Commonwealth Higher Education Management Service benchmarking for management processes (Chapter 15); specifications and expectations of process or outcomes (Chapters 5, 7, 8); grades derived through externally motivated peer review processes (Chapter 6); and qualitative information on organizational and management structures and processes (Chapters 4, 5, 11, 12, 13, 14, 15).

Benchmarks are often focused on performance. While this does not pose difficulties in some areas of higher education, notions of performance related to academic practice are more problematic. One way of circumventing this problem is to define 'performance' in terms of a behavioural descriptor, e.g. 'a smarter way of doing something'. In the longer term, it might be anticipated that benchmarking will encourage academics to think about how they might define their practice in performance terms in order to demonstrate to themselves and others a commitment to continuous improvement within agreed parameters.

Concluding remarks

This chapter is intended to introduce the reader to the idea of benchmarking, the nature of the methodology and the conceptual vocabulary for describing different types of benchmarking activity in higher education. The next chapter considers in greater detail some of the historical and contextual factors that have helped create the conditions for benchmarking in UK HE.

2

Creating the Conditions for Benchmarking: A Brief History of Performance Assessment in UK HE

Helen Lund and Norman Jackson

Overview

This chapter sets out to show how the conditions for contemporary benchmarking in higher education have been established over the last two decades. It demonstrates how external pressure on HEIs in the early 1980s to maximize productivity in both the academic and administrative spheres, while simultaneously cutting costs and maintaining or increasing quality of provision, resulted in a range of review and evaluation mechanisms (summarized in Figure 2.1). There are two main strands to this activity: the first relates to external reviews conducted against various quality criteria and expectations, the second to the development of various statistical and other techniques whereby institutions can assess their own performance. These range from the production of management statistics through the development of 'performance indicators', and culminate in the dynamic process of benchmarking. While it might appear that the individual initiatives and policy drivers have been created in an *ad hoc* manner, the strategic intention to improve system-wide performance and accountability is clear.

Performance assessment in the universities 1980–92

A major factor in the transformation of UK HE during the 1980s was the desire of the Thatcher government to effect a massive expansion in the number of students entering higher education. Between 1980 and 1992, full-time enrolment of 'home' students on first degree and diploma courses rose from approximately 450,000 to close on 800,000 (Smithers and Robinson 1995). This was to be done, however, without committing the government to significantly higher spending on HE. Faced with a progressive reduction in the unit of funding from government sources, institutions sought to

Figure 2.1 Development of performance assessment in UK HE: towards the 'evaluative state'

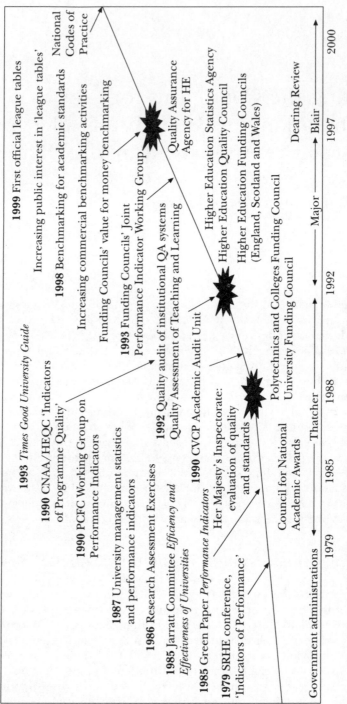

Note: The diagram summarizes key developments in performance assessment in UK HE and the organizations that have promoted this approach. The curve represents the massive change from an elitist to a mass system. While policy initiatives might appear to be *ad hoc*, the overall strategy to create the 'evaluative state' (Henkel 1991) is clear. Important points of change shown on the curve are: 1988 – beginning of expansion of HE system; 1992 – expansion of the university sector; 1997 – publication of the Dearing Report and establishment of QAA.

bridge the funding gap in two ways: by increased efforts to secure income from non-government sources; and through measures to achieve cost savings or 'efficiency gains'. At the same time, institutions were also under pressure to maintain and/or improve the quality of the products or services they provided (whether it be to students, industry partners, or other sections of the university community). The need to combine cost-effectiveness with quality forced HEIs to undertake a systematic scrutiny of academic and administrative performance.

The 1980s, therefore, witnessed repeated attempts by government agencies and the Committee of Vice-Chancellors and Principals (CVCP) to create conditions in which universities would voluntarily engage in systematic assessment of their own performance. Reforms elsewhere in the education system raised fears that if the universities themselves did not take the initiative, the government would intervene and impose some form of regulatory control in order to make them more accountable for the public funds they received. Accordingly, in 1983 the CVCP established an Academic Standards Group (the Reynolds Committee). The committee's report (Reynolds 1986) covered a range of topics relating to quality and standards, for example, the involvement of external peers in the maintenance and monitoring of academic standards. The committee did much to raise awareness of quality assurance as a means of assessing performance in universities and facilitated the exchange of good practice across the binary line. A number of universities responded to the reports of the Reynolds Committee by establishing formal arrangements for the review and evaluation of their provision. In particular, several universities introduced a framework of departmental reviews (see Chapter 3).

Performance assessment techniques

The use of indicators to measure 'performance' within HEIs was already a hot topic by 1979 when the Society for Research into Higher Education (SRHE) made it the focus of their 15th annual conference (Billing 1979). Among the papers given, Sizer (1979: 57) focused on 'indicators in times of financial stringency, contraction and changing needs', while the first keynote speaker, from the Department of Education and Science (DES), attempted to 'identify those [national] indicators . . . likely to be the concern of government over the next few years': manpower need; subject balance; quality of students; first destinations of graduates; continuing education (Thompson 1979: 3). Government interest in 'developing a more rigorous set of procedures for evaluating the performance of higher education' was, however, first publicly expressed in its Green Paper of 1985, which called for 'the construction and regular publication of a range of performance indicators' (DES 1985; Johnes and Taylor 1990: 1). Performance indicators (PIs) have been defined as 'numerical values [that] . . . provide a measurement for assessing the quantitative or qualitative performance of a system'

(Cuenin 1986: 6) or as 'statistics, ratios, costs and other forms of information which illuminate or measure progress in achieving [a] mission and . . . corresponding aims and objectives' (PCFC 1990: 7). The important point is that they are to be distinguished from simple management statistics, in that they 'imply a point of reference, for example a standard . . . or a comparator' (Cave *et al.* 1997: 22). As such their introduction into UK HE represents a significant step along the road towards benchmarking.

1985 was also the year which saw the CVCP respond to a 'wish' on the part of Sir Keith Joseph, the Education Secretary, for an efficiency study in the universities (Cave *et al.* 1997). The Jarratt Committee, which was set up to do this work, recommended, above all, that universities must work to clear objectives and achieve value for money. The report also advocated the development of a range of PIs 'covering both inputs and outputs and designed for use both within individual institutions and for making comparisons between institutions' (Jarratt 1985; Cave *et al.* 1997: 4). It was stipulated that the indicators should be calculable and useable by managers. This work was entrusted to the CVCP and the University Grants Committee (UGC). The idea of annual publication of 'essential data on performance' received a further boost with the government White Paper (DES 1987). In the same year, CVCP/UGC (1987) published the first edition of *University Management Statistics and Performance Indicators in the UK*, comprising 39 sets of comparative data and performance indicators, relating to universities only. The following year, *UMS & PI* increased its range of PIs to 54 with a further 15 added in 1992 (Yorke 1996; Cave *et al.* 1997).

Throughout the late 1980s the emphasis, in developing PIs, had been on quantitative data. Johnes and Taylor (1990), however, criticized the CVCP/UGC approach for its concentration on 'input' (rather than process or output) indicators. The thrust of this study, which focused on four specific indicators in teaching and research activities, was that no one variable (e.g. first destinations, or research ratings) was useful as a PI *per se*. Comparison of differences in outputs between universities was meaningless, and could be seriously misleading, unless allowances for differences in inputs at the various institutions was made. This argument is surfacing again in connection with league tables. Although 'process' indicators (how input factors and resources are combined to achieve an institution's outputs) had been identified by the CVCP/UGC Group, little effort was put into their development.

The quality assurance (QA) movement

During the 1980s, there was no external regulatory authority concerned with the evaluation of teaching and learning in universities. This meant that the introduction of QA arrangements to evaluate academic practice proceeded in a rather *ad hoc* way. In 1988, however, the Universities Funding Council (UFC) made it clear that if universities did not take quality assurance seriously it would intervene. Fearful that the government would impose external regulatory controls, the CVCP established in 1990 an Academic Audit Unit to conduct, through independent and informed peer review, audits of institutional arrangements for assuring quality and standards, and to promote good practice for maintaining and enhancing quality and standards.

Performance assessment in the polytechnics and colleges 1980–92

In contrast to the universities, the polytechnics and most HE colleges had been subject to external regulation and review by the Council for National Academic Awards (CNAA). The CNAA's primary concern related to the quality and standards of programmes. The Council established what now would be called benchmark 'process' standards for programme validation and approval and other institutional regulatory mechanisms, with which polytechnics and colleges whose programmes were validated by the CNAA had to comply. Performance assessment by the CNAA was exercised through validation panels including external peers and through rigorous quinquennial institutional review (Silver 1990). Although the CNAA progressively devolved increasing responsibility for QA to institutions, the culture of collaborative peer review it established exerts a strong influence even today.

Performance assessment techniques

During the 1980s, polytechnics and colleges were also subject to independent inspection by Her Majesty's Inspectorate (HMI), a professional body of HE inspectors with statutory authority to report on the quality and standards of education and institutional arrangements for quality assurance; from 1988, HMI's reports informed decisions on funding above core levels. In 1988, the Polytechnics and Colleges Funding Council (PCFC) was established with explicit guidance from the Secretary of State to encourage institutions to monitor performance systematically, seek improvement and secure greater value for the public investment. State funding policies were geared to expansion of the HE system and the reward for excellent performance (based on HMI quality ratings) was funding for more students! This was the first explicit link between performance assessment, public funding and policy for reshaping the HE system.

The late 1980s and early 1990s witnessed a search for reliable performance measures and methods for evaluating performance in academic and non-academic areas. In 1989 the PCFC established the Morris Committee, which recommended publication of four sets of 'macro' performance indicators: scale and effectiveness; level of resourcing; efficiency; sources of funds (PCFC 1990; Yorke 1996; Cave *et al.* 1997). Three years later, the Scottish Centrally Funded Colleges (SCFC 1992) recommended five 'macro' indicators:

unit costs profile; student success profile; post-course success ratios; client satisfaction; quality of teaching and learning. Of these, the last two depended to a considerable extent on what Yorke (1996: 14) describes as 'judgementally-derived information' and thus a move away from evaluating performance in purely quantitative terms. During this period also, CNAA published papers relating PIs to quality assurance and to course quality (CNAA 1990; Yorke 1991, 1996).

CNAA also joined forces with PCFC to explore the difficult terrain of 'value added'. The idea behind this was to measure student achievement at a particular institution by comparing the exit qualification awarded to students with their entry qualifications at the start of their course. The CNAA/ PCFC study tested six types of 'index' method, whereby scores are attributed to measures of input and output quality and 'value added' is computed by relating the two scores. The report, however, found that such index methods were based on 'arbitrary assumptions on how difficult it is for students to achieve a given exit qualification' and as such, were unreliable. Its authors favoured instead the alternative 'comparative' method, whereby a student's expected exit result (based on an analysis of nationally collected data on the relationship between entry and exit qualifications) would be compared with the actual exit qualification. If a student achieved a much better exit qualification than might have been predicted from his/ her qualifications at entry, then the institution could be said to have performed well in terms of 'adding value' (PCFC/CNAA 1990). The confidence placed by PCFC/CNAA in this comparative value added (CVA) approach was not, however, universally shared and the concept of 'value added' as an indicator of performance remains controversial.

In 1990, HMI conducted a survey of the use of PIs in 43 polytechnics and colleges. The survey (DES 1991b: 1) 'found widespread use of a large number of PIs for a variety of purposes but no systematic approach across the sector'. A third of institutions had made significant progress in the use of a limited number of key indicators to evaluate the achievement of strategic objectives such as cost-effectiveness, income generation, access and quality of provision. Constraints on use of PIs were identified as the absence of comprehensive databases; the high cost of introducing computerized management information systems; lack of staff knowledge about the nature and purpose of PIs; and difficulties of establishing indicators of quality.

Performance assessment in the unified HE system 1992–98

Another government White Paper, *Higher Education: A New Framework* (DES 1991a), laid the foundation for an expanded university sector. Following the Further and Higher Education Act of 1992 the binary system was dismantled and the former polytechnics were given the authority to award their own degrees. Three regional HE Funding Councils (HEFCE, SHEFC and HEFCW for England, Scotland and Wales respectively) were established with statutory responsibilities for ensuring that the quality of publicly funded education was of an appropriate quality and standard. In Northern Ireland, responsibility for these areas lay with the Department of Education for Northern Ireland (DENI). HMI was dismantled (except in teacher education) and each of the Funding Councils established a capacity to evaluate the quality of education (but not academic standards directly).

Under the new system, the established (pre-1992) universities came under the same kind of external scrutiny as that to which the newer universities had been accustomed via CNAA and HMI. This took two forms: institutionally focused quality audits undertaken by a new body, the Higher Education Quality Council (HEQC) and subject-based quality assessments undertaken by the Funding Councils. Self-assessment by institutions and departments of their own quality and performance was an important feature of both review processes.

Performance assessment through institutional quality audit

Quality audit, developed by the CVCP's Academic Audit Unit, was refined and sharpened by HEQC. The process focused on the design, monitoring and evaluation of courses and degree programmes; teaching, learning and communications methods; student assessment and degree classification; academic staff; verification and feedback mechanisms; and institutional arrangements for ensuring that promotional material is not misleading. It involved a self-appraisal by the institution of the effectiveness of its arrangements for maintaining and improving quality and standards; assembly and scrutiny of institutional documentation describing those arrangements; peer review through document audit and interviews; producing a public report. The terms of reference for the audit process were defined in the notes of guidance for auditors and HE institutions typically used the expectations contained in the notes to review and evaluate (benchmark!) their own arrangements. In 1996, HEQC extended the scope of the audit process to overseas collaborative partnership arrangements using the same basic methodology as had been applied in the UK.

Performance assessment through subject quality assessment

The quality assessment procedure adopted by HEFCE in 1992[1] marked an important change from HMI's inspectoral methodologies; academic departments were now required to prepare a self-critical assessment of their own performance (albeit within parameters set by the Funding Council). The self-assessment was then evaluated using a template of questions. If the external assessor considered that there was sufficient evidence to uphold a claim for excellence, the department was subjected to a three-day visit by a small team of subject assessors. This process can itself be seen as a benchmarking exercise in which the department's self-assessment was checked against a set of performance criteria that were not shared with institutions. The HEFCE methodology was subsequently revised (HEFCE 1996a), universal visiting was introduced and a graded profile of 1–4 (unsatisfactory to highly satisfactory) was introduced for six aspects of provision:

- curriculum design, content and organization
- teaching, learning and assessment
- student progression and achievement
- student support and guidance
- learning resources
- quality assurance and enhancement.

The quality assessment reports produced by HEFCE provide an important source of public information on the quality of UK HE and the graded profiles feature prominently in the so-called national league tables produced by commercial interests. By the year 2001 the whole of the UK HE system will have been assessed through the different quality assessment methodologies employed by the three Funding Councils.

Performance assessment through performance indicators

In the mid-1990s responsibility for the development of PIs now rested with the Funding Councils' Joint Performance Indicators Working Group (JPIWG), though the actual collection of 'unified data' on HE was the preserve of the Higher Education Statistics Agency (HESA).

The JPIWG identified three groups as its target audience: the universities themselves which would use PIs for self-evaluation and inter-institutional comparison; the Funding Councils 'to support their operational requirements'; other 'stakeholders' (e.g. students and employers) (CVCP 1995). JPIWG recommended four broad areas of institution indicators (teaching and learning; research; estate management; financial health) plus macro indicators covering student participation and output, financial and space indicators and research (CVCP 1995; Davis 1996). The group recognized that their work represented the first stage in a long developmental process, including in their report caveats on the possible misuse of PIs (CVCP 1995). In 1995 JPIWG was replaced by the new Higher Education Management Statistics Group (HEMS) whose remit was to use data published by HESA 'to devise and recommend for publication, in consultation with the sector, *management statistics* for higher education' [our italics] (Wright 1997). Despite government pressure to publish material which could be treated as PIs, HEMS did not initially generate 'outcomes oriented data' because of the 'very formidable . . . obstacles in the way of doing this meaningfully on the same basis for the entire sector' (Wright 1997). Work by the HEMS Technical Sub-group to overcome these obstacles seems, however, to have been successful; early in 1999 HEMS had already published sectoral statistics on research funding and graduate unemployment rates. One commentator has described the primary aim of this data as being 'for universities to bench-mark their own performance against other institutions' (Elliot Major 1999).

Assessment of research performance

External assessment of research 'output' within the 'old' universities began in 1986 with the first Research Selectivity Exercise, conducted by the UGC (later UFC); a second exercise followed in 1989. In 1992, the research 'performance' of the whole of the newly unified HE sector came under scrutiny with the first Research Assessment Exercise (RAE) conducted by the new Funding Councils (UGC 1986; UFC 1989; Cave *et al.* 1997; HEFCE 1997a); a second RAE followed in 1996. The link between assessment of research performance and funding became overt, with ratings used by the funding bodies to calculate allocations of research funds.

The methodology for assessing research performance changed several times, largely in response to feedback from the sector. The 1986 exercise required institutions to submit data including research staff and student numbers and a maximum of five examples of typical 'best' research from each cost centre. The approach met with strong criticism 'on the grounds of lack of consistency, anonymity and incomplete data' and because 'it in no way met the criteria for proper peer review' (Cave *et al.* 1997: 161). In 1989, universities were rated on an ascending scale of 1–5, on the basis of publications (two nominated by each academic); success in obtaining research grants/studentships and research contracts; the professional know-ledge and judgement of advisory group and panel members and of outside experts, where appropriate (UGC 1988; Cave *et al.* 1997). Criticism this time focused on discrimination against applied research, the retrospective nature of the exercise and the unreliability of some of the publications data. In consequence, the 1992 Research Assessment Exercise (RAE), which now included the former polytechnics (new universities), required informa-tion on *all* publications produced by each individual 'unit of assessment' (cost centre), in addition to the two nominated by each academic. In 1996, the number of publications required from each academic was reduced again (to four) and Grades 3 and 5 were each split into two, with the top grade now being a 5*. Despite this fine-tuning, RAE methodology was still under attack from academics. Grievances included claims that the exercise hin-dered collaboration and interdisciplinary research, led to secrecy and com-petition, and penalized researchers working in industrial collaborations (Royal Society of Chemistry 1995; Cave *et al.* 1997). Following a substantial consultation exercise (HEFCE 1997b) the RAE planned for 2001 will incor-porate 'a number of improvements' including:

- feedback from assessment panels, in the form of a general public report on working methods and findings, plus confidential specific feedback on individual submissions made to the head of each institution

- introduction of a separate form for interdisciplinary projects and more interdisciplinary expertise among panel members
- changes in the methods of appointing assessment panel members and chairs to reduce the risk of bias and improve transparency
- the requirement for panels to consult a corresponding group of non-UK researchers before awarding to any institution the top grades of 5 or 5* which indicate international excellence.

The Funding Councils did, moreover, admit in a report 'announcing key decisions about the next RAE' (HEFCE 1998b), that 'a significant number of HEIs, and some respondents from other sections of the higher education research community suggested that though another RAE is desirable, a fundamental review is needed now to determine whether it will be appropriate to assess research quality differently after the next exercise'. Whatever this 'difference' might entail, it seems unlikely that it would involve a move away from indicators based on measurement of published output.

League tables

The last few years have witnessed another phenomenon: the public evaluation of institutional performance data through commercial publications. Following in the wake of US and Canadian university rankings published by media organizations, the first edition of the *Times Good University Guide* appeared in 1993. Unlike other UK handbooks aimed at prospective students, it not only profiled universities but ranked them in a league table. The guide draws on statistics produced by HESA, the Funding Councils, QAA (Quality Assurance Agency), UCAS (Universities and Colleges Admissions Service), the Standing Committee of National University Libraries (SCONUL) and the universities themselves and covers eight areas (staff/ student ratios; 'facilities' spend per student; graduate destinations; teaching quality assessment; research assessment; points required for entry; library and IT expenditure; proportion of students gaining first or upper second class degrees). For each area, the top-rated university gets 100 points, thus serving as the benchmark for all the others, which get a proportion of this based on their unadjusted scores. A total score out of 1000 is achieved by the fact that two of the indicators are weighted (teaching at 2.5 and research at 1.5); this score gives the university its overall rating.

Like its international counterparts, the *Times* guide is generally not well regarded in the HE sector. An analysis of the 1994 tables (Morrison *et al.* 1995: 128) concluded that 'the table fails to meet any of the technical requirements which would assure its internal construct validity'. Specific criticisms have included past use of a 'value-added' score, reached by subtracting a student's expected degree classification (based on A level scores) from their actual classification; the undue weight that its rankings place on research; and lack of any reference to the educational missions of institutions (Chapter 6). In 1998, the *Sunday Times* and the *Financial Times* also published university league tables. The *Sunday Times* ranking (8 November 1998), compiled using data from HESA, QAA, the Funding Councils and the universities, covers similar ground to the *Times* rankings, excluding entry points, facilities spend and library/IT expenditure. The *FT's* list of the top 100 universities (May 1998) is based on a 'basket' of 20 indicators which include, in addition to those used by the *Times*, ratio of applications to places, percentage of postgraduate and research students, percentage of overseas students, income from industry. Though Wagner (1998) claims that 'league tables are not a serious factor in student choice', the proliferation of such rankings and the fact that the universities themselves publicize a favourable placement in such lists (e.g. UMIST 1998; University of Hull 1998; University of Leicester 1998) suggest that they should not be lightly dismissed.

Institutional quality profiles

Concern over 'misleading attempts to produce league tables' was one of the factors underlying a proposal by HEQC in 1995 to publish a volume of Higher Education Quality Profiles (HEQPs) on UK HEIs. The idea of HEQPs was to 'bring together and publish information about the quality of institutions' provision for the benefit of students and intending students, employers and other stakeholders' (HEQC 1995a). It was proposed that HEQC and UCAS would work together to collate and validate the contents of this volume, which would draw mainly on data already available to these agencies and to HESA. The proposed contents included an institutional profile; data on the student body, subject areas covered, academic structures, graduate outcomes and destinations; information on student facilities and support services, as well as on institutional audits, assessments and other quality reports. In the event, this planned publication did not come to fruition, perhaps in part because HEFCE produced in 1995 the first edition of its own *Profiles of Higher Education Institutions*, which covered some of the same ground, plus details of income and expenditure, academic staff numbers and a summary of the Funding Council's assessments of teaching and research for each institution (HEFCE 1995a, 1997c). Behind both projects, however, lies a shared concern on the part of the sector and its funding and quality agencies that consumers should not be presented with misleading information about UK HEIs and that 'the sector should control as far as possible the use of the information it generates about what it provides' (HEQC 1995a).

Contemporary developments

The mid-1990s witnessed a search for a more integrated (and less burdensome) external quality review process. Two committees addressed this issue between 1996 and 1997: the Joint Planning Group for Quality Assurance in HE (JPG) established by the Funding Councils and HE representative bodies (CVCP 1996), and the National Committee of Inquiry into Higher Education (NCIHE 1997), also known as the Dearing Committee. The Dearing

Report has proved to be the more influential and the committee's recommendations signal a sea change in the structures, mechanisms and approaches used to secure and assure the quality and standards of UK HE. External quality review processes will be refocused on the standards of achievement and institutional competence for making awards, rather than the current priority which is to evaluate the quality of education against an institution's own aims and objectives. Subject-based quality assessment will be replaced by a new quality assurance regime focused on academic standards underpinned by a strengthened system of external examiners, and a national framework for qualifications and credit. The recommendations contained in the NCIHE report are not a blueprint: rather they are intended to steer the HE community and the QAA towards the creation of workable and effective policies. In summary, the key measures include:

1. A national framework of qualifications based on agreed credits and levels of achievement, to be developed and maintained by the QAA.
2. The development of recognized standards of awards and the provision of clear information for students, employers and others about the content, standards and delivery of programmes, and student achievement in respect of these standards. This objective would be achieved via:
   • the creation of benchmark information on standards by subject benchmarking teams, to be used by institutions/teaching teams to inform curriculum design and the drafting of programme specifications
   • clear and explicit, outcome-based programme specifications developed by each programme provider
   • the development of a student progress file containing a transcript and the means by which students can monitor, build and reflect upon their personal development.
3. The adoption of codes of practice by institutions that embrace these expectations and the periodic external review of performance against such codes.

The Dearing Committee also directed funding and HE representative bodies to develop appropriate PIs and benchmarks for families of institutions with similar characteristics and aspirations (NCIHE 1997: Recommendation 58) in order to assist governing bodies in carrying out their five-yearly reviews of institutional performance. The products of development work in this area will result in the first 'official league tables' (Goddard 1999). The tables will provide performance information at institutional and sectoral level, covering:

• broadening participation by under-represented groups
• student progression
• learning outcomes
• learning and teaching
• student employment
• research output.

The purpose of the PIs is to assist institutions in monitoring, managing and improving their performance. These figures will take account of the intake of students to the institution, their educational backgrounds and the subject mix of that institution. The results for an institution can then be compared with the average for similar institutions.

Conclusions

The drive for institutions to establish mechanisms for evaluating their own performance is clearly rooted in the politics of the 1980s, related to government aspirations for a much more cost-effective, publicly accountable and regulated HE system. A look at the HE system of the late 1990s reflects the great extent to which these aspirations have been achieved; clearly, if institutions are to survive and prosper in an increasingly competitive and market-oriented environment, performance assessment will continue to be an essential managerial tool.

The conditions for benchmarking have been created over the last two decades through the parallel development of the capacity of institutions to review and evaluate themselves at all levels and in all functions, and the growth of external quality review processes. There has also been a considerable system-wide effort to develop and apply performance indicators as an aid to good management, and in many areas of HE, criteria, objectives or targets are used as a means of measuring and demonstrating achievement (or performance). Both tendencies result in a more explicit, information-rich environment which managers can exploit; they also raise awareness of the value of reference points against which performance can be measured. Thus, PIs have become progressively more sophisticated and there has been a tendency to place increasing emphasis on outcomes and processes as well as inputs. The creation and use of performance measures, capacities for self-evaluation and external review are features of the 'evaluative state' (Henkel 1991) which is essential for the management of public policy based on the idea of performance contracts (Dill 1998). The Dearing Report (NCIHE 1997: 25 (Summary Report)) commended UK institutions for their 'impressive improvements in efficiency in the face of a dramatic fall in public funding per student over the last 20 years', but added that 'the challenge to find new and better ways of doing things will continue and intensify'. The following chapters demonstrate why benchmarking will play an important role in meeting this challenge.

Note

1. While each of the Funding Councils developed a different methodology, only the methodology employed by the English Funding Council is described in this chapter.

Part 1

Benchmarking to Improve the
Quality of Educational Practice
and Regulate Standards

3

Benchmarking Educational Processes and Outcomes

Norman Jackson

Overview

This chapter provides an overview of the way in which benchmarking is being used to improve the quality of education and regulate the standards of learning. It argues that established collegiate behaviours, like external examining and programme accreditation by professional bodies, are incipient forms of academic benchmarking. All benchmarking activities that are concerned with the quality of educational provision and the standards of learning can be related to three conceptual frameworks. The 'quality' framework is concerned with the relationships between inputs, process and outputs, while the 'academic standards' framework is concerned with the relationship between expectations (learning intentions), process (that enables intentions to be realized) and outcomes (standards actually achieved). The third framework relates to the 'referencing process' that underpins benchmarking activity. This framework provides the basis for describing a range of activities that illustrate how benchmarking is being used in UK HE.

Roots of academic benchmarking

The idea that academics might use benchmarking to understand, regulate and improve their own practice might seem new and innovative but well-established academic processes, like external examining, programme accreditation undertaken by professional and statutory bodies and programme validation and review undertaken by HE institutions, embody notions of benchmarking. However, comparative judgements within such processes are typically made on the basis of experience and impression rather than systematic and explicit information that would enable direct comparisons to be made. Figure 3.1 charts some of the ways in which incipient and more explicit benchmarking has been used to regulate and improve the quality of education and academic standards in the UK. The term regulation is

Figure 3.1 Major influences on academic benchmarking in UK HE

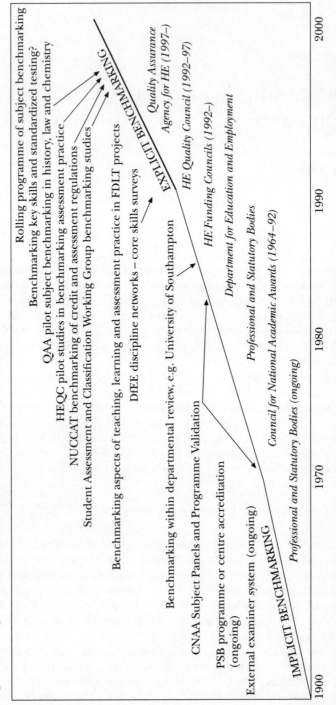

Note: The diagram identifies established academic processes that contain elements of benchmarking within them and contemporary activities that adopt a more explicit approach to benchmarking. Organizations and bodies that have promoted the idea of benchmarking are shown below the curve.

being used to embrace the totality of practices, behaviours, social constructs, written and unwritten rules and codes that determine the character of an HE system (Jackson 1997a). It involves the act of regulating (controlling and adjusting behaviour and practice against explicit or implicit rules) and the state of being regulated (practising within a framework of rules and accepted professional norms and values). It subsumes the ideas of quality assurance and control, quality enhancement and quality management. It can be applied at any level in an HE system from the individual (personal self-regulation), through the activities of institutions to protect their own reputation and standards to the activities of statutory and non-statutory authorities and professional bodies.

External examiner system

Ever since the first half of the nineteenth century when the University of Durham invited scholars from Oxford to help set and mark examinations, external examiners have been the primary means of cross-referencing the standards or outcomes of learning between HE institutions in different subjects. Although the specific duties and functions of external examiners vary between institutions they essentially provide a department or programme team with an independent and objective perspective on the assessment process and outcome standards, by comparing what they see with what they have seen in other institutions. Thus external examiners act as a type of benchmarking agent for an unstructured, unsystematic and largely implicit type of benchmarking process.

Professional and statutory body accreditation and validation processes

Elements of benchmarking can be found in a number of processes operated by professional and statutory bodies (PSBs). The most common process is that of *programme or centre accreditation*. About 65 PSBs are directly involved in programme accreditation (HEQC 1996b) which enables them to exert varying degrees of influence over entry standards to programmes; curriculum content; methods of teaching and learning; the assessment process; resources to support learning including staffing. The process may involve scrutiny of relevant institutional documentation against the standards established by the PSB and may be combined with a visit by an accreditation panel to establish that the appropriate input and process standards are met. A number of PSBs set their own examinations and these act as a vehicle for benchmarking outcome standards across the HE sector. PSBs also create the conditions for benchmarking through the provision of guidance or codes of good practice against which practitioners can compare and align their own practice.

Institutional programme validation processes

The Council for National Academic Awards (CNAA) was established in the 1960s to oversee the quality and standards of awards made by polytechnics and colleges of HE (Silver 1990). Although its function was terminated in 1992 when the polytechnics became universities, the systems it established for programme validation are still used (albeit in a modified form) in many HEIs. The CNAA's approach to benchmarking was to establish a national process standard for the validation and approval of academic programmes. Programme validation involved the preparation of a definitive course document by a course team to a prescribed format which made clear the rationale for the course, the inputs (students, staff, physical resources) and the process – curriculum, teaching, learning and assessment methods. Proposals were vetted by the appropriate CNAA Subject Board to establish whether there was a *prima facie* case for a panel to review the proposal with the course team. The specification of documentation and the standardized formal peer review process involving experienced academics created the conditions for a type of incipient benchmarking.

Contemporary benchmarking – conceptual frameworks

The rapid development of a mass system of higher education in the early 1990s, accompanied by the almost universal restructuring of the curriculum within credit-based modular formats, profoundly affected every aspect of teaching, learning, assessment and administrative practice. The wholesale reshaping of HE in a more competitive and publicly accountable environment is causing academics in UK HE to consider new ways of evaluating quality and standards. Academic benchmarking is a product of this more dynamic, competitive and publicly accountable environment. It is seen as both a means of gaining competitive advantage and of improving the capacity of a diverse, multi-purpose mass HE system to regulate itself.

Benchmarking activities that are focused on the education process might be directed towards:

• the quality of inputs to the educational process
• the quality of the process itself or
• the quality of the outputs from the process (Table 3.1).

The way in which quality is defined will, however, have an important bearing on the way the activity is framed, for example quality may be defined:

• as excellence (equivalent to 'best in class' in the world of profit-making organizations)
• as consistency

Table 3.1   Framework for benchmarking the quality of education

Inputs	Processes	Outputs
Students e.g. entry profiles (gender/ethnicity/origin/qualifications)	**Induction** to the programme/learning environment	**Students** e.g. completion rates, academic standards (degree profiles, value added), employability, progression to further study
Staff e.g. FT and PT establishment, individual and collective expertise, experience, qualifications (both academic and teaching), age, recruitment, appointment, induction, preparation for teaching and development	**Design of curricula and assessment** **Teaching and learning** e.g. strategies and methods; effectiveness, innovation	**Staff** e.g. SSRs, productivity and creativity – teaching and administrative workloads, research productivity, supervisory workloads
Physical resources e.g. accommodation, facilities, specialist equipment, library and information technology resources	**Student guidance and support** e.g. academic and personal tutor systems, careers advice, handbooks and other information, project supervision	
Financial resources e.g. costs per student; costs per staff	**Student record systems** e.g. recording and reporting achievement	
External inputs e.g. involvement of employers, use of external facilities or equipment	**Management and administrative systems** **Review and evaluation processes** e.g. peer review, student feedback, employer feedback	

- as fitness for purpose
- as value for money or
- as the capacity to transform learners (Harvey *et al.* 1992).

Benchmarking processes that are focused on the standards of learning might be directed towards:

- the expectations for learning (what is it that learners will be expected to know and be able to do?)
- the means by which learners will be enabled to achieve the expected outcomes (the curriculum, teaching and learning methods, and support and guidance systems)
- the means by which learners will demonstrate the achievement of specified educational outcomes and the actual standards they achieve (Table 3.2).

Table 3.2 Framework for benchmarking the standards of learning

Expectations of learning	How standards are achieved and demonstrated	Achievement
Award descriptor – statement about what a learner who has met the requirements for an award would be expected to know and be able to do	**Design of curricula –** match to learning intentions; match to learner abilities; innovation	**Quality of evidence that outcomes have been achieved**
Levels descriptor – statement about what a learner studying at a specified level would be expected to know and be able to do	**Teaching and learning methods –** link to learning intentions; effectiveness; innovation	**Assessment criteria, grading and marking schemes –** the basis for judging whether the learning intentions have been realized and the level of attainment
Subject expectations/ outcomes – statements developed by subject benchmarking groups about the qualities, skills, capabilities and values that a learner can expect to gain from a programme in that subject	**Assessment methods –** link to learning intentions; reliability; validity; innovation	**Regulatory and discretionary controls** – over threshold and other levels of attainment
	Guidance and support – effectiveness of academic and personal tutor systems; careers advice; handbooks and other information; project supervision	**Standard assessment tests –** that can be used across departments in the same or different institutions to enable standards of attainment to be compared
Programme/module learning outcomes – specific statements about what a learner completing a particular programme or module of study should know and be able to do		**Student record systems** – recording and reporting achievement; personal profiling

The relationship between these dimensions of learning are complex and they are not easy to understand or explain. The strength of benchmarking as an academic process is that it provides a vehicle for peer communities to apply their research skills to examine such complex relationships in order to gain a better collective understanding of how inputs and processes combine to produce an outcome.

The third conceptual idea that might be used to explain and understand academic benchmarking is the nature of the referencing process through which quality and standards are compared and evaluated (Table 3.3).

Table 3.3 Benchmarking typology based on the referencing process

Surveys supported by discussion	Performance criteria, scoring systems
TVU modular curriculum study (Ch. 4)	CHEMS criterion referencing (Ch. 15)
TRIADS learning outcomes in Earth Science (Ch. 3)	QAA subject benchmarking (Ch. 7)
SACWG assessment practice (Ch. 6)	Key skills standards using national criteria (Ch. 8)
NUCCAT credit and assessment regulations (Ch. 3)	Standardized testing (Ch. 3)
EPC assessment practice (Ch. 5)	
Descriptors, codes, specifications and exemplars	**Performance indicators, statistics and data sets**
Levels descriptors (Ch. 3)	University of Southampton Departmental Review (Ch. 3)
EPC academic management specification (Ch. 5)	Degree performance data (Ch. 6)
Institute of Physics specification for accreditation (Ch. 3)	Module assessment data (Ch. 6)
QAA subject benchmarking (Ch. 7)	'League tables' (Ch. 6)
ASSHE Inventory of Assessment Strategies (Ch. 3)	Student perception questionnaires (Ch. 6)
	Student recruitment (Ch. 10)
	Student retention (Ch. 6)

Benchmarking against descriptors, specifications, codes and process exemplars

In this type of benchmarking an individual, teaching team, department or institution reviews and adjusts practice or performance against information that is provided in a written descriptor, specification or code of practice or exemplar of practice or process. This type of referencing process is an important feature of benchmarking for regulatory purposes. It is likely to become an important institutional process as codes of practice are developed by the Quality Assurance Agency (QAA 1998a). When linked to performance specifications this approach also underpins the idea of regulating academic standards through subject benchmarking or national key skill standards (Chapters 7 and 8).

Benchmarking using levels descriptors

Levels descriptors are general statements about what it is that students are expected to know and be able to do at different stages in their learning. The expectations they embody can be used by academics to guide the design of curricula and assessment and to inform decisions about the award of credit for experiential learning (Shaw and Stoney 1995, 1996; Lyons and Bement 1996; Moon 1996).

Benchmarking using examples of practice

The creation of directories or online databases of examples of practice provides another source of information which academics can use to benchmark their own practice. A good example of this type of practitioner database is the ASSHE Inventory (Hounsell *et al.* 1996) which contains over 300 examples of assessment practice each described in a standard format. This approach might also be taken up by subject groups to support the improvement of practice in the discipline.

Benchmarking using a specification

The Engineering Professors' Council (EPC) coordinated the production of a specification for a departmental *quality management system* (Burge *et al.* 1996; Chapter 5, this volume) that attempts to codify what academic staff would consider to be good professional practice in the main areas of academic management. Each element of the specification attempts to create a 'good practice' benchmark against which departments can compare and develop their own practices for the management of quality and standards.

Use of a specification for programme accreditation

The *Core of Physics and Graduate Skills Base* document produced by the Institute of Physics (IoP 1998) provides an example of subject benchmarking information that is used as the basis for accrediting physics degree courses. The five-page document defines the core concepts and skills base that physics programmes seeking accreditation would be expected to embody. It identifies a set of objectives for accredited physics programmes; a set of generic skills (mathematical; analytical, information-handling; computer literacy; communication; organizational and personal and interpersonal); subject-specific skills; the core concepts and the knowledge base for physics graduates. The *Core of Physics* contains a set of seven major headings with examples of material that should normally be covered. It is not a syllabus but a set of core concepts that should be familiar to a graduate in physics. Departments that seek accreditation are expected to demonstrate how their programmes meet the expectations contained in the specification and a simple audit tool is used by IoP reviewers to check that the expectations can be satisfied. The Quality Assurance Agency is currently developing an infrastructure to support the benchmarking of subject outcomes across the UK and the results of early development work are described in Chapter 7.

Benchmarking through surveys and action research

In this type of benchmarking an individual or group creates a research strategy in order to compare/evaluate aspects of its practice, processes or performance. The process may involve an individual, department or institution identifying the partners, or it might involve a group of individuals, departments or institutions working together. In the case of a forum the members agree what to benchmark and identify the main enquiry themes and research questions. The information is used as the basis for discussion and comparative evaluation with a view to gaining a better collective understanding of practice and process, the meaning of 'performance' and the directions for change to improve 'performance'. Practice is then adjusted using the knowledge and insights gained. Some examples of both types of approach are outlined below.

Benchmarking the curriculum framework

The curriculum framework is central to the way an institution provides its education. Chapter 4 describes the benchmarking exercise undertaken by Thames Valley University (TVU) to inform the development of a new curricular environment. Eleven institutional partners were identified using criteria that related to the institution's own interests. The objective was to gain a better understanding of the organization, administration and infrastructure underpinning different approaches to learning in a modular regime. Information on different institutional approaches and operational systems was summarized in a report that was made available to benchmarking partners. It identified a number of strategic changes that have since been implemented by the university.

Benchmarking subject learning outcomes

The Fund for the Development of Teaching and Learning (FDTL) was established by the Higher Education Funding Council for England (HEFCE) to promote innovation and improvement within subjects and encourage the dissemination of good practice. A number of FDTL projects have incorporated benchmarking-type activities within their methodology. The Earth Science TRIADS project (Tripartite Assessment Delivery System) aims to improve assessment in higher education by promoting a learning outcomes-based approach and by providing computer-based tools to facilitate the assessment of outcomes (Boyle and Paul 1998). In order to develop computer-based assessment (CBA) it was first necessary to identify the generic subject outcomes. This was achieved through a simple survey instrument that enabled subject outcomes to be identified for common Level 1 (Year 1) modules in each department. When the data were collated it became apparent that there was substantial agreement on what the generic outcomes were. The design of CBA based on such generic outcomes would enable departments to benchmark their academic standards directly against group test scores for other departments and against the performance of previous cohorts in their own institution.

Benchmarking assessment practice

One of the best examples in the UK of survey-based benchmarking is provided by the Student Assessment and Classification Working Group (SACWG). The benchmarking forum, which has representatives from seven post-1992 universities, has conducted a number of comparative studies (see Yorke *et al.* 1996, 1998; Woolf *et al.* 1997; Chapter 6, this volume). In one study (Yorke *et al.* 1996) the frequency distribution characteristics of over 90,000 undergraduate module marks in eight subjects were pooled and examined. The study revealed systematic differences in the distribution of marks in different subjects. Such patterns reflect deep-rooted marking traditions that transcend institutional cultures or regulatory regimes and which ultimately give rise to the well-known variations in degree classifications in each subject (Chapman 1994; HEQC 1996d).

A complementary study compared the effects on student outcomes of different institutional algorithms used to classify honours degrees (Woolf and Turner 1997). The study revealed the complex interrelationship between modular structures, the rules for aggregating and discounting marks and the treatment of borderline candidates (students whose performance was just below the accepted boundary for a particular classification but who are considered for the higher classification on the basis of their overall performance). Using a 'what if' approach, SACWG demonstrated that a hypothetical set of module results would generate similar overall outcomes (degree classification profiles) in five institutions but that the overall results tended to be higher in one institution and lower in another compared to the group of five. The study concluded that 15 per cent of students would receive a different classification if they were subjected to another institution's assessment algorithm.

A third benchmarking study (Yorke *et al.* 1998) focused on outcome standards in three subject groups: history (four institutions), computer studies (two institutions) and business studies (five institutions). Each subject group was facilitated by a SACWG coordinator but the groups determined their own strategy and focus. The study confirmed the complexity and difficulty of creating the information bases that would permit judgements to be made on the comparability of outcome standards and demonstrated the inadequacy of current information systems to support this type of standards-focused enquiry. It also raised questions about the differential demand on learners of different assessment methods and strategies used in broadly comparable study units at the same stage in a programme.

Benchmarking credit and assessment regulations

The Northern Universities Consortium for Credit Accumulation and Transfer (NUCCAT) is one of five regional consortia in the UK. Its membership is drawn mainly from registrars, heads of academic development or heads of modular schemes in 35 universities and it acts as an important forum for debate on all matters relating to modularization, credit-based learning and the regulation of assessment. In 1997 the consortium undertook a major benchmarking exercise to examine systematically the way in which credit was being used in member institutions (Margham 1998; NUCCAT 1998). The NUCCAT survey provided information on the range and norms of practice in respect of:

- *the academic year* (length of the undergraduate and postgraduate year; timing of semesters or terms; number of notional learning hours at undergraduate and postgraduate levels)
- *rules for using credit* (number of credits required for an award; size of undergraduate and postgraduate modules; number of credit levels)
- *the regulation of assessment* (extent to which institution-wide regulations are developed at undergraduate and postgraduate levels; contribution to honours classification of marks at different levels; module pass mark; rules for compensation or condonement of failure; progression with module failure; rights to reassessment; extent to which failed modules can be substituted; structure of assessment boards; and deployment of external examiners).

The main lesson to emerge through the benchmarking survey was the sheer diversity 'in fundamental approaches, regulations and credit conceptions between the 29 universities who contributed to the study' (NUCCAT 1998: 57). The results of the survey provide an important resource for institutions within and outside the consortium and the knowledge and understanding gained through the exercise was disseminated nationally via a major conference. The results and methodology are now being used by the Quality Assurance Agency to help develop a national framework for credit and qualifications: a good illustration of how benchmarking for self-improvement can also improve the capacity of a system to regulate itself.

Benchmarking using performance criteria and scoring systems

There are a number of ways in which this type of referencing process is being applied. The first approach is to incorporate criteria and scoring devices into survey instruments in order to demonstrate the extent to which certain 'ideal' conditions or performance are achieved. The application of this approach to evaluating the quality of HE management is described in Chapter 16 but it has yet to be applied to academic management. However, as academic management becomes more systematized (Chapter 5) it becomes possible to apply criterion referencing within a benchmarking strategy. The second application of criterion referencing in the benchmarking of education is to provide a consistent basis for the measurement and comparison of 'subject-specific' or 'generic key skill' standards. At present there are relatively few examples of these applications (see Chapters 7 and 8) but this is likely to become an important feature of regulatory benchmarking.

Benchmarking through standardized testing

There is growing interest in the idea of using standardized testing as a means of benchmarking the standards of literacy and numeracy in HE (and possibly generic discipline-based outcomes in subjects like engineering). In North America such tests are used extensively in the field of 'general education' and for entry to post-graduate education. Nene University College is evaluating the potential for adapting a North American standard assessment test for literacy (M. Daniel, personal communication). The testing agency provides a test score for individual students; statistics on test scores by programme; statistics on test scores by institution; and statistics on test scores across all institutions. The tests (and scores) offer the potential to compare the educational effectiveness of an individual programme or institution with that of others. In North America the availability of such data has also resulted in the sharing of information between comparable institutions to facilitate inter-institutional benchmarking at programme level. The tests are also used by some institutions to show the value they are adding between test scores at entry and test scores on completion of a programme. Again this provides comparative information that can be used to benchmark institutional (or programme) effectiveness.

Benchmarking using performance measures

This approach is focused more on the inputs and performance end of the educational continuum than on the process of education.

Benchmarking departmental performance

Departmental review is an established process in many UK universities. The University of Southampton was one of the first institutions to develop this type of review and incorporate benchmarking into the self-evaluation process. The process involved the preparation of a Departmental Profile and Critical Self-Evaluation (Gregory 1991; Anon 1992). The profiles seek to compare departmental performance directly with identical cost centres in peer institutions. Typically a department would discuss its position, compared to similar departments in five peer institutions. The analysis would be based on indicators such as full-time equivalent (FTE) staff; total student load; postgraduate research students; ratio of student load to FTE teaching staff; expenditure per FTE academic; expenditure on support staff per FTE academic; expenditure on equipment per FTE academic; research ratings; research income; PhD submission rates; and publication rates.

Benchmarking degree performance

The UK honours degree is divided into four classes (first, upper second, lower second and third). Degree performance data can be used as an aid to benchmarking the outcome standards of different subjects and departments (Chapman 1994; HEQC 1996d; Chapter 6, this volume). Chapman (HEQC 1996d) studied the pattern of degree results between 1973 and 1993 in eight subjects (civil engineering, French, physics, history, biology, accountancy, politics and mathematics). Some subjects have more compact distributions of degree classifications than others, e.g. social sciences, languages and humanities relative to the physical and mathematical sciences which have a higher proportion of firsts and thirds. But there are significant changes in the pattern of awards through time with all subjects (except for civil engineering) showing a progressive increase in the proportions of 1/2i at the expense of 2ii/3. The study demonstrates how this type of information can be used to:

- develop national profiles of degree results for each subject
- produce anonymous profiles showing departmental performance in degree results through time compared to national averages
- provide an indication of the educational value added by a programme by comparing the input standard (expressed as GCE A level point Z-scores) and the output standard (expressed in terms of the first and upper second class degree Z-scores).

The same types of variations in assessment outcomes were noted by Margham and Jackson (1999) in a study of module assessment data in science, technology and humanities subjects in a single university. The internal benchmarking exercise raised questions relating to variations in the use of norm versus criterion referencing and highlighted issues of equity of outcome when students combined subjects from different subject fields in a single programme.

Coda

The examples cited above are intended to provide a flavour of the way benchmarking can be used to understand and improve the quality of education, the standards of learning and the quality of academic practice and performance. The chapters that follow develop these themes further through case studies and more detailed analysis.

4

Benchmarking the Learning Environment

Rikki Morgan

Overview

This chapter describes how a university used benchmarking to understand and learn from the modular policies and practices in 11 other HE institutions. The benchmarking survey underpinned a strategic move towards restructuring the undergraduate curriculum and the development of a new, more flexible learning environment. The products of the exercise provided a valuable resource for working parties to use during the planning and development stage of this innovative approach to learning. It illustrates how an institution might use benchmarking to achieve its own strategic objectives.

Introduction

Modularization of the curriculum was introduced at Thames Valley University (TVU) in 1992. In broad terms, the TVU Modular Scheme required the unitization and semesterization of existing courses and the accommodation of their specific regulations to the general scheme regulations. Pre-existing programmes remained largely intact except for the compulsory introduction of an element of free choice (two elective modules at Stage 1 and one elective after Stage 1). While this structure represented the minimum possible disruption to courses converting to modularization it introduced a series of tensions relating to issues such as the ownership of modules and student expectations of choice. There was also tension between the learning intentions of programmes of study leading to an award and modules, which might be contributing to a range of awards as well as being available across the university as electives. Such tensions associated with the introduction of modularization are well documented (HEQC 1994; HEQC 1996f; HEQC 1997c, 1997d).

It became increasingly apparent that difficulties in operating the modular scheme were symptoms of more fundamental structural issues inscribed within the design of the scheme itself. Student feedback had shown that the scheme could not deliver the range of choice it appeared to offer – mainly due to the inevitable constraints of timetabling and financial imperatives that required a minimum number of registrations to make a module economically viable. The *Review of Module Registration 1994/95* (by Indepen Consultants) identified a range of problems associated with operating university-wide module choice, registration and timetabling, as well as identifying a lack of ownership of the scheme within the university at large. At the heart of this were a series of tensions at a structural and management level between schools and the centre, and at an academic level between programmes of study and modules/subjects. Fundamentally the review highlighted the need for 'clarification of the context, concept and policies relating to TVU Modular Scheme(s)'. In short, it asked, 'What kind of scheme(s) do we want at TVU?' (Indepen Consultants 1995: 18).

This fundamental challenge was addressed in the Vice-Chancellor's paper, 'Towards a new learning environment: developing the educational strategy of TVU', which focused, *inter alia*, on the need for provision for lifelong learning, increased participation and flexibility, and the erosion of the distinction between part-time and full-time study (Fitzgerald 1995). The university had already initiated a series of fundamental debates to enable TVU to formulate its educational strategy for what became known as the 'new learning environment' or 'NLE'. The benchmarking exercise was intended to inform and extend these debates and to provide practical advice and example material that could be drawn upon by the various working groups charged with the development of the new curriculum framework and its implementation.

Benchmarking study

The benchmarking study involved a survey and analysis of the modular schemes at 11 HE institutions identified by TVU as having features that were of particular interest to the development of its own curriculum framework. The benchmarking exercise was designed to encompass matters of policy, structure, operation and administration and its focal points reflected the key points of tension and structural and operational detail which had already been identified as problematic at TVU (Table 4.1). In planning the survey four main lines of enquiry were identified. The first consideration was the size, type and educational missions of institutions, the different conceptual and operational contexts, and the philosophies and principles on which modular schemes were based. The second focal point for study was the structural and organizational factors of schemes including such matters as the size and number of modules, levels, credits, etc. and the nature of the programmes and awards offered. The third line of enquiry related to the mechanisms for planning, management, development, infrastructure and key operational processes and practices. Finally, the survey

Table 4.1 Summary of the main design features of the benchmarking survey of modular schemes in 11 HE institutions shown in relation to the particular issues

Starting points and issues for TVU	*Specific focal points for study*
Conceptual context TVU mission New learning environment Philosophy and structure	Institutional mission Guiding principles underpinning modular scheme Operational context (size, historical factors, etc.)
Modular scheme structure	**Organization of scheme** Modules; levels; credits **Programmes** Awards; combinations; choice **Planning** Development and introduction of modular scheme Annual planning cycle
Management structures	**Monitoring and development** Management structure Relationship between centre and schools/ departments Controlling devices **Academic and quality management** Academic management structure Quality assurance processes
Operational issues	**Operational management and processes** Responsibilities; registration process; timetabling Infrastructure Information Systems; communications
Teaching, learning and assessment in the new learning environment	**Delivery of curriculum** Delivery patterns Approaches to learning and teaching Assessment patterns and processes

explored a number of areas relating to teaching, learning and assessment within a modular framework. The specific focal points relating to each of TVU's main areas of interest and concern are summarized in Table 4.1. A set of target information was identified within each of these areas and this was expanded and refined in the course of carrying out the research. These focal points and their associated target information provided a framework for the research process and the analysis and evaluation of information.

Eleven HE institutions (Table 4.2) were identified and contacted to see if they would be willing to participate in the benchmarking exercise. All the institutions were of interest from the point of view of examining the structure of their modular schemes, programme packages and the interface with operational systems and practices. But some institutions were targeted because of specific features of their schemes that were of interest to TVU's development plans. In selecting partner institutions a variety of criteria were used which reflected their potential interest to TVU, e.g.:

- similar structure or contrasting structures
- long-term operation
- range of subjects
- progression structures and requirements
- academic, administrative, IT and curricular support structures.

In each case the partner institution provided documents about its scheme and participated in discussions. These discussions normally involved the scheme director but in some cases other staff with particular responsibilities within the scheme were involved and students on the scheme were consulted. The key research questions that were used as the basis for discussion were:

- What are the principles that underlie the modular scheme?
- How is it structured and organized?
- How is the scheme managed academically and operationally?
- How is the curriculum delivered and assessed?

Research findings

The detailed findings of the benchmarking survey were presented in a report for the university (TVU 1996). Some of the main structural, organizational and management features of the 11 institutional schemes are summarized in Table 4.2. Features of particular interest to TVU were presented in terms of the relative advantages and potential disadvantages of the different structures, processes and procedures observed at the institutions visited. Some of these are described below to give a flavour of the insights gained through the study and the way in which the information was used.

Academic year structure

The issue for TVU was what the most appropriate structure would be to support the new learning environment. All but two institutions were semesterized but the length and positioning of the semesters had a number of permutations. Semester length ranged from 15 to 16 weeks, with a preference being for 15 weeks. In one institution, the academic year was organized around three terms. However, each term was treated as a separate entity and full-time students normally took, completed and were assessed on three modules in each term. Full assessment boards took place at the end of each

Table 4.2 Partner institutions in the benchmarking survey and examples of information that was gathered

Institution and date scheme introduced	Number of students on scheme	Teaching pattern Semesters or terms	Number of UG levels	Number of modules in full-time year	Types of module	Module credit values	Credits per year of FT study
Bath CHE *Sept 1994*	800 (95/96) rising to 3000 (98/99)	2 × 15-week sem (13 teaching + 2 assessment)	2	6 (3 per sem)	Compulsory Optional Elective	20	120
Cheltenham and Gloucester CHE *Sept 1990*	4500	2 × 15-week sem	3	10 (5 per sem)	Core options Level 1 'workshop' modules	1	10
Coventry University *1990*	15,000	Year-long	3 + 'H' for HNC/D	8 year-long	Mandatory core options Free choice	15	120
University of Derby *Oct 1991*	12–1300 UG	2 sem	3	9 (Stg 1) 8 or 9 (Stg 2) 8 (Stg 3)	Core choices Electives	15	120
Liverpool John Moores University *Oct 1990*	15,000	2 sem	3	10	Cores Electives Free electives	3	30
London Guildhall University *Oct 1992*	5700	2 sem	3	8	Cores options Free choice	15	120
University of North London *1988*	7500	2 sem	3	8 (4 per sem)	Core Designated options Non-designated (free choice)	15	120
Oxford Brookes University *1980*	6031	3 terms	2	9 (3 per term) extra 1 in year 1	Compulsory options Free choice	15	120
Sheffield Hallam University	700	2 sem	planned: 3 'cycles'	6 (3 per sem)	Negotiated programme	20	120
Wolverhampton University *Oct 1991*	16,492	2 × 16-week sem	3	8 (4 per sem)	Compulsory options	15	120
Worcester CHE *Oct 1993*	1700	2 sem	2 (but Yr3 work double-weighted)	8 per year	Cores Options Free choice	15	120

term and students were given their results before the start of the next term. The turnaround for this was extremely tight and its apparently successful operation reflected a culture where strict adherence to deadlines is the accepted norm. Students generally applauded the choice the modular scheme afforded, but had reservations about the length of the modules and frequency of assessment.

At the other extreme, students in another institution took eight year-long modules. Assessment boards only occurred at the end of the year; the disadvantage of this model was the lack of opportunity for students to amend their programme of study halfway through the year and the difficulty of offering multiple entry points (an important objective for a flexible curricular environment). The advantage of the year-long model, however, was the reduction of the administrative workload associated with two major sets of assessment board meetings each year and the gentler learning curve for students. After a lengthy consideration of the possibility of a return to the year-long model, TVU finally opted to keep the most widely accepted semester model in the interests of flexibility (including student mobility between institutions and countries) and operational efficiency in a flexible learning environment.

The starting date for the year had also been a matter of concern to TVU. Like a number of other institutions it had experienced the problems associated with a 'limping' week after the Christmas vacation and the difficulty of completing marking and assessment boards in order to make results available to students before Semester 2. A range of patterns operating elsewhere was noted, including the early start adopted by two HEIs to allow for completing both teaching and assessment before Christmas. An advantage of the pre-Christmas finish was that assessment boards had more time to conduct their business and the results from Semester 1 could be readily communicated to students before they embarked on Semester 2. However, it was also apparent that such systems created two major pressure points: August/September and December. The August/September pressure focuses on recruitment and admissions and, significantly, the two institutions that had opted for the early start did not recruit large numbers of students through the clearing system; this was not the case for TVU. In December, the pressure is on students to sit examinations without a revision period. While it might be argued that pre-Christmas examinations enable staff to mark papers during the Christmas break, it was felt that the timescale (taking into account vacation time during this period) was likely to be as tight as in a post-Christmas marking period. As no significant improvement to the status quo was to be achieved by any of the feasible options, TVU maintained the existing arrangement.

Size and credit weighting of modules

Similar discussions of the pros and cons of different approaches to the number and credit weighting of modules, notional study hours and levels (including the specific problems relating to university-wide levels for languages) were also offered in the report. The survey of other HE institutions showed that just over half of the institutions visited curretly operated a structure of eight modules per full-time year. But other models were also apparent among the institutions surveyed including: six modules per full-time year (three 20-credit modules per semester), and ten modules per full-time year, although these differed in their delivery and credit tariffs. Notwithstanding the differences in number of modules, the principle of taking 360 credits for an honours degree (120 for Certificate, 240 for Diploma) is clearly the most widely accepted. As a strategic measure to ensure the financial viability of the institution and its undergraduate operations, TVU adopted the six-module structure where each module would represent 20 study credits. However, this shift was to be accompanied by an educational strategy designed to promote flexible learning, increased participation and the development of independent learners. Teaching contact time would remain constant for the module and the university would make a strategic move towards promotion of active learning skills and materials, supported by directors of study who would be responsible for overseeing the development of independent learning skills in support of the curriculum. In the light of its own and other institutions' experience of the complexity introduced into modular schemes by the existence of differently sized modules, the model adopted by TVU was one of standardization. All modules would be packaged in 20-credit units, the only exception being Level 3 dissertation/project modules which could, where academically appropriate, be double modules (i.e. 40 credits), although few areas of study adopted this option.

Organization of programmes

Another major area of concern for TVU was to address the existing tension between subjects and programmes of study. The survey showed that, with the exception of one institution surveyed, modular schemes were structured around the subject. The meaning of subject ('subject area', 'subject field' or 'field of study') was broad and encompassed a range of interdisciplinary areas and combinations (e.g. health studies, cultural studies, global futures, etc.), as well as more traditional disciplines such as history, biology, etc. Each institution took a slightly different approach to the designation of its subject areas, but a consistent pattern emerged. The organization of programmes by subject field (which may in turn contain a number of different pathways) had a range of implications for the management of quality and standards, administration and other operational issues. Some of the difficulties encountered at TVU (e.g. timetabling and the management of quality and standards) became less complex issues within subject-based schemes. A possible disadvantage to this was the structural barriers that might be created which would inhibit cross-subject curriculum development.

The notion that modularization leads to 'pick and mix' degrees was not borne out by the study. Students tended to be recruited to programmes based in subject areas or 'fields' but could opt for different 'routes' within the field. The identification of building blocks of study within each subject field, however, enabled students to opt for a single-subject/field programme or to combine two (or possibly three) smaller blocks. The level of 'control' and guidance over student choice within subject areas was variable. For example, each subject might designate a set of modules (including cores and options) for each of the routes it offers (single, major, joint minor programme). Target numbers for recruitment were normally set within each of the fields of study and by route.

Pathways

The issue for TVU was how to organize pathways and routes through the scheme. A 'Russian dolls' model was adopted whereby the minor pathway is an integral part of the major. Where there is a specialist or 'full' route, this is an extension of the major: A and B are the two minor modules at each Level; A, B, C and D constitute the major; A, B, C, D, E and F comprise the full pathway. This model facilitates 'upgrading' and 'downgrading' between major and minor pathways as students will have studied modules that are common to both, as well as bringing about economies of scale. The disadvantage of the structure is a perceived rigidity, particularly in the case of Level 1 foundation pathways.

Foundation courses

The isssue for TVU was whether to provide a small number of Level 1 foundation programmes that prepared learners for study within specified pathways at Level 2. Very few institutions in the survey were offering any form of core course at entry level that served a range of higher level academic routes. One exception was a modular scheme that was organized on a faculty basis. In this case an applied social science scheme had a common 'preliminary level' programme for all students enrolled on programmes within the faculty. The four foundation modules in Semester 1 focused on transferable skills applicable to the subject areas they served. Another of the universities surveyed was considering, and subsequently moved to, a similar 'Cycle 1' structure within which a limited number of foundation modules provided the basis for students to progress to a range of pathways across the university at Level 2. Another university had considered and experimented with the idea from time to time, but their experience was that foundation modules serving a number of pathways did not provide an adequate basis for progression to the next level. Another institution had introduced a policy whereby all Level 1 students took two 'study and transferable Workshop' modules but other modules were taken from the subject.

TVU decided to adopt a flexible approach to this matter and the pattern of Level 1 studies introduced in 1996–97 was variable. In some areas each Level 2/3 pathway had its own Level 1 feeder pathway (e.g. languages, digital arts). In other areas a common Level 1 foundation programme of study was developed to prepare students for a range of Level 2/3 pathways (e.g. social sciences common Level 1 pathway provides the foundation for sociology, history and economics as well as for the interdisciplinary Level 2/3 social sciences pathway; the newly-developed creative and cultural studies Level 1 foundation is designed to serve English, American studies, cultural studies, creative writing and journalism).

Student choice

The issue for TVU was how much choice should be designed into the scheme. Choice within subject areas tended to vary from institution to institution – some being more rigidly structured in terms of core and pre-requisite modules than others. For example, one institution had few core modules in most areas and students were able to gain access to the next level of study from a range of different modules. Many institutions had reduced the amount of choice at Level 1 – often permitting no choice in the first semester for both educational and administrative reasons. Many schemes offered a Level 1 structure that permitted students to take two or three subjects, thus keeping their options open for Levels 2 and 3. The general principles that underpinned all the schemes studied was that options should be kept open at Level 1 and that there should be greater choice within the subject areas in the later stages of a programme. As far as free choice electives are concerned, all the schemes offered the possibility of selecting some 'free-floating' modules (i.e. not part of a subject package), but their experience seemed to be that students more frequently opted for a 'minor' package rather than for randomly selected modules.

TVU finally opted for a small number of specialist programmes of study (known as pathways), mainly in vocational and professional subjects such as psychology and law and subjects that are by their very nature already inter- or multidisciplinary, such as business studies. The bulk of the undergraduate curriculum was to comprise a series of major and minor pathway building blocks of uniform size. Pathway combinations would only be possible in major/minor pairs where the major is four modules per full-time year and the minor two. The apparent (though often inoperable) choice of the previous scheme was reduced within the pathways, with alternative module choices only available at Level 3 and elective modules eliminated.

Timetabling

Timetabling had been identified as one of TVU's most persistent and fundamental operational difficulties, exacerbated by limited availability of accommodation. The modular scheme brought this problem into particularly sharp focus because of the need to publish a university-wide timetable. Although at one point a blocked timetable was planned for TVU, the difficulty with implementing it lay in the fact that it was difficult to know which clashes had to be avoided: for many areas, modules were being shared by a number of programmes. In most of the institutions visited, the timetabling problem was considerably eased by the fact that their schemes were organized around subject areas/fields of study. Once institutional decisions had been made about which subjects should be designated as viable combinations, all subjects could be grouped according to the timetable clashes that needed to be avoided. The use of a blocked or slotted timetable then permitted cores to be entered into clash-free zones and options positioned for optimum viability for students taking likely combinations. A variety of IT packages were in use for timetabling purposes at the institutions surveyed, and a number of these were integrated with student record systems/modular scheme management packages. Some were able to group students within modules (i.e. allocate them to seminars, practical classes, etc.). The insights gained helped TVU develop its own specification for the IT timetabling package: it opted for the purchase of a timetabling system for both the construction of the university timetable and the production of individual student timetables.

Module registration

Another key operational issue for TVU had been the process by which students registered their module options and accessed advice on which to base their choices. At most of the institutions visited, module registration was largely a matter of pre-registration by completing and handing in a form. This was relatively straightforward for continuing students and done by post as far as possible with new students. Given the large percentage of students recruited to TVU via clearing, pre-registration by post would be unsuitable for many programmes. Each case study institution had arrangements for handling registration for late recruitment on site (particularly where large numbers are expected through clearing). This typically involved intensive activity and advice sessions from directors of study and paper-based registration systems that were subsequently recorded on the university's electronic record system. One of the universities studied had recently introduced a system for induction week where students had access to checking and amending their module registrations online (the initial data being entered manually). Although academic staff are on hand to advise students on these amendments, the students' records still need to be checked over the following weeks by programme leaders; the system did perform this task automatically.

The design of the new learning environment modular scheme at TVU and the elimination of choice within pathways at Levels 1 and 2 considerably reduced the need for module registration. This would now be limited to Level 3 modules which continuing students would select (by completing and submitting a form) during the course of the previous academic session. Students would receive details of their pathways in *Pathway Handbooks* and the constituent modules in *Module Study Guides* for each component of the course. The information gathered in the survey provided a useful set of contacts and a starting point for matching the purchase of an electronic timetabling system to TVU's own needs. In particular the 'functional fit analysis' used at one institution was used to help select an appropriate system.

Scheme management

Modularization has often been associated with the more 'purposefully managed' university curriculum demanded by financial imperatives, but often perceived as a threat to the professional autonomy and judgement of academics (Watson 1989). Finding the appropriate balance between centralization, ownership and participation has clearly been an issue for many of the institutions consulted in this study and was also highlighted as a matter to be addressed at TVU. Such tensions appeared to be relatively minimal in scheme structures that demand an extremely high level of institutional self-discipline in order to adhere to the academic year cycle of termly assessment boards and other administrative deadlines and where there are strictly observed procedures for amendments to the scheme itself. A number of the studied schemes were initially quite centralized, or at least were perceived as such, and have subsequently adjusted management structures and roles to arrive at a more acceptable and productive model of central coordination and a wider sense of ownership. The recent experiences of two universities demonstrated that getting the balance right is not an easy matter. Like TVU, both institutions were in the process of reviewing the structure and operation of their respective modular schemes. In both cases, the outcome was likely to be a shift towards greater participation by schools/departments in the decision-making processes and wider consultation, alongside a strong administrative infrastructure.

Following the benchmarking survey, a further analysis of the strengths and weaknesses of the modular management structures at TVU was undertaken in the light of the case study material and the new insights gained. It seemed significant that in all of the case study institutions that had experienced serious problems with modularization, a relatively weak university-wide modular management structure had been superimposed over a historically strong set of vertical school-based structures. While the centre was unable to ensure adherence to university-wide regulations and procedures, the independent vertical management structures were neither configured nor resourced to fulfil the necessary university-wide functions on which a modularized curriculum depends. More successful modular structures tended to be characterized by a strong, central regulatory authority that ensured adherence to standard structures and procedures across the institution. Academic management emphasized the importance of subjects, rather than programmes, and was well connected to consultative and decision-making processes in the modular scheme.

TVU's restructuring for the new learning environment introduced a matrix structure comprising schools with academic responsibility and accountability for the quality and development of subject areas, and three university-wide colleges at undergraduate, postgraduate and further and continuing education levels. In addition to the regulatory function typically associated with modular scheme centres, the colleges have also been charged with a strategic planning role in relation to the development of the curriculum. In consultation with the schools, the College of Undergraduate Studies, through its Board of Undergraduate Studies (including membership from all the academic schools) will steer the shaping and development of the undergraduate curriculum at a university-wide level.

Conclusions

The main aim of the benchmarking survey was developmental: to help the university achieve its strategic objectives. The process of benchmarking was not simply a matter of identifying best practice. Rather it was a matter of looking systematically at, and learning from, the practices and experiences in other universities and colleges of HE and evaluating their feasibility for the TVU context. Many of the areas explored in the initial survey required further research and development work to provide the level of detail needed to create new structures and processes for TVU. One of the most valuable outcomes of the benchmarking survey was the fact that it placed the operational difficulties faced by TVU in perspective, increasing the visibility of the shared nature of challenges posed by the changing face of higher education.

5

Benchmarking to Improve Departmental Systems for Managing Quality and Standards

James Tannock and Norman Jackson

Overview

This chapter describes how six university engineering departments (see Acknowledgements, p. 66) used benchmarking to improve their capacity for managing the quality and standards of the education they provide. Two different benchmarking methods were used as part of a strategic change process. The first involved creating a specification based on codifying good practice in the academic management and administration of taught programmes. Each department evaluated and compared its own practice against the expectations contained in the specification and made the necessary changes to meet the good practice benchmarks. The second approach used benchmarking to research how departments assess learning. The case study demonstrates the value of benchmarking as an aid to departmental learning and development while improving departmental capacities for self-regulation.

Introduction

The Engineering Professors' Council (EPC) has been responsible for leading a number of projects within the HE engineering community directed towards improving quality assurance and quality management in engineering education (Burge and Tannock 1992; Tannock and Burge 1994). The project described in this article sought to develop and implement a specification for a quality management system in six engineering departments. The project had the support and financial backing of the four major professional engineering institutions and national quality assurance agencies (see Acknowledgements). Information on the background to this work, project methodology and evaluation report are given by Burge *et al.* (1996), Jackson *et al.* (1996), Jackson *et al.* (1997) and EPC (1998 [online] available

Figure 5.1 Summary of the process of creating and implementing the EPC specification

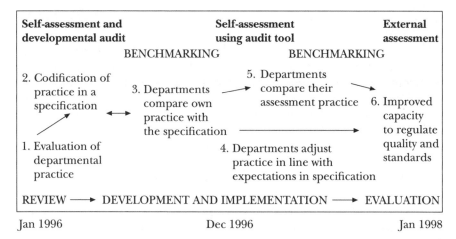

Self-assessment and developmental audit	Self-assessment using audit tool	External assessment
BENCHMARKING	BENCHMARKING	

2. Codification of practice in a specification

3. Departments compare own practice with the specification

5. Departments compare their assessment practice

6. Improved capacity to regulate quality and standards

1. Evaluation of departmental practice

4. Departments adjust practice in line with expectations in specification

REVIEW ⟶ DEVELOPMENT AND IMPLEMENTATION ⟶ EVALUATION

Jan 1996 Dec 1996 Jan 1998

Note: The diagram shows that benchmarking was part of an integrated strategy involving a number of review, developmental and evaluation activities.

at http://www.nottingham.ac.uk/meom/epc). Although not conceived as a benchmarking exercise the development process involved applying two different benchmarking methods within an integrated review, evaluation and improvement-led strategy (Figure 5.1).

Developmental review and self-assessment

The development process for each department began with a comprehensive review of the existing arrangements for managing educational provision and related activities using a questionnaire prepared by the project facilitators (two university-based, one a member of the Higher Education Quality Council's Quality Enhancement Group). This was linked to a visit to each department by two of the project facilitators who systematically worked through the self-assessment with members of the department to construct an overview of current practice. The developmental review therefore contained four elements:

- departmental self-evaluation of current arrangements using a standard survey instrument
- collection of sample documents to illustrate how such arrangements worked in practice
- discussions involving departmental and institutional staff and two project facilitators
- feedback reports for each department and a summary report that provided an overview of current arrangements and highlighted noteworthy practices.

The developmental review laid the foundation for benchmarking because it:

- established a collaborative working relationship between participants and facilitators
- introduced the idea of systematic self-appraisal guided by survey instruments
- encouraged departments to be open and to share their practices with each other
- created a format for reporting that enabled departments to compare practices in a systematic way.

Codification of practice through specification

A quality management framework is the means by which a department satisfies itself that the quality of the education it provides is being maintained and improved, and appropriate academic standards are being achieved. Frameworks for the management of quality and standards in UK HE must also be designed to meet the expectations and requirements of external subject-based quality assessment, external and internal audits of practice, processes and performance and, where appropriate, accreditation by professional bodies. The specification that was created through this project (Burge *et al.* 1996) sets out a comprehensive standard of recommended practice covering the way a department manages the education it provides. It does so without adopting a prescriptive position on academic matters relating to curriculum design, teaching, learning or assessment, but instead focuses on the quality management and improvement processes which promote both academic excellence and educational effectiveness. The creation of a specification (based on Tannock and Burge 1994) was an iterative process undertaken by the project facilitators in collaboration with the representatives of each department. The development process took account of the growing body of literature and guidance on quality assurance produced by national agencies (e.g. HEQC 1995c, 1996c; HEFCE 1996a), and the expectations of accreditation processes of the engineering institutions. The specification also sought to address issues emerging from a national debate on academic standards (HEQC 1997a).

The specification identifies the elements of a departmental system for managing education in terms of:

- its policies and objectives
- how it is organized for managing quality
- its quality assurance system and documentation
- the means by which it seeks improvements
- the way it relates to the rest of the university and external constituencies
- how it assures its academic standards.

Table 5.1 Areas of academic management included in the EPC specification

1. Design of programmes of study
2. Admissions and entry standards
3. Delivery and management of programmes of study
4. Student guidance and support
5. Service support of programmes of study
6. Staff–student communication
7. Problem reporting and corrective action
8. Assessment and academic standards
9. Research supervision
10. Review of quality and standards
    (a) Review of programme elements
    (b) Review of programmes of study
11. Collaborative arrangements
12. Staffing
    (a) Recruitment, induction and probation
    (b) Staff appraisal and development
13. Control of the quality management framework
    (a) Document control
    (b) Records and evidence
    (c) Review of the quality management framework

Each element of the specification attempts to create a 'good practice' benchmark (derived from the expectations contained in external review processes, professional body accreditation requirements and acknowledged good practices within the collaborating departments) against which departments might judge their own processes and performance.

The specification codifies good practice in all significant academic management activities (Table 5.1). A concise set of expectations is presented for the practices, procedures and activities required to support quality, professionalism and appropriate academic standards. The educational process can be visualized as a cycle of activities the most important stages of which are planning, curriculum design, delivery, student assessment and the regulation of standards. This cycle of activities lies at the heart of the quality management framework. It is supported by review processes in which self-critical evaluation leads to improvement-led or developmental activities.

The maintenance of records which demonstrate the effectiveness of systems to plan, control and validate the design and review of programmes of study, staff development, admissions policy, etc. is emphasized in all relevant sections of the specification. An example of the type of expectations that are embedded in the specification is given below.

Assesment and academic standards (Section 3.10 of the specification)
It is expected that a department will establish, maintain and document its policies and practices to ensure the equity and integrity of the assessment process, considering:

(a) The alignment of assessment purpose, range, balance and work-load to the overall learning objectives of programmes and programme elements.
(b) The validity and reliability of assessment and the impartiality, accuracy and consistency of marking standards. This process should take account of the views and comments of external examiners, where appropriate, on examination papers, marking schemes and coursework assessments.
(c) Progression of students through each programme of study, taking account of all relevant university regulations and the requirements of professional and statutory bodies where applicable.

A key focus of departmental assessment systems should be the application of appropriate academic standards in modules and awards. This will require:

(a) The documentation of staff and external examiner roles and responsibilities, and of committee terms of reference relating to standards, and the discharge of such responsibilities effectively.
(b) Explicit assessment and marking criteria at module/unit level as a basis for judgements about standards (e.g. examination marking schemes and documented benchmarks/exemplars for student achievement levels in coursework essays or projects).
(c) Consistency in the operation of examination boards and the application of assessment regulations to ensure that overall standards in the award are maintained.

It is expected that opportunities will be provided for internal and external examiners to review and evaluate the assessment process and share their perspectives on academic standards. Documented procedures should be in place concerning external examiner selection and appointment (including guidance, induction and training) duties and reporting requirements. Procedures for considering and responding to external examiners' comments and recommendations should be defined and incorporated into the annual review process.

Using the specification to benchmark practice

The developmental review was used to formulate departmental action plans aimed at:

• demonstrating that departmental approaches to the management of quality and standards met or exceeded the expectations in the specification
• identifying the ways in which a department's approaches to managing quality and standards would be changed or new measures introduced in order to align better with the specification.

The action plans also indicated where advice would be sought from project facilitators, the resources that would be committed to supporting the plan and the timescale for implementation. While it was necessary for the facilitators to provide guidance on the ways in which systems and practice might be developed, care was exercised to ensure that each department developed systems that suited its particular needs and circumstances. The dialogue between departments and facilitators and between key staff in each department continued throughout the development process. Periodically, departmental representatives met as a group to share their experience. A mid-project review was also held to check progress, aid the development of each department's capacity for self-audit, identify development issues and the reactions and responses of departmental staff to implementation of the system. The evaluation exercise was conducted as a departmental self-audit against a comprehensive 94-item checklist (Tannock *et al.* 1999) which encouraged departments to evaluate the extent to which they felt they met the expectations (fully, partially and yet to be developed) contained in the EPC specification. This was the most systematic benchmarking exercise conducted against the final specification. At this stage no independent evaluation of departmental self-appraisals was undertaken but the information was used as the basis for the end-of-project evaluation.

Benchmarking assessment practice

The motivation, commitment and ownership of the project by departmental participants and their willingness to exchange information and share their experiences provided the stimulus for a proposal to conduct a benchmarking exercise. Five of the six departments that participated in the main project agreed to participate in the exercise. In addition, the home departments of the two university-based facilitators also participated in the exercise. Given the emerging national focus on academic standards in HE (HEQC 1997a), it was agreed that the exercise would concentrate on student assessment and its link to academic standards. It was hoped that the process would illuminate the ways in which the relevant expectations in the EPC specification were addressed by departments. It was also recognized that the experience gained through the benchmarking exercise would help refine the advice given in the specification on the assessment of learning and the construction, application and review of academic standards.

A detailed description of the benchmarking process is given by Jackson (1998c). An initial meeting of departmental representatives led to the identification of a number of primary research questions of the type:

- What are we assessing (knowledge/skills/capability/attitudes)?
- Why are we assessing (formative/summative/other)?
- How are we assessing (exam/coursework; types of assessment instrument/ questions)?

- How do we measure the level of attainment (marking and grading criteria)?
- How valid and reliable is the process?

Using these questions as a guide a survey instrument was constructed which focused on:

- guidance on assessment and the preparation and development of staff
- relationship between educational expectations–objectives and the assessment process
- assessment methods
- the means by which the validity, reliability and rigour of assessment was ensured
- workloads and costs.

Participants prepared their responses on an electronic template and these were compiled into a feedback report and used as a basis for discussion at a second meeting. The information provided was treated as confidential to the forum and the standard protocol of using letter codes to identify departmental responses was adopted. Having completed a baseline survey a more detailed survey of a specific aspect of the assessment process was undertaken. The final level (year) individual student project was chosen as the target for this enquiry. A second survey instrument was prepared and revised after consultation with the group. This questionnaire was designed to gather information on, and evaluate the relationship between:

- the educational objectives or learning outcomes of the honours project to the overall objectives or outcomes for the programme
- the educational objectives and learning outcomes for the honours project and the marking/grading schemes and criteria used to measure performance
- the means by which departments share understanding of standards in project work
- the marking and moderation practices to ensure that project assessment is accurate, valid and reliable
- the relationship between performance in the project and the overall performance in the BEng award.

The second questionnaire was completed by four participants and the data summarized in a feedback report which provided a starting point for discussion at a third meeting.

Example responses

Many of the questions in the survey instruments could appear deceptively simple to answer. Frequently a question could be answered at many different levels and an important feature of benchmarking is the attempt to penetrate these levels to expose and share underlying meanings, assumptions and interpretations. An example of a typical response is given below.

'*In your judgement, what is the general level of knowledge and expertise of staff about assessment in your department?*' Respondents were encouraged to make an honest self-critical appraisal of the general level of professional expertise in assessment within the department's teaching staff. The responses indicated that the level of expertise in assessment-related matters among staff was generally adequate to good, e.g.:

'Knowledge within the department varies, but it is nowhere inadequate.'
'Almost without exception, the performance of the staff in assessment tasks is wholly satisfactory.'
'The general level (of knowledge) is very good. In many cases there is a common approach to assessment, but staff are encouraged to be pro-active in experimenting with new methods and discussing the results with colleagues.'

But these general endorsements of professional skill and behaviour must be tempered by comments such as:

'Staff are very good at traditional formal methods of assessment and major individual projects. However, they may be considered only adequate at continuously assessed work where collusion can spoil the value of formative feedback.'
'Staff generally have a limited view of assessment possibilities, based on their past experience going back to the assessment they themselves were subjected to as students. The result is generally adequate but dull and traditional, with scope for improvement in a number of modules.'
'Staff in general are more interested in their teaching materials and methods than in assessment.'
'A major theme in deciding on the type of assessment to be used is the amount of marking time involved. Staff will tend to resist more student-centred formative assessment methods when these involve greater marking time.'
'Assessment practice is highly variable with considerable scope for development.'

Research findings

The process of identifying key research questions and designing a questionnaire to gather appropriate information was instructive in illuminating the complexity of the assessment process. All participants recognized an assessment process model with the following features:

1. High-level expectations (e.g. overall programme educational aims).
2. Module or unit learning objectives broadly related to the high-level expectations.
3. Assessment methods and marking schemes that tested achievement of the learning objectives.
4. Processes and procedures to moderate and confirm judgements on outcomes.

It was recognized that assessment is not a science and that the academic standards emerging through the process were both personal and social constructs. These are developed within a particular learning context and were informed to a substantial extent by external perspectives from peers working in academia and professional practice, mediated by external examining processes and the accreditation processes of the professional engineering institutions. There was considerable commonality in engineering assessment practice, even between sub-disciplines (for example civil and mechanical engineering) because the Engineering Council has in recent years operated to coordinate the assessment standards set by the various engineering institutions for accredited courses. It was also apparent that many of the individuals participating in the exercise already had considerable detailed experience of assessment in departments other than their own, gained mostly through external examining.

While there were well-developed and understood systems to ensure that the assessment process was valid, reliable and rigorous, methodologies for systematically linking formal programme aims with the educational and personal qualities, skills and attributes the programme is intended to develop were not well developed. In addition, the translation of programme aims into practical module/unit learning objectives was typically a matter of professional skill and judgement and individual staff had considerable autonomy in this process. Much reliance is placed on the expertise and professionalism of staff individually and collectively (including external examiners) to ensure that these vital relationships are sustained.

It was also found that there was relatively little in the way of formal and systematic evaluation to ensure that the overall assessment process actually tested the achievement of the educational objectives of the programme. Interestingly, no participating department highlighted the importance of programme validation and approval processes in evaluating this relationship (revealing that the detailed design of assessment is not part of the curriculum design process). Departments indicated that although there were no formal and consistent processes for considering this important area, in reality effective checks and balances exist through module review, student feedback, boards of examiners (including external examiners), departmental management boards, boards of studies and from the relevant engineering institution via accreditation processes.

A surprising discovery was that assessment (apart from regulations) did not appear to figure prominently in the university or departmental teaching and learning policies. A recurrent theme in discussions was the appropriate balance and relationship between the different purposes of assessment. These were felt to be encouraging and promoting learning; providing evidence of learning; and ranking students according to their abilities. Although formal statements on the purposes of assessment were rare, there was convergence of views among the participating departments which amounted to an implicit set of principles captured in one response: 'Assessment is primarily to assess learning, secondarily to assist learning.'

An overarching theme was the relationship and balance between formal regulatory mechanisms and trust in the professionalism of staff. It was acknowledged that assessment practice should be guided by departmental and university frameworks and guidelines, but opportunities also need to be provided to prepare academic staff for assessment and to enable them to share and calibrate their perspectives and judgements. The benchmarking information suggested that skills in assessing learning were developed implicitly through engagement with peers in the assessment process, rather than through a systematic and deliberate process of preparation and development within the department or university. Only three departments required new staff to participate in formal teaching development programmes, while three used a 'mentoring' system. One department deliberately paired new staff with more experienced colleagues within the assessment process. This is one area where a more deliberate approach within departments might bring benefits.

Benchmarking 'graduateness'

An attempt was made to identify the key qualities, skills and attributes developed through BEng degree programmes using the Graduate Attributes Profiling tool (adapted from HEQC 1997a). The version of the GAP tool that was used (Jackson 1998c) contained 38 attributes (educational outcomes) in five categories (subject mastery, intellectual skills, subject practical skills, self-individual skills and qualities and social qualities and skills). Every component of the attributes matrix (except for spatial awareness and ethical practice) was awarded points by at least six of the seven respondents suggesting that virtually all the attributes listed are considered to be desirable in the make-up of a graduate engineer. An indication of the relative importance given by participants to different parts of the attributes matrix can be gained from the average scores for each section of the template. In order of importance these were:

Intellectual/cognitive skills	29.0
Subject mastery	25.4
Practical skills	16.9
Social/interpersonal skills/qualities	14.9
Self-skills/qualities	14.7

There were significant variations in the values placed on individual GAP attributes by respondents. For example, score ranges of 0 to 6 or 1 to 5 were not uncommon. The highest mean scores, reflecting a consistent view across departments, related to:

Ability to reason critically	6.3
Capacity to analyse	6.0
Knowledge of the subject's conceptual basis	4.7

Ability to conceptualize/apply concepts	4.0
Ability to communicate	4.0
Ability to work as part of a team	3.8
Knowledge of subject methodologies	3.7
Knowledge of contexts in which subject is used	3.7
Ability to synthesize knowledge/information	3.6

Use of the GAP tool in this way illustrates how a simple tool can be developed to facilitate benchmarking. It provides a starting point for teaching teams to consider how the assessment process relates to the development of these essential educational and training goals. The GAP tool also provides a useful device to enable a department to identify and evaluate any mismatches between the individual and collective views of its members on the outcomes of the education they are providing. The exercise described above has now been completed by over 50 engineering departments with similar results (Tim Whiteley, personal communication), suggesting that the approach does have validity within a broad disciplinary field.

Assessment of final year projects

As the single most important assessment item in the typical BEng honours programme, the final year project was the focus for the second stage of the benchmarking exercise. For the student, the final year project is the single most significant and sustained investment of time, intellectual and creative effort, being weighted at 25–38 per cent of the total learning effort for the final year. Considerable staff effort is expended in the supervision, assessment and moderation of projects, and particular care is taken to ensure marks are accurate and reliable. These projects also feature strongly in the judgements of standards made by external examiners, and performance in the project is often used to resolve borderline classification issues. A strong correlation was found between the performance in the project and the overall performance in the award, as reflected in honours classification.

It was found that departments had no systematic formal way of relating the overall educational goals of the programme to the assessment process, or of checking this relationship. Considerable similarities in the skills, qualities and attributes to be promoted by the project were found between departments, but a diverse range of methods were used to demonstrate attainment of project goals and enable staff to evaluate this level of attainment. The traditional project report remained the primary contributor to the overall mark, but this is supplemented by presentation, poster displays, short papers, vivas and oral examinations.

It was concluded that the project provides an important vehicle for developing and maintaining the social construct on which a department bases its academic standards. All the participating departments used double-blind marking as an essential quality control mechanism (which is not often the case for written examinations). In addition, most departments undertake an internal moderation exercise and utilize their external examiners as a further reference point in the setting of standards.

Conclusions

The process of developing and implementing the EPC specification demonstrates the value of benchmarking as an aid to departmental learning and development. Benchmarking was deployed within an integrated strategy involving other development and review activities. Thus the products of developmental review across all the departments helped create the specification which was then used as the basis for benchmarking practice in each department. Similarly, the developmental process of implementing the specification was aided by detailed benchmarking of the chosen area of assessment and the products of this exercise could then be used to refine the specification and provide tools and aids to good professional practice (Tannock *et al.* 1999).

Engagement in the process revealed to participants that qualitative benchmarking is a proper academic process with valuable academic outcomes. The group was able to identify key research questions, construct appropriate research tools, synthesize information and provide it in ways that facilitate comparative analysis. The information generated in this way provided the basis for discussion and enabled a deeper understanding of the relationship between academic practice, processes and context. In engaging in the process participants created the space to reflect on their own departmental assessment practices and enabled them to gain a better appreciation of the range and norms of practice and to consider alternative approaches to common problems.

The process of enquiry forced participants to think in a comprehensive, systematic and holistic way about the nature of the assessment process and its relationship to the construction of academic standards. The systematic and deliberate way in which questions about the assessment process, and its relationship to standards, had to be considered was challenging in its own right. Respondents perceived that the benchmarking process extended their capacity to evaluate themselves critically in a non-threatening way. The main benefit of benchmarking to individuals derives from the process of discourse within a well-informed and motivated group of peers.

Independent evaluation of the whole project (Edwards 1997; EPC 1998) demonstrated unequivocally that the objectives set by the steering group 'to develop and implement a quality management framework' had been realized and benchmarking had played an important role within the overall strategy for achieving these objectives. In the view of the facilitators there is no doubt that benchmarking contributed to improving each department's capacity to manage and regulate the quality of its provision and its academic standards.

Acknowledgements

The EPC project was supported and funded by the Higher Education Quality Council (HEQC), the Higher Education Funding Council for England (HEFCE), the Engineering Council, the Royal Academy of Engineering, and four major UK engineering professional institutions (Electrical Engineers, Mechanical Engineers, Civil Engineers and Chemical Engineers). It involved the University of Cambridge (Engineering Department); Heriot-Watt University (Department of Mechanical and Chemical Engineering); University of Northumbria at Newcastle (Department of Electrical Engineering); University of Portsmouth (Department of Mechanical and Manufacturing Engineering); Queen's University of Belfast (Department of Chemical Engineering); University of Surrey (Department of Civil Engineering); Lancaster University (Department of Engineering); University of Nottingham (Department of Manufacturing Engineering and Operations Management).

6

Benchmarking the Student Experience

Mantz Yorke

Overview

This chapter outlines some of the ways in which the student experience can be benchmarked. Two types of benchmarking are distinguished: 'developmental benchmarking' is characterized by voluntarism, mutual trust, and a primary commitment to self-determined improvement, whereas 'regulatory benchmarking' is primarily motivated by an externally driven desire to ensure that learning experiences in, and outcomes of, higher education conform to specified standards or criteria. Examples of benchmarking are drawn from student satisfaction surveys, assessment outcomes and non-completion rates. League tables of universities are discussed from a benchmarking perspective. It is argued that developmental benchmarking is likely to do more for the enhancement of quality and standards than will regulatory benchmarking.

We have been speaking the prose . . .

Like Monsieur Jourdain in Molière's *Le Bourgeois Gentilhomme,* we in higher education have been speaking the prose of benchmarking for many years without apparently realizing it. Procedures for the validation and approval of programmes have often involved external advisers (and continue to do so) in order that the curriculum under consideration can be judged against expectations held by other institutions. External examiners have for a long time been used to test whether the standards achieved by students are consonant with those from elsewhere. Many institutions use cross-institutional student feedback questionnaires, allowing them the opportunity to make relevant internal comparisons. Until recently it would not have occurred to us to construe such activities in terms of benchmarking, though – with varying degrees of precision – that is what we have been doing.

Activities such as these relate to three of the four categories of benchmarking proposed by Camp (1989):

• benchmarking against internal operations (an example is student feedback data, treated comparatively by department)
• benchmarking against external direct competitors (e.g. programme validation/approval, and use of external examiners) and
• benchmarking against industry functional leaders (having an eye to the quality of provision of, and standards set and achieved by, the leading institutions as far as the particular function is concerned – two examples are institutional access provision and the adoption of problem-based learning in curricula).

The fourth of Camp's categories, benchmarking generic processes that cross different types of organization, is relatively underused in UK HE, though this kind of benchmarking can be expected to increase as higher education comes to terms with the need to be more businesslike in its operations.

The philosophy underlying Camp's (1989) perception of benchmarking is that it is a process that is conducted with the intention of assisting improvement. It is typically a voluntary activity from which all the partners in the exercise intend to derive benefit. It also requires mutual trust of those involved if it is to be successful. In this chapter the term '*developmental* benchmarking' will be used where voluntarism, trust and a commitment to improvement are the primary features.

. . . but the prose now has a wider meaning

However, and particularly following the Dearing Report (NCIHE 1997), benchmarking in UK higher education is acquiring another meaning. The second meaning, which Alstete (1995) disavows, relates more to notions of regulation and conformance with a pre-specified standard than to self-determined development. This is apparent in the Quality Assurance Agency's (QAA) expectation that threshold academic standards can be identified and used as benchmarks to help guide and evaluate institutional performance. Failure to attain the benchmark (one of the indicators of standards, and in some circumstances implicitly of the quality of provision also) may lead to sanctions (QAA 1998b). The term '*regulatory* benchmarking' will be used to describe this notion of benchmarking, whose primary characteristic is an orientation towards control.

There is an obvious tension between developmental and regulatory benchmarking, even though both have within them an orientation towards improvement. The tension arises because, in each, the benchmarking exercise is being driven by different imperatives. Developmental benchmarking is driven by the need of an institution or part of an institution to improve its activities and hence improve its competitive position. In contrast, regulatory

Figure 6.1 Internal and external perspectives on quality and standards

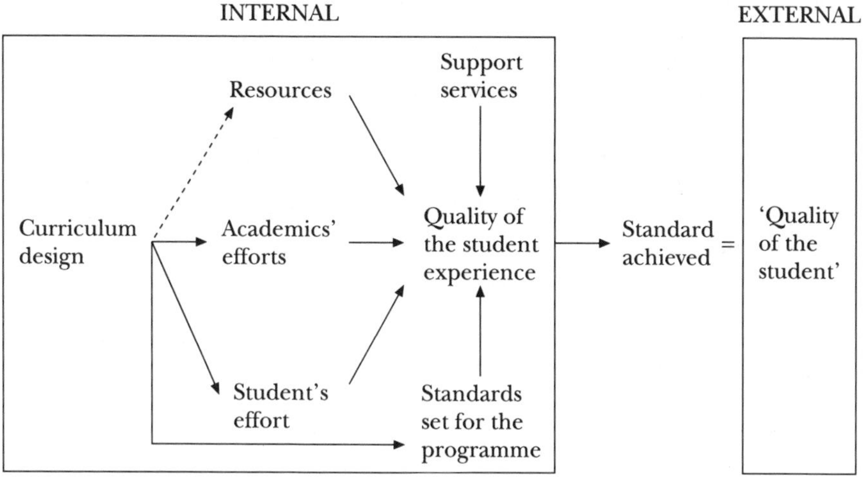

Source: Yorke 1997a

benchmarking is driven by the desire for quality control to demonstrate to various stakeholders that higher education provision and outcomes meet at least minimum acceptable standards.

Quality and standards

Much of the benchmarking activity relating to the educational process has, in one way or another, been about the student experience, whether it has been about the quality of the student experience or about the maintenance of expected and achieved standards. It is important to be clear about the terms 'quality' and 'standards' since both bear on the concept of 'the student experience' and at times the ways in which the terms are used do not differentiate well between them. Here the term 'quality' is being used to denote the processes that underpin the student experience, while the term 'standards' refers to the anticipated and actual outcomes (Figure 6.1). The term 'student experience' refers both to study units (modules) and the totality of a student's programme of study.

Performance indicators and the student experience

Both Camp's and the QAA approach to benchmarking necessarily involve the use of performance indicators. The indicators may be quantitative (e.g. distributions of student performances; ratings on feedback questionnaires; gradings from teaching quality assessments)[1] or qualitative (e.g. judgements

by validation panel members and external examiners). One of the problems with performance indicators is that they may be used for purposes for
which they were not designed. A particularly relevant example is the use of
a derivative of the Course Experience Questionnaire (Ramsden 1991) – an
instrument which, though technically flawed,[2] is of value for teaching improvement purposes – to obtain, on a national scale, graduates' evaluations
of the programmes they experienced (see, for example, Johnson 1998).
The problem of misuse is compounded when CEQ data are converted into
star ratings, like those given to hotels, in Ashenden and Milligan's (1998)
guide to Australian universities.

   Performance indicators in the area of the student experience tend to be
fuzzy (Yorke 1998a). Entry and exit qualifications are subject to more inherent variation than the casual observer might think and the variability is
compounded where 'value added' is concerned; peer assessments of teaching quality are shot through with subjectivity and methodological difficulties;
and data relating to retention and completion are not free from ambiguity.
These kinds of indicator are often given an aura of objectivity that is not
warranted[3] and their detachment from the student experience itself con-
tributes to this objectivism. Higher education is still some way from identifying indicators of the extent to which students are stimulated by their
academic experiences, or are helped to become autonomous, lifelong learners:
students' self-reports can help in this regard, but are necessarily 'soft' kinds
of indicator. The closer one gets to the student experience, the 'softer' (but
perhaps more valid) the important data become. On the other hand, the
further one gets from the source of the data, the greater the inferential
leap and hence, arguably, the greater the threat to validity.

Benchmarking aspects of the student experience

This chapter examines the notion of benchmarking in so far as it relates to
a number of aspects of the student experience, namely student perceptions
of the quality of their experience; academic standards (aspirational and
achieved); non-completion; and, at a more overarching level, league tables
of universities.

Student perceptions of the quality of their experience

Many institutions conduct surveys of student opinion. These surveys are
used to identify aspects of provision that stand in need of improvement and
to demonstrate to students that the institution takes seriously what they
have to say. The use of student feedback contains an inherent ambiguity:
on the one hand, it has for academic staff a simple enhancement-oriented
purpose, whereas on the other it allows their managers to identify the
performance levels of components of institutions and to instigate action.

The late 1980s and early 1990s saw considerable development of student feedback systems, some of which was stimulated by the increase in pressure on institutions to demonstrate the effectiveness and efficiency of their quality assurance systems. In the UK the former Council for National Academic Awards (CNAA) sponsored work on indicators of programme quality (Yorke 1996) and the system in use at the University of Central England (UCE: see Green *et al.* 1994) was one which gained national exposure. Similar developments took place in Australia where Ramsden's Course Experience Questionnaire was first tested as a national level performance measure (Linke 1991).

Consumer power

There are various ways in which students can be asked about their perceptions of study programmes: each has its strengths and weaknesses, as any reasonable text on survey design will show.[4] Standard questionnaires provide more general information than invited feedback gained orally from students at the end of teaching sessions.

A particular feature of the UCE questionnaire-based system is its request to students to indicate not only their level of satisfaction with aspects of their experience but also the importance that they attach to each aspect. The combination of the responses into a two-dimensional plot of satisfaction versus importance allows the university and its component parts to infer where the priorities for action might lie.[5] The method has the potential to serve both developmental and regulatory benchmarking.

Figure 6.2 shows clearly the importance that students from one university attached to the provision of learning resources of various kinds (i.e. Learning Resource Centre materials and IT provision), yet a relatively modest degree of satisfaction was expressed. Here there seems to be a pointer to the need to seek improvement (a matter, given the increasing trend towards open learning, that the institution ought to be addressing anyway). The figure also suggests that the institution might wish to consider doing something to improve its provision of childcare facilities, since it appears in the 'higher importance, lower satisfaction' quadrant. There are no grounds for complacency about a number of other aspects of provision, even though satisfaction levels lie above the mid-point of the scale that runs from 1 (low) to 5. In interpreting data such as these, however, one needs to be cautious when ratings are close to the mid-point. The mid-point can be a kind of 'dustbin' rating into which can be tossed, for example, genuine neutrality of opinion, 'don't know' responses, and acknowledgements that the item is irrelevant to the respondent. Sports facilities and childcare facilities are of high importance to a fraction of the student body, and other items such as the university's environmental policy and practice and even its Student Charter may impinge very little on the average student's consciousness.

Even simple plots of student perception ratings of their overall learning experience provide useful information for benchmarking. For example,

Figure 6.2   Results of a survey of student satisfaction

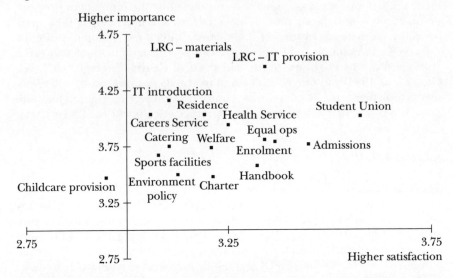

Note: This is a representation of feedback data from a university's undergraduates, cast into a scattergram of importance versus satisfaction, in a manner analogous to the way it is done at the University of Central England. In this instance the data-points are clustered fairly closely together and hence attention is concentrated on only the relevant area of the complete plot of importance versus satisfaction.

Figure 6.3 provides data from one university's 1996/7 postgraduate student feedback questionnaire which relate to three different academic areas. The data are presented in greater aggregation than would be typical of the institution concerned, but illustrate the capacity of such relatively simple data to assist in the generation of questions about aspects of institutional performance.

Some questions almost beg to be asked, for example:

- Why are satisfaction levels for area A on the whole much higher than those for the other two, and what (if anything) is special about the teaching in this area?
- Why does teaching accommodation seem to be so much of a problem for areas B and C, only one of which is technological in character?
- Why are the organization of the programme and the quality of feedback on assignments in area B seen as markedly less satisfactory than those in the other two areas?
- Why is it that training in the use of information technology is not rated highly in all three areas, and does the evidence indicate some general institutional weakness in provision at a time in which the global importance of IT is clearly manifest?

When the data were disaggregated by mode of study, the ratings for part-time students were consistently about half a scale point higher than those

Figure 6.3 Student perception ratings of the overall quality of their learning experience from three professional areas (A, B and C) given by all postgraduate students in 1997

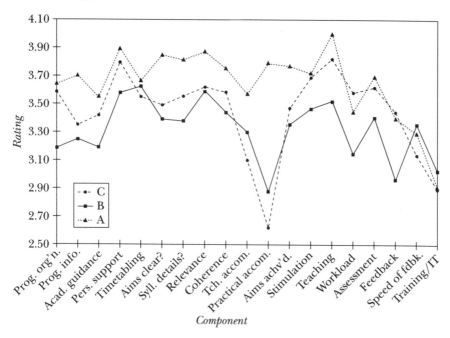

for full-time students. This set of differences in itself raises questions, but there is not the space to pursue them here.

Broad-brush questionnaires are designed to highlight areas for further enquiry rather than to provide detailed answers. Some answers may be identified by staff from within a particular area: for example, it may be relatively easy for them to identify problems relating to teaching accommodation. Other answers may require further exploration with colleagues from different academic areas, with whom contact may not be a normal feature of academic life (particularly if they are geographically distant) – and/or with students themselves. The improvement of feedback on assignments would seem to be a natural candidate for this kind of activity. It is clear that student perception surveys can contribute to improvement of the student experience through internal benchmarking (in both developmental and regulatory senses).

Academic standards

The benchmarking of academic standards has two obvious foci: on the one hand, the validation and accreditation of programmes and, on the other, student outcomes. These form the two ends of the student experience on a programme.[6]

Validation and accreditation of programmes of study

Validation and accreditation[7] typically involve the scrutiny, by a panel, of the proposed programme and of the resources that will be available to support learning. In my own institution, which is not untypical of new universities in this respect, the panel will contain 'home' academics from different parts of the institution who can bring to bear expertise in cognate disciplines and/or in teaching/learning. It will also include external members who may be academics with disciplinary expertise and, where appropriate, representatives of professional and statutory bodies and of employers. A central question that the panel has to address is whether the proposal is congruent with the quality of educational provision and aspirational standards elsewhere: if there are any doubts in this respect, then the proposal will be referred back for further work.

The validation/approval exercise is based on the judgements of experienced academics and others. Sometimes the criteria for judging quality and aspirational standards will be explicit (Chapter 3) such as the specific requirements of a professional body: if these are not met, then approval will not be given. Some institutional criteria are much less explicit. Although in the past programme validation and accreditation have not been described in terms of benchmarking the processes clearly align with the notion of regulatory benchmarking. A proposal document is essentially a design sketch that will take its actual form only when the programme is running. Document-based validation involves a considerable amount of inference in order to assess whether the proposed programme is consistent with similar programmes elsewhere. The panel will probe, on a sampling basis, to see if the inferences made prior to the review meeting accord with what the proposers actually say in elaborating it. This process helps to refine the inferences and allows the panel to come to a judgement on the balance of evidence. Again, there is a kind of benchmarking going on, but one in which there is a fair degree of inference: in this case it is a much 'softer' version of regulatory benchmarking.

Outcomes of learning

The outcomes of learning can be benchmarked in various ways, the context determining whether this is regulatory or developmental. External examiners of programmes will, *inter alia*, look at the profile of outcomes (e.g. proposed degree classifications) and express a view if the profile is out of line with what they construe as the appropriate norm.[8] Again, the 'soft' version of regulatory benchmarking seems to be operating. It should, of course, be noted that deviations from the norm are not necessarily 'wrong', since particular groups of students may be exceptional in one way or the other. The basic point is that there does exist some kind of a norm to which reference can be made – and the data now available from the Higher

Table 6.1 Honours degree classifications in selected degree subject areas, 1997

Subject area	Class of honours degree, 1997 (by %)				
	First	2.1	2.2	Third	Pass
Biological sciences	8.1	49.0	33.8	7.1	1.9
Physical sciences	10.5	36.9	37.0	12.7	3.0
Computer science	9.5	32.8	37.9	15.1	4.7
Engineering and technology	11.4	31.9	34.8	15.6	6.3
Social, economic and political studies	4.9	46.6	40.7	5.4	2.4
Law	3.9	48.8	39.3	5.1	2.9
Business and administrative studies	3.5	38.5	43.5	9.4	5.1
Humanities	7.3	55.8	32.5	3.1	1.2
Creative arts and design	8.8	44.9	37.0	7.3	2.0

Source: HESA (1998)
Notes: 1. 'Unknown' degree classifications included in 'Pass' column.
 2. The category of lower second class (2.2) degrees includes 'undivided seconds'.

Education Statistics Agency (HESA) makes the identification of a norm much easier than it used to be.

Developmental benchmarking can come into play when the results from a programme are set in a broader context. There are two main kinds of comparison – with cognate programmes running in other institutions and with different programmes running in the same institution.[9] Chapman (1994) and in HEQC (1996d) has shown convincingly that there are differences in the profiles of degree classifications across a number of subjects and between institutions. There is no indication in these studies as to what the norms should be, and hence Chapman's findings raise the question of why the differences are as they are. This is something that statistical analysis cannot uncover and that needs inter-institutional discussion for its elucidation. One might speculate that the differences reflect differing approaches to the subject (for example, whether it is more or less mathematical), programme structures, learning experiences, assessment requirements and so on. Even this short list is indicative of the complexity that might underlie the diversity of outcome profiles. Table 6.1 illustrates the variation in degree classifications between subjects. It is clear that the physical sciences and engineering have higher proportions of first class and third class degrees than do areas such as the humanities and law. Outside scientific and technological studies, art and design has a noticeably higher proportion of first class degrees than subjects in the humanities and social sciences. There are likely to be many underlying variables – for example, the extent to which an answer can be adjudged right or wrong, the marking tradition in the subject area, and student intake.

The HESA data align with earlier work conducted by the Student Assessment and Classification Working Group (SACWG: a voluntary benchmarking group which is interested in assessment). Yorke *et al.* (1996) found, *inter alia*, that the spread of grades in mathematics and statistics and in computer studies was significantly higher than that of other subjects and that marks tended to be relatively higher in fine art.[10] Yorke *et al.* (1996) and Bridges *et al.* (1999) demonstrated that the combination of modules taken by a student may influence the class of degree awarded. None of this will come as a surprise to anyone who has been involved in examination boards that cover more than a single subject, but studies such as these are necessary to address issues of equity, particularly in combined subject programmes.[11] The benchmarking interest in SACWG's work, whether directed towards inter- or intra-institutional comparisons, is related to the clarification and improvement of practice and hence is consistent with developmental benchmarking. The question of why there is divergence between sets of outcomes can only be answered with reference to underlying variables, of which one is the nature of the assessment involved.[12]

Assessment and its methodology

During 1997/8 SACWG led a pilot investigation into the benchmarking of academic standards in three disciplinary areas with different characteristics – history, computer studies and business studies (Yorke *et al.* 1998). This work involved volunteer groups of staff from the respective areas digging beneath the surface of relevant curricula and coming together to discuss their findings. A number of features of assessment were identified as having a bearing on standards:

- possible variability in assessment demand for broadly common modular content
- variation in assessment method (e.g. examinations; assignments; multiple-choice papers; group presentations; and combinations drawn from these and other methods)
- weighting ratio of examination to coursework
- procedure adopted by staff when grading work
- 'local freedom' to vary assessment tasks as long as these were consistent with stated learning objectives
- the use, in some modules only, of marking schemes and model answers
- variation, across institutions, in the profile of outcomes from broadly similar modules.

The underlying complexity of module assessment data can be illustrated using the data from business studies Level 1 modules in quantitative techniques (Figure 6.4).

A module on quantitative techniques (or similar title) at Level 1 is 'core' to the BA in business studies (BABS) in Institutions A, C and D, but is optional in Institution B. Both Institutions A and C used closed-book examinations at the end of the module, but Institution C used two open-book

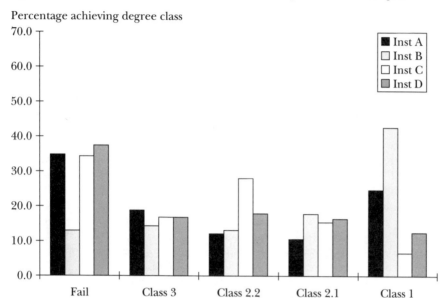

Figure 6.4 Performance data for Level 1 modules in quantitative techniques

examinations during the module as well. Institution B used a multiple-choice examination at the end of the module. Institution D used a mixture of examination (weighted at 60 per cent) and coursework (40 per cent). The results profiles for the four institutions show that Institutions A, C and D have a relatively large number of failures, whereas Institution B has a preponderance of first class outcomes (Figure 6.4). At least three possible causes may be operating to produce the marked disparity.

1. The multiple-choice examination in Institution B may be intrinsically easier than the assessment instruments used in Institutions A, C and D.
2. The data from Institution B relate to BABS students only, whereas the students in the other three institutions were taking the module as part of a business-related degree (not necessarily BABS).
3. The students taking the module in Institution B were in any case self-selected and may have opted for it on the basis of their competence in mathematics, hence making it more likely that the distribution of outcomes would be skewed towards the upper end.

These differences (and those relating to other modules that were appraised) came to light as the staff involved in the group shared their data. There is no 'right answer' to the question of which institution has the best approach to standards, but the inter-institutional discussion of practice and its underlying rationale gave everyone who participated a clearer understanding of the complexity that underlies the benchmarking of academic standards.

Non-completion

The withdrawal of a student from an HE programme may be an important indicator of the quality of that student's experience, or it may be a manifestation of other factors that are not directly related to the HE experience. In recent years the retention of students and the level of non-completion of programmes have become issues of concern in the UK (though interest in such matters has for many years been routine in the United States). Part of the interest has been driven by bodies such as the Committee of Vice-Chancellors and Principals which are concerned about the impact, on students and on institutional finances, of the tightening constraint on student support. In addition, the Funding Councils are concerned about the national cost of non-completion (and hence the efficiency with which the national investment in the sector is being converted into outcomes).

A study conducted for HEFCE by Yorke *et al.* (1997) showed that the wrong choice of field of study and financial problems were jointly the most salient factors influencing non-completion in six institutions in the North West of England. However, dissatisfaction with the quality of 'human contact' within the student experience was not far distant in third place, with about one-quarter of the respondents citing this as influential in their withdrawal. The provision of facilities was much less influential in student withdrawal. An almost identical set of results was obtained from a replication study in five of the original six institutions. Together, the two studies generated questionnaire responses from 2151 full-time and sandwich-course[13] students.

Analysis of these responses showed that, while there were variations between age groups, men and women, social classes and so on, there were some interesting variations between academic subject categories (ASCs) as far as the quality of the student experience was concerned.[14] Table 6.2 shows the mean frequencies of citing, across all ASCs, of a number of possible influences on withdrawal: notable deviations from the mean are also shown.

The data in Table 6.2 suggest quite strongly that the influences on withdrawal vary between subject discipline. Subject difficulty is to the fore in engineering and related disciplines. While this may be connected in part to the calibre of entrants, it may also stem from the ways in which the disciplines are taught.[15] In contrast, social science, humanities and education have a lower than average chance of the quality of teaching being cited as an influence on non-completion. The data in Table 6.2 do not prove that some subjects are, as far as teaching and learning are concerned, 'better' than others – not least, it must be emphasized, because the responses were only those of students who had left before completing their programmes. The data do, however, allow institutions to ask themselves why it is that, say, the quality of teaching in humanities is less likely to appear as an influence on non-completion than it is, say, in art, design and the performing arts, or why the difficulty of programmes is more likely to be cited as an influence

Table 6.2 Means for academic subject categories (ASCs) against the all-ASC mean for each of the selected items

Variable	Mean % citing	Academic subject category													
		1 Clinical and pre-clinical	2 Allied to medicine	3 Science	4 Engineering and technology	5 Built environment	6 Maths, IT, computing	7 Business and management	8 Humanities	9 Social science	10 Art, design, etc.	11 Education	50 Mixed arts	51 Mixed sciences	52 Mixed arts and sciences
Teaching did not suit me	31	**	–		*	*			–		**	–			*
Insufficient academic progress	30	**	–		**						*	–		*	–
Organization of the programme	27	**		*		–			–	–	**		*	*	*
Lack of personal support from staff	24	**									*	–			*
Inadequate staff support outside timetable	24	**		*	–	*					*	*			
Quality of the teaching	23	–	–		*	*			–	–	**	–	*	**	
Stress related to the programme	22	**	–	*	*	–		–			–	–		**	–
Difficulty of the programme	21	**	*		**	**	**		–	–	–	–	–	*	*
Workload too heavy	17	**	–	**	**	*	–			–	–	–	–	*	–
Lack of study skills	17	*	–	**	**					–			–	*	–
Class size too large	16	–	–	**	**		–			–		–		*	–
Lack of personal support from students	15	–	*	*		–				–		–	**		–
Timetabling did not suit	11	–	–		*	–	–		–			–	*		**
Inst'l provision of social facilities	9	–			*	*	*		–		*	*		**	
Inst'l computing provision	9	–			*	*	–	**	–		*	–		**	
Inst'l library provision	8		–		*	*		*	–	–	*	–	*	**	–
Inst'l provision of specialist equipment	7	–	–		**	*		*	–	*	**	–		**	*

Note: * indicates 120–139% and ** indicates at least 140% of the all-ASC item mean.
– indicates 61–80% and – – indicates at most 60% of the all-ASC item mean.

on withdrawal from engineering than from social science. Table 6.2 can, of course, be replicated at the level of the single institution, and at a finer level of discrimination than that of the relatively crude ASCs.[16]

League tables

League tables containing various indicators of institutional performance have, in recent times, become a feature of the landscape of higher education around the world. Their inadequacies have been discussed by a number of authors:[17] the league tables of universities in the United Kingdom are dominated by research performance that seems to correlate with resourcing and reputation. The more recent tables have incorporated externally conducted assessments of teaching quality which are relevant to the theme of this chapter.[18]

Subject quality assessments (also known as teaching quality assessments and 'subject reviews') are based on the peer review of institutional documentation and direct observation of teaching and other pedagogic activities. In essence, they take the curricular aims and assess the extent to which they are being realized, drawing on qualitative and quantitative evidence. The reader of a league table (and particularly one from outside HE) could be forgiven for believing that the column in a league table which lists scores based on subject quality assessments provides valid and useful indications of the relative standing of institutions and, in benchmarking terms, of the extent to which an institution measures up to best practice. In reality, the reader receives very little information that is useful, for a number of reasons, including the following:

- The quality assessment grade is based on scores across the subject areas that happen to have been assessed, and may bear no relationship to the quality of teaching in a particular discipline.
- Grades are based on institutionally generated aims and objectives, and hence it cannot be said that, across the sector, like is being compared with like (Alderman 1997), even at the level of the subject discipline. The grades are however an indicator of the extent to which the institutional educational objectives in a subject discipline are being met.
- The quality assessment process is not the same across the whole of the United Kingdom (nor has it been across time).

None of these criticisms of league tables necessarily undercut the value of the quality assessment process itself which, for those in the assessed institution, provides an opportunity to test their, and their students', achievements against the perceptions of knowledgeable peers.[19] The institutional mission is of particular relevance to the reader of league tables. For example, a community-based institution may gain few points for student accommodation since its students will tend to commute and not require institutionally provided accommodation: in contrast a resource-rich university attracting students from a national market with good campus-based accommodation and facilities will gain more points. Similarly, a research-led university is likely to spend more per enrolled student on its library resources than one whose mission directs it to invest in other types of learning resource. However, institutional mission does not appear in the league tables themselves.

The production of league tables constitutes a kind of benchmarking exercise of aspects of the student experience: after all, that is how the compilers expect them to be used. However, league tables do not really fit either of the main categories identified at the beginning of the chapter since the voluntary element of developmental benchmarking and the defined performance criteria of regulatory benchmarking are both lacking.

What can be learned from these examples?

Seen from afar, benchmarking the various aspects of the student experience might seem to be simple and straightforward. Standards ought to be identifiable and their attainment verifiable. It should be relatively easy to make comparisons relating to aspects of process. A closer inspection, however, shows that benchmarking academic aspects of higher education is a much more subtle and complex matter than benchmarking non-academic aspects of performance (premises-related expenditure and so on) or benchmarking industrial processes. The complexity derives from the sheer number of variables that impinge on the students' experience. When one approaches benchmarking from a transnational perspective the complexity is even greater.[20]

Where outcome standards are concerned, the Graduate Attributes Profile (HEQC 1997a; Chapter 5, this volume) shows how complex student performance is. Institutions, subject areas and individuals vary (explicitly or implicitly) in the levels of emphasis that they give to different components of performance. There is, therefore, no single benchmark that can stand as a reference point of excellence or threshold standard. One solution to the problem would be to prescribe in detail a set of expected learning outcomes for the student in subject X. This, however, would have a number of adverse effects, among them the following:

- The precision in specification would, in practice, be unwieldy and acknowledged more in the breach than in the observance. It would rerun, in a slightly different form, the behavioural objectives approach to higher education that was tried in the United States in the 1960s and which relatively quickly collapsed.
- Statements of benchmarks on their own are probably insufficient to convey what is intended (see Wolf 1995).
- The use of tightly framed learning outcomes would constrain students' freedom to explore their subject(s) of study: this would sit uncomfortably within a higher education system in which learner autonomy is increasingly being advocated.

- If undertaken on a national basis, then a tight framing would constitute a move in the direction of a national curriculum. National competitiveness might be disadvantaged if students' development were to be standardized across the country.
- No account is taken of the evolution of standards over time, nor of preferred modes of assessment (see, on this point, Elton 1998).

The difficulty in specifying benchmarks for academic standards is evident from the pilot studies being carried out, under the aegis of QAA, in chemistry, history and law. These show that such benchmarks are inherently judgmental: they are relatively high-inference attributes that are open to a variety of interpretations. The issue for those engaged in benchmarking academic standards is not so much whether a programme or the students' performances explicitly meet a set of precise criteria, but rather an assessment of whether, all things considered, these match up to normative (and substantially tacit) expectations. The pilot studies will, of course, help to bring into debate a number of features that had previously been taken for granted, and thereby help to sharpen the quality of the benchmarking judgements that are made.

When one turns to aspects of academic process, the problem of precision again raises its head. Data such as those presented above can certainly expose differences between academic areas in their treatment of students. The evidence, however, merely signals that there may be good reason to ask why some parts of an institution are apparently performing less well in certain respects than others: it does not provide information as to what should be done to improve matters. For that, one has to turn to other modes of inquiry and professional judgement regarding any necessary action.

The theme of regulatory benchmarking is developed elsewhere in this volume (Chapters 3, 5, 7 and 8). Too high an expectation is being placed on the idea of regulatory benchmarking if it is construed in terms of conformance to performance criteria in the field of academic endeavours. It is like trying to close an over-filled suitcase: if one can get one side of the case closed down, one finds that the clothes have somehow burst out of the other side. To argue thus is not to suggest that benchmarking can offer no real purchase on academic matters: quite clearly, the detailed examination of quality and standards can help to refine understandings about what higher education involves and hence assist the improvement of practice. The argument thus curves back towards developmental benchmarking in which groups of individuals voluntarily work together in order to share information for the purpose of self-improvement and collective improvement. The studies conducted by Yorke *et al.* (1998), Morgan (Chapter 4, this volume) and Tannock and Jackson (Chapter 5, this volume) testify to the value of sharing and comparing information. The importance of discussion among peers is captured in a report on assessment:

> . . . research suggests that administrative procedures and documentation, designed to make standards explicit, can contribute only a limited

amount to reliability; and what is really important is the nature of assessor networks. Consistent assessment decisions among assessors are the product of interactions over time, the internalisation of exemplars, and . . . inclusive networks. Written instructions, mark schemes and criteria, even when used with scrupulous care, cannot substitute for these. A fragmented assessor system which relies on documentation produces judgements which, on different sites, are markedly different in where they place substantive boundaries.

(HEQC, 1997b: 11)

The same point applies with respect to other aspects of the student experience, in which students will be drawn more directly into the debate.

To the observer from outside higher education, developmental benchmarking applied to the student experience might seem to be woolly and self-indulgent. It certainly could be so. However, if it is conducted with a serious commitment to improvement it is a systematic and searching process that might well achieve more than regulatory benchmarking. As far as the student experience in a diverse system goes, there is no easy way of identifying the best academic practice or the highest educational efficiency. However, a professional commitment to understanding and improving practice using techniques such as benchmarking can go a long way towards ensuring that students have an experience of high quality and that the standards expected of them – and that they achieve – are high. Ultimately, the standards that students achieve depend, of course, not only on the quality of the programme but also, and crucially, on their own commitment to their studies.

The problem with the benchmarking examples set out above is that, useful as they may be for various purposes, they inevitably miss out a lot of the essence of the truly *higher* education experience.[21] This essence includes being excited by learning, being prepared to wrestle with problems of various kinds, and being motivated towards learning throughout one's life. How much goes on in higher education that is routinized in one way or another; how much is dull and uninspired? No one knows – and anyway, the question can really only be answered at a finer level than can probably be picked up by most benchmarks (and certainly by those that might be used by external agencies as performance criteria). Sometimes one can get a clue from unlikely sources. I remember sitting in a lecture theatre at a conference a few years ago and glancing at the bench in front of me. Gouged into its surface, in large capital letters, were the words 'SMILE YOU MISERABLE GIT'. Now that is an unambiguous benchmark of the student experience!

Acknowledgements

Many colleagues have worked with me on the various projects on which this chapter is based and, while I must take responsibility for the content, it is appropriate that their contribution should be acknowledged. My thanks, therefore, go to the following. *Members of SACWG*: Bernard Bourdillon, Paul Bridges, Debbie Collymore, Angela Cooper, Wendy Fox, Chris Haines, Paul McHugh, David Turner and Harvey Woolf.

Benchmarking generally: Norman Jackson. *Benchmarking in business studies*: Bernard Boudillon, Margaret Price, Julie Lydon, Saundra Middleton, Kate Murray, Mark Price and Caroline Woodhead. *Student feedback*: John Minten and Susan Troilett. *HEFCE non-completion study*: Robin Bell, Alan Dove, Liz Haslam, Heather Hughes Jones, Bernard Longden, Catherine O'Connell, Rose Typuszak and Julie Ward.

Notes

1. In the system previously run by HEFCE, and now known as 'subject review'.
2. For a critique, see Yorke (1996: Appendix 6).
3. In another context Mintzberg (1994: 97) referred to the soft underbelly of hard data.
4. Some of the considerations are discussed in Yorke (1996: 109–12).
5. See Green *et al.* (1994: 103) for an accessible illustration of the plot.
6. They may, however, only constitute a phase in lifelong learning.
7. The points being made apply, *mutatis mutandis*, to the review of existing programmes.
8. It has to be noted that some external examiners may not have a full understanding of the span of student performances (particularly in multi-subject schemes) and may concentrate on the assurance of processes at final award level.
9. A further issue in the benchmarking of academic standards is the way in which students' performances are cumulated into degree classifications. A survey by NUCCAT (1998) has confirmed, on a wider basis, earlier investigations by SACWG which pointed to considerable inter-institutional variation in classification algorithms (Woolf and Turner 1997).
10. The Kendall coefficient of concordance was computed for the rank orderings of subject standard deviations because the institutions involved used incommensurate grading scales.
11. Where students took single-subject degrees the issue of equity was less obvious.
12. There are, of course, a number of wider curricular issues which can be explored.
13. Sandwich-course students spend a period, usually of a year's duration, in a work-related environment during their programme of study.
14. For a fuller account, see Yorke (1998b).
15. Seymour and Hewitt (1997) showed, from a large qualitative study in the United States, that the ways that students in science, mathematics and engineering were treated were often inimical to student learning and progress. A pertinent question is whether these findings transfer to the United Kingdom and elsewhere.
16. If the data are disaggregated too finely, then random fluctuations may obscure the true situation.
17. For example, Machung (1998), Morrison *et al.* (1995), and Yorke (1996, 1997b).
18. Other variables included in league tables and which bear on the student experience are the spending on library and computer equipment: one issue is the extent to which these are meaningful for students.
19. Whether the teaching quality assessment process represents value for money is another question.
20. See, for example, Lonbay (1994), Resnick *et al.* (1995), and Vroeijenstijn *et al.* (1992).
21. In a series of books Barnett (1992, 1994, 1997) has stressed the importance of critical thinking to higher education, in contrast to other levels of education.

7

Benchmarking the Outcomes of Learning

Norman Jackson and Vaneeta D'Andrea

Overview

The comparability of academic performance in undergraduate education has become an increasingly important issue in the transformation of UK HE from a highly selective elitist system to a more accessible, multipurpose mass system. Notions of comparability of standards are being redefined in terms of developing the capacity to compare the outcomes of learning in the belief that it will eventually be possible to create threshold (or minimum) standards for degrees in a subject. This chapter[1] describes the initial steps towards the development of subject-based threshold standards that are intended to provide benchmarks for institutional standards. Used in this sense benchmarking is being employed to help improve the capacity of academic communities to regulate their standards and provide more explicit information on what people who possess an HE award might be expected to know and be able to do.

Rationale for subject benchmarking

The social fabric of UK HE is derived from two sources: the cultures, traditions and missions of each institution and the value and belief systems of subject-based academic communities. Institutional cultures influence the nature of the provision (e.g. research-led or vocationally oriented), the way it is organized, administered and regulated. They may also influence particular approaches to learning, for example a commitment to the development of general transferable skills (like communication and team working). Subject-based communities exert a strong influence on the nature of learning in the subject and the way academic standards are created (manifested through the products of research and scholarship, examination and other forms of assessment). The idea that academics inhabit one or more 'tribes and territories' (Beecher 1989), each with its own set of norms, traditions and values, is one that is widely recognized in UK academe. Subject cultures are promulgated both formally and informally by immersion in the learning traditions of the subject, by research-led activities within specialist interest groups and by familiarity with the educational debates within discipline networks. Subject cultures are also promoted through the programme accreditation activities of professional and statutory bodies and through the external examiner system. The pervasive influence of subject communities on academic standards is revealed in studies of the variation of degree classifications with time (Chapman 1994; HEQC 1996d) and the marking/grading profiles of subjects in different institutions (Yorke *et al.* 1996). Such empirical evidence suggests that interventions designed to influence academic standards are most likely to be successful if applied through the subject community. This is the fundamental premise on which subject benchmarking is based.

Origin of subject benchmarking

Professional and statutory bodies (PSBs) with responsibilities for protecting the standards of the professions (and in some cases for conferring a licence to practice) have for decades used the idea of benchmarking to regulate subject standards. HE institutions wishing to offer programmes in such subjects must submit periodically to a formal accreditation process. About 65 PSBs are directly involved in programme accreditation (HEQC 1996b). This process enables them to exert varying degrees of influence over the entry standards to programmes; curriculum content; methods of teaching and learning; the examination and assessment process; the accreditation of prior certificated and experiential learning and the resources to support learning including staffing levels, library and technical support. Some PSBs may also influence the appointment and practice of external examiners.

More explicit benchmarking is now seen as one way in which institutions might enhance their capacity for comparing and improving academic practice and standards (Jackson 1998d, 1998e). In 1996/7 HEQC initiated two lines of development work:

1. A pilot project on benchmarking assessment practice (QAA 1998c).
2. Work with a number of subject communities to examine the feasibility of using the concept of 'graduateness' (the attributes that a person graduating with a degree might be expected to possess) (HEQC 1995b, 1996e, 1997a, 1997b).

The products and insights gained through these projects are now helping to shape the QAA's conception of subject benchmarking.

First steps in developing subject threshold standards

The creation of national policy on subject benchmarking stemmed from Recommendation 25 of the National Committee of Inquiry in Higher Education (NCIHE 1997). This directed the Quality Assurance Agency to 'work with institutions to establish small, expert teams to provide benchmark information on standards, in particular threshold standards . . .'. The policy steer was influenced by the findings of the Graduate Standards Programme (HEQC 1997a) and by the Chair of the Committee of Inquiry (Sir Ron Dearing) who had seen the work of subject benchmarking groups in Australia (see Chapter 15, this volume).

HEQC began working with subject communities on the feasibility of establishing threshold standards in 1995 with a consultative study involving the fields of art and design, biology, business and management, English, music and drama (HEQC 1997a). Findings from this study confirmed the diversity of HE curricula within subject fields and the resistance of academics to any suggestion of convergence around common curricula. However, subject groups considered that there was scope for defining threshold standards in terms of generic (academic and employment-related) attributes or educational outcomes.

The second stage of HEQC's work involved 14 subject communities (accountancy; art and design; biological sciences; classics; communication and media studies; economics; English; European studies; French; geography; history; hospitality management; law and philosophy (QAA 1998f). Each group explored its own 'territory' in a way that had not previously happened. This was an important prerequisite for creating the conditions for subject benchmarking and for demonstrating the potential of benchmarking methodologies to subject communities. Six out of the 14 subjects reported significant progress in identifying and gaining agreement on the attributes acquired and developed by undergraduates in their subjects. The report for history provides an example of the outcomes of this process (HUDG 1997). The historians considered that by requiring students to attempt to understand, interpret and explain past human experience, the discipline encouraged the development of two distinct but related areas of cognitive expertise: analytical thinking and creative thinking (Table 7.1). In addition the communication and presentation of work in written and oral forms was integral to the development of an analytical and creative historical mind.

Biological sciences took the idea of benchmarking 'graduateness' a step further by identifying the attributes considered to be essential to the graduate and comparing these with the attributes that are actually assessed (Table 7.2). A survey of 103 departments (Jordan and Withnall 1997) revealed that different departments expected their graduates to acquire more or less the same set of attributes. They also assessed honours graduates by weighting the attributes in similar ways and used similar assessment methods and instruments to provide evidence that these attributes had been developed.

Table 7.1   The main cognitive skills of the historian

Characteristics of analytical thinking – ability to:

- gather, sift, select, organize and synthesize large quantities of evidence – literary, visual, physical, quantitative, or oral;
- discriminate between what is relevant and irrelevant, essential and peripheral for the task in hand;
- appreciate the range of problems involved in the interpretation of complex, ambiguous, conflicting and often incomplete material;
- appreciate the limitations of knowledge and the dangers of over-simplified explanations of cause and effect;
- understand and evaluate the range of conceptual frameworks and theoretical perspectives through which such material is explained and interpreted;
- arrive at and justify their assessment of the validity and merit of contrasting scholarly opinions and theories;
- question received scholarly wisdom and develop and defend their own opinions.

Characteristics of creative thinking – ability to:

- make the imaginative and empathetic connections without which unfamiliar structures, cultures and belief systems of the past cannot be properly understood;
- solve problems by devising and formulating the appropriate questions to ask of the evidence;
- overcome the deficiencies of the sources by devising well-informed working hypotheses to bring to bear on existing evidence;
- be flexible and adaptable in their thinking and remain open to new types of evidence and methods of analysis and to original and challenging interpretations.

Source: HUDG 1997

Fourteen attributes were recognized as being essential to the make-up of a graduate and the rank order was similar regardless of institutional type. There were, however, significant differences between the list of attributes deemed to be essential for the graduate biological scientist and the list of attributes which staff felt were actually being assessed. Such differences reveal a tension between the value systems that recognize the importance of the acquisition and demonstration of intellectual skills and the assessment systems that are still heavily focused on knowledge and subject mastery.

Studies such as these demonstrate that there is a basis to the idea of 'graduateness' and that different subjects are seeking to develop a broadly similar set of qualities, skills and attributes, although these were manifested differently in different subjects. The pilot studies also demonstrated that with relatively little support an appropriate infrastructure could be developed to enable subject communities to research and share their practice and educational outcomes.

Table 7.2 Comparison between valued and assessed educational outcomes in biological sciences (rank order based on average scores)

Expected attributes	Assessed attributes
1. Critical reasoning	1. Subject content and range
2. Subject's conceptual basis	2. Subject's conceptual basis
3. Investigative skills	3. Critical reasoning
4. Intellectual analysis	4. Intellectual analysis
5. Communication	5. Laboratory and/or field craft skills
6. Data/information processing	6. Data/information processing
7. Subject content and range	7. Subject methodologies
8. Laboratory and/or field craft skills	8. Investigative skills
9. Subject methodologies	9. Originality
10. Teamwork	10. Synthesis
11. Independence	11. Context in which subject used
12. Professional skills	12. Communication
13. Time management	13. Reflection/evaluation
14. Synthesis	14. Subject's relation to other subjects

QAA conception of subject benchmarking

The Dearing Report (NCIHE 1997) placed responsibility on the Quality Assurance Agency for creating the infrastructure and parameters within which subject benchmarking will be conducted. It will be some years before the full potential of subject benchmarking will be realized and only the initial development work, undertaken between May and December 1998, will be considered in this chapter. Information on the subject groupings, the method of creating a Subject Benchmarking Group (SBG), the definition of the task and the potential use of benchmark information can be found in QAA 1998a and 1998b. The initial task of SBGs is to produce 'statements that represent general expectations about standards at the threshold level, for, in the first instance, the award of honours degrees; and relevant comparative information that can guide the quality control and assurance processes of programme design, approval, accreditation, examining and review' (QAA 1998a: 11). Benchmarking information is intended to focus on the general intellectual outcomes of learning in a subject rather than defining curricular content (i.e. the role of SBGs is not to establish national curricula). In trying to understand how this process might be used to benchmark academic standards it is helpful to develop a process model to show how such standards are created (Figure 7.1).

Subject benchmarking can be applied to each part of the model:

- to identify a set of common expectations or learning outcomes
- to identify the ways in which these expectations might be realized through different teaching, learning and assessment methods and
- to facilitate a more consistent approach to setting standards.

Figure 7.1   Process model for making academic standards more explicit.

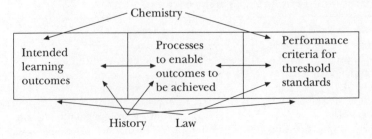

Figure 7.2   Method of producing benchmark information for history, chemistry and law (steps 1 to 4) and how it will be used by HE institutions and external review processes (steps 5 to 7)

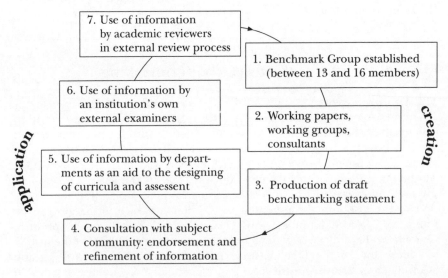

The guidance given to SBGs would allow them to address all parts of the model but the initial intention was to focus on the two ends of the model, i.e. the expectations of learning and the performance standards that would be used to judge the attainment of outcomes. Three subjects (law, chemistry and history) are pioneering the approach (Bell 1999; Haines 1999; QAA 1999 and online (http://www.qaa.ac.uk). A generic model for the way in which the benchmark information has been created is given in Figure 7.2. The main features of the three subject benchmarking statements are summarized in Table 7.3. Different benchmarking groups emphasized different parts of the outcomes model in their statements.

Table 7.3 Summary of the main features of the benchmarking statements for law, history and chemistry benchmarking groups

Nature of information	Law benchmarking statement	History benchmarking statement	Chemistry benchmarking statement
Length	18-page document	16-page document	7-page document
Application	Programmes containing more than 180 credits (50%) of law	Single honours programmes	Honours degrees in chemistry
Specification of expectations/outcomes	23 learning outcomes organized within 7 categories	16 learning outcomes – not categorized: supplemented by a list of desirable qualities and skills of the mind and behaviour that a history programme is intended to foster and inculcate	23 skills-based learning outcomes in 3 categories. 14 areas of core knowledge defined
Position of threshold statement	Bottom of third class honours	The standard achieved by the typical student	Criteria given suggest threshold i.e. when most outcomes achieved at performance equivalent to 2ii)
Specification of performance standards to meet expectations	Generic criteria in the form of: • modal statements of performance linked to 7 categories of expectation • example guidance for degree classifications • criteria at pass, proficient and very proficient performance linked to 7 categories of expectation	Generic criteria for examination by essays written under timed conditions for each class of the honours degree. Criteria address: • structure and focus • quality of argument • range of knowledge	Generic criteria for 5 levels of performance (equivalent to honours classification). Criteria address: • knowledge/understanding • problem solving • subject/experimental skills • generic skills

Table 7.3 (cont'd)

Nature of information	Law benchmarking statement	History benchmarking statement	Chemistry benchmarking statement
Opportunities for achieving expectations	No specification of content, mode of study or teaching or learning methods	Specification of 6 basic requirements which might be classed as design principles for the history curriculum, teaching and learning	Content specified in terms of 14 areas of subject knowledge. No information on teaching and learning
Opportunities for demonstrating achievement	No specification of assessment modes or methods	7 expectations defined for the assessment process	Identifies 5 types of assessment that should be used to provide evidence of achievement and 6 other types of assessment that might be used
Information on the nature of evidence to demonstrate achievement of outcome	Nature of evidence of achievement of outcomes to be determined by each institution: some guidance on how some of the outcomes might be demonstrated	Nature of evidence of achievement of outcomes to be determined by each institution; expectations of assessment methods provide guidance on how outcomes might be demonstrated	Not specified

Note: Based on information available in January 1999.

Law benchmark information

The law benchmarking information comprises an 18-page statement in three parts (Law SBG 1998):

1. A set of subject outcomes (termed areas of performance).
2. Guidance notes to help academic staff interpret and implement the outcomes statement.
3. Guidance to aid the assessment of performance in the form of three appendices.

The statement of learning intent represents the minimum expectations of achievement (threshold standard) of a graduate with a Bachelor honours degree in law or legal studies. It is intended to apply to all programmes containing 180 credits or more of law (e.g. single-, major-, joint- and combined-subject programmes in which law comprises 50 per cent or more of the programme).

The statement of threshold standards for law graduates is set at the bottom of the third class honours degree. The statement does not specify the mode of study or learning methods by which a student is able to achieve these outcomes, although the accompanying notes provide limited guidance on how particular learning outcomes might be demonstrated. The law benchmark statement indicates that in devising statements of learning outcomes for their own programmes of study, institutions will be expected to include all of the features listed.

Each institution will have to develop its own assessment criteria, appropriate to the activities through which students are expected to demonstrate their achievement in each of the performance areas identified. These criteria will provide the objective basis on which an institution can claim that its students have reached the requisite standard for the award of an honours degree in law or legal studies. The benchmarking statement offers guidance on the general criteria for achievement of the threshold standard based on 'a student satisfactorily demonstrating achievement in the area of performance on a sufficient number of occasions or over a sufficient range of activities to give confidence that they have the ability or skill which is claimed for graduates in law'. Guidance on what might be deemed 'sufficient' is provided in the form of generic performance criteria that might be expected at the threshold standard in each of the seven areas identified in the benchmarking statement. The criteria are quite different to those that are traditionally used for the classification of honours degrees. Overall the information produced by the law benchmarking group focuses on the expectations and outcome standards of the model shown in Figure 7.1.

History benchmark information

The history benchmarking group produced a 16-page statement (History SBG January 1998). The statement of learning intent represents the minimum expectations of achievement of a typical graduate with a Bachelor honours degree in history. Although the information is primarily directed to single-subject honours programmes it might also be applied more broadly to joint programmes. The benchmarking statement is written in the form of a list of 16 uncategorized learning outcomes but these are supplemented by a list of skills and qualities of mind that a history programme is intended to foster and inculcate and more explicit expectations that relate to the assessment of communication and information technology skills. The history benchmark information differs from that produced by chemistry and law by specifying 'criteria for content' of programmes, teaching, learning and assessment in the form of six design principles. These cover:

- time depth
- geographical range
- contemporary sources
- reflexivity
- diversity of specialisms
- an extended piece of written work.

It also provides guidance on the assessment process and generic assessment criteria for the examination of essays written under timed conditions. The history benchmark information is distinctive in emphasizing process.

Chemistry benchmark information

The chemistry benchmarking information comprises a six-page statement (Chemistry SBG 1998) with information on:

- the main aims and purposes associated with Bachelor honours degree programmes in chemistry
- the essential subject matter (main components that might be expected to be covered in all study programmes leading to such degrees)
- the abilities and skills to be developed in students through the study of chemistry at Bachelor honours degree level
- assessment procedures and performance criteria.

The outcomes statement lists 23 generic learning outcomes in three categories. It also provides information on the main areas of knowledge that a degree programme should enable students to develop (14 areas identified) and the assessment procedures that should/might be used.

The statement does not include information on the teaching and learning methods that might be used to enable the outcomes to be realized. All students graduating in chemistry are expected to demonstrate that they have acquired and demonstrated skills and competencies in all the areas identified. A set of generic performance criteria are provided covering five levels of attainment (which relate to the four honours classification bands and the category of degree without honours). If the threshold standard is interpreted as satisfactory achievement of most of the learning outcomes then the most appropriate criteria occupy the mid-point of the five sets of criteria (equivalent to the lower second class division in honours classification).

Commentary and critique

The idea of subject benchmarking is pivotal to the idea of creating threshold standards and to strengthening the formal involvement of subject communities in creating and assuring academic standards. This commentary is intended to promote understanding of the nature and potential use of the information that has emerged through the process. It attempts to identify and address some of the concerns that have been raised (QAA 1998b) and to highlight possible ways in which the process might be developed. Any discussion must begin by recognizing that creating subject threshold standards for a diverse HE system is inherently difficult (HEQC 1997a) and that the pilot exercises described above are only the first step in a long development process. Ideas on subject benchmarking are evolving rapidly as the SBGs explore their remit and as other parts of the QAA policy framework (like academic review and programme specifications) develop.

Consistency and utility of benchmarking information

It has become increasingly clear that benchmark statements might contain three types of information (Figure 7.1). This information relates to:

1. The valued educational outcomes resulting from learning in a subject.
2. Guidance on the teaching, learning and assessment methods that might be used to enable particular outcomes to be achieved and demonstrated.
3. Generic criteria for setting performance standards at the threshold level of achievement and guidance that would support consistent interpretation of these criteria.

The three subject benchmarking groups were encouraged to examine the idea of outcomes-based benchmarking in their own way. Consequently, the benchmarking statements contain different types and levels of information; they emphasize different aspects of the process of creating standards and address the matter of threshold standards in different ways (Table 7.3). Such inconsistency, it might be argued, is a weakness, but at the development stage of any process it is helpful because of the additional insights it brings. Nevertheless, the matter of consistency of information will need to be addressed. For example, the law and chemistry benchmark statements identify significantly more educational outcomes in the subject than the history statement, which focuses more on the process to enable outcomes

Table 7.4   Learning outcomes that are common to history, law and chemistry

---

1. Subject knowledge/understanding (specified to varying degrees chemistry>law>history)
2. Subject specific skills
3. Capacity to learn
4. Capacity to access/manage/deploy/discriminate/compare different sorts of information
5. Ability to synthesize/analyse/evaluate/interpret information and reflect critically
6. Skills in presenting information/providing reasoned arguments
7. Capacity to plan, design, research/study in depth
8. Ability to apply knowledge/understanding to the solution of problems within the subject
9. Ability to communicate effectively in a variety of modes/media
10. Ability to use information technology
11. Proficiency in numerical skills appropriate to the subject
12. Ability to work independently and collaboratively (teamworking)

Note: Based on data available in January 1999.

to be achieved. The statements differ in the extent to which knowledge is specified: the chemistry statement identifies 14 areas of knowledge required by a graduate, law defines three general fields of knowledge and history six principles to guide curriculum content. There are also substantial differences in the way different subjects address the matter of performance criteria. However, in spite of the differences in presentation and detail noted above, a number of common outcomes emerge from the pilot exercise (Table 7.4). These are perhaps the generic learning outcomes that will characterize most of UK undergraduate education.

The utility of the information depends on who will use it for what purpose. The two intended purposes are:

• to inform the design of programmes so that they make provision for the acquisition and development of the specified learning outcomes and
• to facilitate the evaluation of the standards of attainment in the subject so that a level of comparability can be demonstrated (particularly the minimum standards for an award).

Learning outcomes are statements of learning intent that describe what learners will be expected to know and be able to do as a result of learning. They are expressed in ways that make it clear how their achievement can be assessed (Melton 1997: 29). In the case of law and chemistry the statements are written in the form that makes it clear how achievement might be assessed. They could therefore be used as the basis for a minimum set of programme learning outcomes. This is not the case with history where the 'outcomes' are more an expression of aims. Only the law statement attempts to link performance criteria directly to the constituent elements of the benchmark statement and specifically to identify criteria for the threshold level of performance. It is clear that the different approaches will have important consequences for the way the statements are applied by teaching teams and academic reviewers. The public and academic perceptions of such differences have yet to be evaluated but they are likely to be important.

Subject definition and level of specification

The definition by QAA (1998b) of 42 subject categories as the basis for subject benchmarking is essentially one of administrative convenience rather than an attempt to reflect accurately the subject base for UK HE which recognizes several hundred subjects. This categorization of subjects can be criticized from two standpoints. The first is that there are too many subject categories. This line of reasoning argues that the most appropriate level for the definition of learning outcomes and generic performance criteria are the broad fields of learning like science, engineering, humanities and the arts. This level of specification would be relatively easy to achieve and it would permit greater freedom of expression at the level of the programme. The contrary position, expressed by subject categories where there is an enforced union of different learning cultures and constructs, is that there should be more subject categories to reflect more faithfully the knowledge base for learning. While the advantage of this is greater specificity, relevance and ownership of the benchmarking information, it would effectively impose a tight specification on programmes. While this might be an advantage in some subjects, particularly those that are linked to professions where accreditation by a professional body is essential, it might be unhelpful in other areas. One solution might be to create subject-specific information that could then be aggregated at the level of a major field of learning to identify the generic features that should underpin all programmes in the field. This would enable subjects to choose between two levels of specificity according to their particular needs. Figure 7.3 provides a graphical illustration of what might be termed 'top-down' and 'bottom-up' approaches to subject benchmarking with reference to the field of engineering.

There must be an optimum number of major outcomes for any programme. Example programme specifications that have been produced in chemistry, history and law list between 11 and 25 separate outcomes (12–20 history, 21–25 chemistry, 13–14 law). The subject benchmarking statements that have been produced list between 14 (history) and 37 (chemistry) learning outcomes. It stands to reason that the more detailed and comprehensive the specification of outcomes at subject level the less room there will be for the expression of programme-specific outcomes. In some subjects (such as those with strong professional body affiliation) it might be appropriate for such convergence but in others it might lead to a level of prescription at the programme level that would not be in the interests of higher education. The level of specificity indicated in Table 7.3 for a major field of learning

Figure 7.3 Two models for subject benchmarking

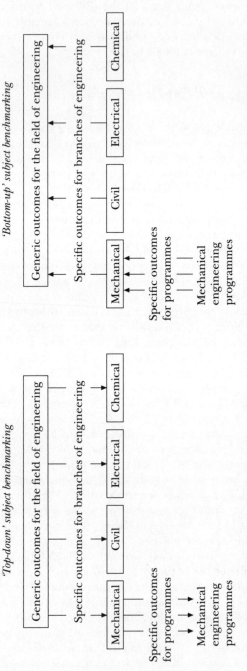

'Top-down' subject benchmarking

'Bottom-up' subject benchmarking

Note: The 'top-down' approach takes as its starting point the major field of learning containing cognate subjects (e.g. engineering). It creates generic information that relates to *what it is to be an engineer* and perhaps more specific information that relates to *what it is to be a civil, mechanical, electrical or chemical engineer*. The 'bottom-up' approach takes as its starting point the specific field of learning called the subject i.e. *what it is to be a mechanical engineer*. It defines specific learning outcomes relevant to the subject. As this information becomes available for each subject within the major field of learning the generic outcomes can be identified.

might therefore be the most appropriate level at which to benchmark learning outcomes and generic performance criteria relating to such outcomes. This combination would provide for a basic set of threshold expectations but would enable teaching teams to be creative and innovative beyond the basic expectation.

Subject benchmarking and interdisciplinary programmes

The administrative framework for subject benchmarking does not cater for interdisciplinary programmes like sports science that have effectively created new subjects in their own right (a well-defined field of learning and application). There are a number of options. The first would be to locate the interdisciplinary subject within one or more major fields of learning to which the generic outcomes might be expected to apply. The second approach might be to create a hybrid set of outcomes from the individual subjects that form the field of interdisciplinary study. A third approach would be to create a benchmarking group specifically for the field of study. A fourth approach would be to gather information on generic outcomes through the programme specification. This would be a cost-effective way of creating benchmarking information and it would be truly 'bottom-up'.

Subject benchmarking and multidisciplinary programmes

A more difficult matter to resolve is the ability of subject benchmarking to relate to multidisciplinary programmes in which there may be little or no connection between the subjects comprising the programme. The key organizing principle for such programmes is breadth rather than depth of study. The Scottish Ordinary degree where a student might study 10 different subjects spanning three or four major fields of study provides a good example of this type of programme. Subject benchmarking could relate to such programmes in one of three ways. First, a set of generic outcomes could be established for all multidisciplinary programmes based on the distinctive educational aims that underpin them. Generic outcomes could be created through an *expert group* or by gathering information from academic staff using a survey instrument, like the Graduate Attributes Profiling Tool (see Chapter 5), or the programme specification template. The alternative way of looking at such provision is to argue that if the subjects comprising the programme have been referenced to appropriate benchmark information then the overall standard of the programme should also be appropriate. The use of subject-level descriptors (expectations of learning in a subject at different stages of a programme) could provide another reference point for the formulation of outcomes at the level of study units and modules.

Work-based learning (and learner-managed programmes in general) pose a particular challenge to subject-based benchmarking since every programme is unique to the learner and the standards achieved are also unique to the individual. Such fields of applied learning could be supported by a dedicated benchmarking forum which could research the processes of learning and accreditation and provide examples of credit-rated learning that could act as system-wide benchmarks.

Impact on teaching, learning and assessment

If the outcomes identified in the subject benchmarking statement become the core outcomes for programmes in the subject they will effectively become the main organizers for teaching, learning and assessment. In order to demonstrate (to learners, teaching teams and quality assurance processes) that programmes in a subject provide opportunities for the subject-specific outcomes to be achieved it will be necessary for teaching teams to show how the outcomes are developed/taught, practised and assessed. Such a referencing process is illustrated schematically in Figure 7.4. The most economical way of showing this relationship is through the use of curriculum and assessment mapping tools such as those described by Jenkins *et al.* (1994), Jenkins (1997) and QAA (1998d). It might therefore be anticipated that the production of outcome-based benchmark information will be accom-

Figure 7.4 Possible use of subject benchmark information by a teaching team to inform the design of curricula and assessment and evaluate student performance

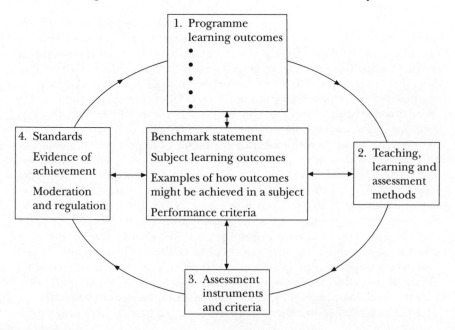

panied by the development of curriculum mapping techniques to enable the information to be applied. It is this combination of processes (benchmarking and curriculum mapping) rather than benchmarking alone that will lead to a more explicit environment in which the dimensions of standards and the ways in which they are achieved and assessed are made clearer. This line of reasoning suggests that the need to provide learning and assessment opportunities to demonstrate achievement of the subject outcomes may have considerable implications for staff development.

Assessment of thresholds standards

The absence of an assessment model that would underpin a consistent approach to threshold standards poses a major challenge to the proposition that benchmarking information can be used to set threshold standards in subjects. The current assessment model in UK undergraduate education is linked to the honours system of classification (the five levels of performance recognized in the chemistry benchmarking information reflects this system, i.e. four pass and one fail category). It is based on an assessment regime in which the idea of grading upwards from a minimum standard to excellence is alien to marking traditions and where there has been a relatively loose linkage between the instruments of assessment and the educational aims and objectives. Fundamentally, it is based on marking traditions that compensate for strengths and weaknesses across the overall performance of a student and where grading of the quality of performance, rather than a concern for establishing that a minimum standard has been met, is the priority. It can be argued (Jackson 1998f) that a commitment to applying benchmarking information to secure subject threshold standards will require a new type of assessment model. Such a model would assume a more direct relationship between learning intentions and the assessment of learning, i.e. between the outcomes for a programme or module and:

• the overall assessment strategy
• the assessment instruments
• the performance criteria.

Subject benchmarking provides a means of promoting large-scale movement towards a criterion-referenced system but, given the tradition of operating a norm-referenced compensation assessment model, a pure threshold criterion-referenced model, in which all the learning outcomes have to be achieved at the specified standard, is unlikely to be successful. Such reasoning suggests that any new assessment model would need to incorporate an element of academic discretion to enable compensation to be applied for weakness in some outcomes at the threshold/pass level of performance. This accepts that assessment of higher level learning is not a precise science and that there is an important element of professional judgement involved in determining standards. The law benchmarking information provides an

Figure 7.5   Referencing processes used in benchmarking

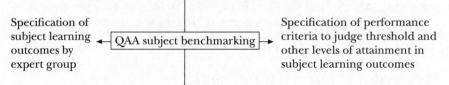

Surveys of practice supported by discussion
(e.g. surveys of outcomes, teaching, learning and
assessment methods, performance and criteria)

Specification of
subject learning
outcomes by
expert group

QAA subject benchmarking

Specification of performance
criteria to judge threshold and
other levels of attainment in
subject learning outcomes

Performance measures (e.g. degree results,
module assessment data, value added, progression
to employment or further study, student and
employer satisfaction data)

Note: Subject benchmarking currently focuses on the horizontal dimension of this diagram
but there is the potential to exploit all the referencing processes.

example of how this might be achieved by bundling learning outcomes into
one of seven 'areas of performance'. The threshold standard for the award
is based on satisfactory performance in each area rather than achieving the
individual learning outcomes that make up each area of performance. Having developed criteria to guide judgements on achievement, at the threshold level of achievement the next logical step for subject benchmarking is
to provide guidance and exemplar materials that will facilitate consistent
interpretation and implementation by assessors, external examiners and
academic reviewers.

Conclusions

Subject benchmarking, as initially conceived, is a device to support self-
regulation within a diverse, multi-purpose national HE system. The initial
development work has demonstrated the possibilities of the method and
exposed difficulties and limitations in applying the concept. It has confirmed that different subjects approach the idea of benchmarking in different ways and that the products reflect these differences. Ultimately, such
differences will exert a strong influence on the way the information can
be applied and on public and political perceptions of the utility of the
method for improving the capacity of the system to regulate standards. The
referencing framework for benchmarking developed in Chapter 1 (shown
in Figure 7.5) indicates that the initial development work on subject benchmarking is utilizing only two of the four referencing processes (specification of outcomes and performance criteria). The full benefits from subject
benchmarking will perhaps only be realized through a more holistic approach

involving surveys of practice, the identification of good practice within the discipline and research directed to understanding the reasons for differences in outcome data. It is worth noting that this more holistic approach, albeit undertaken in a much smaller HE system, characterized subject benchmarking in Australia – one of the triggers for UK policy on subject benchmarking. The possibility exists to connect the process and products of regulatory benchmarking to more developmentally focused research and support activities such as might be associated with the subject centres proposed by HEFCE (1998d). This would improve the capacity of the subject to regulate standards and also promote a strong subject-based developmental agenda.

Note

1. Norman Jackson is expressing his own views which are not necessarily the views of the Quality Assurance Agency.

8

Benchmarking Key Skills Using National Standards: the Open University Experience

Linda Hodgkinson

Overview

Key skills are those personal and cognitive skills and abilities that people use in carrying out a wide range of tasks and activities and in learning new things. National standards have been created for six key skill areas: Communication; Application of number; Information technology; Improving own learning and performance; Working with others; and Problem solving. This chapter describes how key skill standards can provide benchmarks to aid the design of curricula and assessment and improve learning. The process of benchmarking course outcomes against key skills standards is illustrated with reference to the design of an Open University mathematics course.

Introduction

When people talk about 'improving the quality of learning in higher education' they generally mean one of two things: either that students may successfully be taught more facts and skills within particular disciplines, or that they may learn to use their minds more effectively so that they can continue to learn better in all areas of study. To improve the former requires more efficient instructional skills; but improving students' ability to learn effectively offers a far more efficient way of raising long-term achievement. It requires a different, and for many academics a radically new, approach to curriculum design, teaching, learning and assessment. Improving the capacity of learners to learn by designing opportunities for the development of key skills (formerly known as core skills) was the objective of an Open University (OU) initiative (Hodgkinson 1996). The process of designing curricula with reference to key skill national standards can be viewed as a type of benchmarking exercise.

The Open University is the largest university in the UK (160,000 students) with a world class reputation for high-quality undergraduate courses delivered through distance learning. The OU has long been a pioneer in innovative practices in teaching and learning, not least because it has an open access policy for adult learners. Indeed, its world class reputation is founded on an organizational climate that promotes the evaluation of new ideas and research findings in the field of education and training. It was this concern to experiment and embrace new ideas that led the OU to research the idea of embedding opportunities for key skills in the HE curriculum.

National skills agenda

During the last decade UK HE (with other parts of the education system) has come under increasing pressure from government and the employer community to give greater attention to the development of skills that will improve the employability of graduates. The government's strategic objective has been promoted by reports, policies, funded initiatives, research and development work, sponsored mainly by the employment department arm of what is now the Department for Education and Employment (e.g. DES 1985 and 1987; EDG 1990; NCC 1990; Oates 1991; DfEE 1994 and 1998a). The ideas for improving graduate skills embedded in these reports were strongly endorsed by employer and HE representative bodies (CBI 1989; AGR 1995; CVCP 1998). Emerging from these strategies and debates has been the idea that all learning should be underpinned by a set of key skills, although the idea is not without its critics (Hyland 1998; Hyland and Johnson 1998). Key skills are those personal and cognitive skills and abilities that people use in carrying out a wide range of tasks and activities and in learning new things.

Early development work on a set of core or common skills (NCC 1990; BTEC 1992) has been refined into a set of detailed specifications and performance criteria for six key skill areas: Communication; Application of number; Information technology; Improving own learning and performance; Working with others; and Problem solving (Oates 1991). Responsibility for maintaining and developing the national key skill standards now resides with the Qualifications and Curriculum Authority (QCA), and key skills units and qualifications are an important part of the qualifications framework managed by QCA. The Dearing review of higher education (NCIHE 1997) encouraged HE to give greater attention to the development of key skills. Many universities and colleges have created opportunities for the explicit development of a range of personal and social skills (including key skills) within their programmes but very few have used the QCA standards (Murphy *et al.* 1998).

Applying key skills standards in HE

The key skills were originally described in units that related to five levels of progression (Levels 3, 4 and 5 are most relevant to HE). These initial

Table 8.1 Format of the key skills specification for Communication Level 3 as used in the OU development work

---

Element 3.2: Produce written material

Performance criteria – A student must:
1. include information which is accurate and relevant to the subject
2. check that text is legible and the meaning is clear, correcting it if necessary
3. follow appropriate standard conventions
4. present information in a format that suits the audience and purpose
5. use structure and style to emphasize meaning

Range
Subject: straightforward, complex
Conventions: spelling, punctuation, grammar
Format: pre-set, outline, freely structured
Audience: people who are familiar with the subject and who are not familiar with the subject and people who know the student and do not know the student

Evidence indicators
At least six pieces of material on different subjects, of which four pieces should include evidence that the student is able to write about complex subjects. Four pieces should demonstrate that the student is able to organize and present information in an appropriate and freely structured format.

Note: The format of these specifications was revised in 1998; see Figure 8.1.

specifications have been modified in the light of further development work and feedback from practitioners. The assessment framework differs from the traditional norm-referenced approach usually found in universities as key skills units involve the collection and judgement of evidence against nationally defined criteria. The specifications effectively constitute a type of benchmark information against which a study unit can be designed, the performance of individuals can be judged or individuals can evaluate their own progress towards achieving the specified standard. An example of a keys skills specification is given in Table 8.1 to illustrate the principles of design.

OU approach to key skills

In 1995, the OU began a major programme of research and development work aimed at embedding key skills in the curriculum. The work was largely carried out through a development project funded by the Employment Department to investigate the extent to which the QCA framework of key skills could be embedded in university Level 1 courses in mathematics, science and technology. The approach adopted has been to work towards explicit integration of specific key skills into the subject context and to use, as the organizing principle for learning, the model represented by the key skill, Improving own learning and performance. This embraces the idea of consciousness or awareness of an individual's own learning processes. The theoretical models behind this approach are those associated with reflective learning. Such models foster learning as understanding as compared with 'superficial or surface' learning and recognize the importance of metacognition in learning and in adapting one's thinking/learning strategies to new and different contexts (Boud *et al.* 1985; Schon 1987).

The initiative was such a radical departure from existing practice that the OU Vocational Qualifications Centre provided specific briefing and training to all tutors on key skills, learning outcomes and assessment methods appropriate to a learning outcomes-based approach. In addition, tutors were given the opportunity for more detailed training and assessment to Training and Development Lead Body (TDLB) standards leading to an assessor award. Mechanisms were also established to allow students the option of external key skills assessment and certification through the Royal Society of Arts accreditation scheme.

Why mathematics?

A number of OU-specific factors, combined with wider changes in education and training in the UK, created a climate in which new ideas for restructuring entry-level mathematics courses were welcomed by academic staff. The mathematics and computing faculty needed to update the content and approach of the entry-level provision as well as address issues of extending access, reducing early drop-out, improving the gender balance and broadening achievement through its new suite of courses. In addition, a goal of the faculty was to promote a deeper understanding of learning mathematics, and to move away from learning materials that focused on the correct following of certain routine procedures and algorithms. Against the backcloth of changing demands from students, employers and the institution itself, the OU sought to promote curriculum change that fostered ideas fundamental to key skills. That is, supporting the development of learning skills, such as reflecting, questioning, challenging and analysing; helping individuals gain self-awareness, ownership, personal responsibility and autonomy in their learning; and promoting the application and transfer of learning. The integration of key skills into the learning programme at Level 1 was therefore designed to improve the quality of student performance in mathematics and specific key skills and to make them better learners.

Particular features of the mathematics course

MU120 was to be the first of the new suite of mathematics courses designed to provide access to mathematics to people who had previously had little opportunity to develop and improve their mathematical abilities. The course had to make the study of mathematics both accessible and attractive to a large and diverse constituency (2500 students in the first cohort). For many students MU120 would be their first OU course and would represent a return to study after many years' absence. It was therefore important that the course enabled students to learn and gain confidence in their mathematical ability and to 'learn how to learn' effectively at a distance. Integrating the key skills of communication and improving own learning and performance was adopted as a design principle at an early stage to help create a different kind of learning environment, where the learner is placed centre-stage. It was intended that learners would be given the confidence and power to use their mathematical skills and abilities in a wide range of contexts, from music to warfare. They would also be involved from day one in thinking about, reflecting on and taking responsibility for their own learning, and monitoring and improving performance through target setting using the framework of key skills.

Conceptual framework for benchmarking key skills

The process of designing a curriculum which provides opportunities for developing and demonstrating key skills is outlined below and described in detail by Hodgkinson (1996). In essence a teaching team takes as its starting point the specification for the particular key skills that will be developed and assessed and defines a set of outcomes that reflect the elements of the specification but are set in the context of the subject. These effectively become the organizing principles on which the curriculum, teaching, learning and assessment methods are based. Similarly, the performance criteria (what students need to know and what they must do) and guidance on the evidence that might be used to demonstrate the acquisition of the skill can be used to guide the design of subject-specific assessment criteria. Figure 8.1 illustrates schematically the process of benchmarking a course design process against the national key skills specification.

Development process

The OU uses a team-based approach to course design supported by specialist advisory groups like the Vocational Qualifications Centre. The process of explicitly integrating key skills into the mathematics curriculum began with the identification and adoption of a number of principles that characterize effective programmes of learning for the development of skills, knowledge and understanding including the ideas that:

• skills need to be developed through all components of the course with opportunities for skills to be both taught and developed, recognizing and using prior experiences

Figure 8.1 A process model for benchmarking key skills

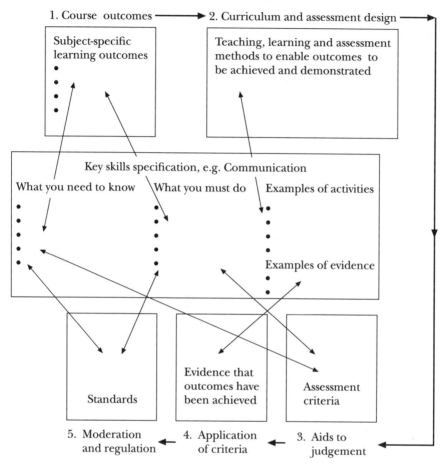

- theoretical ideas need to be linked with practice components that involve skills
- opportunities need to be provided for skills to be practised through a variety of activities of varying demand
- opportunities need to be provided for modelling the selection and use of learning strategies and accurate feedback given on performance
- skills of application and 'transfer' integral to the key skills need to be explicitly developed and practised
- students need support and feedback on accurately judging and assessing their own work
- opportunities need to be created within the assessment strategy for skills to be demonstrated and assessed.

Curriculum design process

The production of a new OU course involves a number of stages including detailed planning, drafting of materials and editing and printing of the course. The early discussions on the design of MU120 focused on the overall aims of the course and the main concepts to be covered in each unit and block. This enabled progression strands and integrative themes to be identified. Decisions were taken as to which key skills were to be included and the specification of these within the planned learning outcomes of the course. These course outcomes were then linked to particular blocks and appropriate descriptors identified (Stages 1 and 2 of the model illustrated in Figure 8.1).

To highlight the importance of key skills within the course, it was agreed that all aspects of the teaching and learning would support the students' acquisition of skills using a variety of methods including exposition, multimedia components and 'interactive' activities in the text. Activities would be followed by comments providing teaching and development points for students. From the beginning students were to be encouraged to think about the quality of their learning and performance, how they were learning, and how they could improve. Thus the notion of using 'specified standards' was highlighted as a teaching and learning strategy. This philosophy demonstrates that national standards and benchmarking are to be viewed from a multi-level perspective. In the curriculum design process, key skill standards can be used as a design aid and/or audit tool. They provide a set of benchmark statements against which course outcomes can be modelled, enable checks to be made on the opportunities for developing skills in the course and provide a quality assurance tool to demonstrate that sufficient opportunities for skill development are created. For students, the key skill standards can be used as part of their own self-assessment and self-audit activities as well as the basis for tutor assessment of achievement against the intended course outcomes. Thus the use of national key skill standards is both multi-layered and multifunctional within the curriculum.

Incorporating the key skills standards into course-based activities proved to be complex and time-consuming. Learning activities had to be designed to help students move from the instrumental aspect of a key skill standard, for example in communication, towards an understanding of the analytic and communicative conventions within the discipline. In order to do this it was necessary to create a learner-centred environment. Students were invited to take ownership of the key skills from the outset, to self-assess against the given criteria for the standards and, ultimately, to take responsibility for their own learning.

As part of the planning and design process and to provide an overview of all the skills being developed in a way that would facilitate links to content, a skeleton matrix was created, which showed the different key skills and learning strategies planned for each quarter of the course. This became a working document, which highlighted the different progression strands in the development of key skills and provided, along with other documents, an ongoing skills audit, which helped maintain continuity of skills development. It also proved to be a useful tool for matching opportunities for skills development with course content. An extract from a working version of the matrix for the course is presented in Table 8.2.

The planning stage was difficult and it required considerable time and effort. The course team had to interpret key skills specifications that were largely untested at HE levels and were grappling with the complexities of meshing a key skills matrix with a subject content matrix across a range of course components. Eventually, the key skills unit, Improving own learning and performance was adopted as the overarching organizing principle which was to support all the other skill strands and provide the underlying rationale for the change in learning environment. On completing the course, students should be able to:

- begin to identify how they learn effectively within a distance-learning environment and so understand more about how they learn
- use different learning styles and strategies to achieve effective performance in mathematics at this level
- recognize and demonstrate improvement in their own learning and performance in mathematics
- use their awareness of the processes relating to learning and improving performance by applying them to future work.

In designing the course to achieve these intended outcomes, the approach adopted was to introduce students to the power of learning mathematics through application. Topics were presented through a problem-orientated approach involving familiar everyday contexts. Students were encouraged to engage in activities in a systematic way and make conscious links between prior knowledge and understanding and current tasks. This was designed to provide opportunities for students to reflect on how they were learning mathematics and to provide opportunities to use and respond to a wide range of different types of learning milieu. In the final stages of production, the key skills standards were used extensively as an audit tool to help check for coherence of skills development between course components, and to check and ensure appropriate progression opportunities between the course units.

The process of designing and producing the assignments was an integral part of the curriculum design process (Stage 2 in Figure 8.1). Key skills are described and specified in terms of learning outcomes, and assessment is criterion-referenced. Such an approach is incompatible with the traditional norm-referenced approach to grading students. For MU120, the challenge was not only to design appropriate criterion-referenced assessment instruments for key skills attainment, but to couple the assessment with more traditional academic assessment requirements (Stage 3, Figure 8.1). Criterion-referenced assessment sits uneasily with the principle of compensation, which is widely applied in the assessment of individual pieces of work and in the

Table 8.2 Part of the matrix for one block of MU120

Unit	Learning how to learn	Communicating mathematics	Improving own learning
1. Mathematics everywhere?	Introduction to course components	Produce written material – paragraphs	Directed in study skills
2. Prices	Statistical ideas and techniques	Define given mathematical terms Present data Use and draw tables, graphs, diagrams	Plan study Use calculator for exploring and learning Identify areas of difficulty
3. Earnings	Statistical ideas and techniques	Define given mathematical terms Produce written material – paragraphs – summary Discuss mathematical ideas	Plan and monitor study Identify progress – things that were straightforward, difficult
4. Health	Consolidation of statistical ideas and techniques	Define given mathematical terms Read for learning Identify key points from a text	Plan and monitor study Identify areas for change and implement changes
5. Seabirds	Use and identify stages in the statistical problem-solving cycle Think about process in learning mathematics	Define given mathematical terms Produce written material	Plan and monitor work Identify progress – areas for development
		REVIEW	
General outcomes for block	Learning supported Techniques given Increasing number of techniques through block	Communicating *about* mathematics Produce written material in mathematics *for self and tutor* – paragraphs – summary – produce and use tables – read for learning	Directed in study skills Plan and monitor work Identify strengths and areas for development Provide ideas for improvement and suggest change

computation of overall grades. A student's overall performance or grades may include poor performance, or even failure, in one area compensated for by good performance in others. The strategy that was adopted involved total integration of academic and skills assessment, with the option of disaggregation for the purpose of certification of skills attainment. Each of the tutor-marked assignments that students completed on a regular basis included a skills component with target criteria. The final summative assessment required students to bring together their previous skills response sheets and to analyse and reflect on their learning throughout the course in a way that produced evidence of 'improving own learning and performance' as well as subject knowledge (Stage 4 in Figure 8.1). The outcome was graded and the evidence of learning provided material from which attainment of the required key skills criteria could be judged. Overall it was felt that the key skills framework helped the course team to specify those skill elements amenable to assessment and provide assessment criteria that were relevant in HE, but considerable work was required to develop a workable assessment strategy.

Lessons from benchmarking key skills standards

The OU's experience of integrating key skills into its new generation of Level 1 courses has been a learning experience for all involved and has had many and varied unforeseen effects on all parts of the institution. A number of lessons have been learned through the experience of applying the key skill national standards.

1. Many HE staff are not familiar with using an outcomes-based key skills framework for curriculum design. Most academic staff in HE are used to working with a content-led or syllabus-based curriculum. This approach emphasizes what has to be taught rather than what students can do with their knowledge, and the assessment strategy is a way of checking that some of the content has been successfully transmitted. Even when learning outcomes (based on the QCA specifications) were agreed and contextualized in a subject, it was not immediately obvious what teaching and learning opportunities needed to be provided within the programme to achieve them. This required considerable discussion to raise awareness of possibilities.
2. Key skills descriptions to support effective learning are as much about the process of learning as the content. They require consideration of how learning takes place as well as what is covered. The quality of the teaching and learning are central to integrating key skills into programmes.
3. Assessment has to be intimately linked to the development of course learning outcomes, with alternative methods for assessment being developed where necessary. The methods of assessment may be further complicated by the need both to measure the achievement of course

outcomes and relate these to the subject benchmarks and to provide
useful descriptors of achievement that are structured and validated for
the student.

4. Widespread curriculum changes are unlikely to be effectively implemented
   unless a major programme of staff development is in place. Developing
   learning outcomes, using national standards in key skills and designing
   subject benchmark statements should be part of a strategic development
   plan.

5. Development and change on the scale described above is resource-
   intensive and needs to allow for systems modifications.

Conclusions

The development work undertaken at the Open University has helped to
demonstrate that key skill national standards can provide a set of benchmark statements against which course outcomes can be referenced. The
process and the effects of such benchmarking activity are multi-layered. For
staff, the key skill standards can promote more systematic coverage and
opportunities for skill development and progression. For managers, they
offer a quality assurance tool to enable checks to be made that sufficient
learning opportunities are provided. But perhaps the real net gain is for
students who benefit from improved opportunities for learning and develop
important generic skills through studying their subject.

Part 2

Benchmarking to Improve the Quality of
Administrative and Business Processes
and Services to Support HE

9

Some Approaches to Administrative Benchmarking

Helen Lund

Overview

This chapter discusses some recent and current projects within UK universities that have applied benchmarking techniques to administrative functions. These range from the publication of management statistics for comparative purposes to benchmarking in its fullest sense – the analysis and comparison of performance within a group of 'peers' in order to identify 'best practice' and adopt it or adapt it to particular institutional needs. It also discusses some of the barriers that have prevented benchmarking by UK HEIs and asks whether this situation might be about to change. Where sources are not specifically cited, information was provided as a personal communication to the author.

Benchmarking: awareness, attitudes and deterrents

A telephone survey by the Commonwealth Higher Education Management Service (CHEMS) in autumn 1997 to the registries of about 60 per cent of UK universities suggested a considerable variation in regard to familiarity with the concept of benchmarking and attitudes towards it. In some institutions there was immediate recognition and referral to the institution's benchmarking champion(s); in others, the term needed further explanation, even at senior management level (Lund 1998a).

When invited to join a benchmarking project, university responses tended to be informed by pragmatic considerations. The timing of a request, so as not to coincide with a particular division's busiest period, was crucial. It helped if the questionnaire was clear and not too long. More than one respondent believed that a questionnaire alone was not sufficient for a good benchmarking exercise: follow-up visits were essential. Universities needed to feel that they were getting enough out of a benchmarking exercise to warrant the time and resources spent on contributing data. One administrator implied a greater readiness to respond if the invitation came from another HEI, rather than a firm of management consultants.

The main obstacles to benchmarking seemed to be difficulty in collecting data, even at the level of mapping internal processes, and the time and money involved. For example, one registrar at a research-intensive university expressed interest in the concept of benchmarking, but said that lack of resources prevented the institution's involvement. Another pre-1992 institution had begun to establish PIs relating to a range of activities within the registry and estates departments, but this had been curtailed as too time-consuming. One 'new' university cited shortage of time and resources, together with a lack of manual skills and data to explain why neither construction of PIs nor internal comparative evaluation of departments had been undertaken, despite awareness of its necessity. Some institutions were at the stage of mapping internal processes and hoped to progress from this to benchmarking with other HEIs.

In terms of comparative evaluation, several HEIs preferred to 'benchmark' their performance, in areas such as estates management or library services, against statistics produced either by commercial companies or professional bodies, rather than join benchmarking groups or clubs. Many respondents mentioned the perceived difficulty of obtaining a genuine comparison of 'like with like'.

There are signs, however, that, since then, attitudes may be changing, and that benchmarking within small groups or 'consortia' is beginning to gain wider acceptance. For example, one 'new' university reported that it had previously considered it to be more cost-effective to evaluate its performance through internal Value for Money (VfM) studies and to compare performance against publicly available information (statistics from local government and the National Health Service (NHS) as well as HESA) than to benchmark through visits to other institutions. By the end of 1998, however, the need to produce specific VfM studies had lessened. This was partly because the outcomes of previous studies were now embedded in the university's routine activities and its internal programme of audits, and partly because the university was able to draw on VfM work done by the Higher Education Funding Council for England (HEFCE; see Chapter 13) and other HE agencies. In view of this the university took the decision to join an informal benchmarking group of seven 'similar' institutions.

Benchmarking via existing consortia/regional groups

Given the collaborative nature of benchmarking and the degree of openness and trust involved, it is not surprising that universities have often sought benchmarking partners within well-established groups or consortia, founded on common interests arising either from regional location or broad institutional type.

94 Group

In November 1997, the 94 Group (14 smaller research-based 'old' universities) produced the first edition of a volume of comparative management statistics. Based on published data produced by bodies like HESA and UCAS, it covers four main areas: students; finance; staff; and quality assurance. Each university can see its own data set against that of other 94 Group members and against the UK average, where this is available (University of Essex 1997). This is intended to be an annual publication.

Midlands universities

In the Midlands, KPMG in Birmingham have, since 1992, run an annual Value for Money study for a small regional consortium of four 'old' universities. Both quantitative and qualitative data are collected and topics have included space utilization, provision of engineering/building workshops, administrative computing services and procurement management. This last study focused on analysis of purchases at departmental rather than institutional level with the aim of identifying top suppliers so as to negotiate better discounts. Past studies are reviewed to get feedback from users. KPMG in Birmingham has also conducted benchmarking studies for a group of nine 'new' universities (not a formal consortium) which meets annually to identify a topic of common interest. Each study takes about a year to complete and areas covered so far include: catering management; business planning; print and reproduction; and sickness management (Lund 1998a).

Southern Universities Management Service

The Southern Universities Management Service (SUMS) is a management consultancy service run on behalf of approximately 30 institutions. SUMS has previously undertaken one-off pilot studies to develop PIs, using quantitative data and covering topics such as staffing, personnel, and the effectiveness of printing units (Lund 1998a). It has now moved on to process-based benchmarking using a consortium approach.

Two pilot projects have been undertaken. The first study focused on graduation. The topic was chosen by the participants, a group of seven academic secretaries and registrars, as being reasonably self-contained and, therefore, suitable for a pilot. Areas for benchmarking were identified and defined in terms of 10 objectives, such as 'increasing academic staff participation at graduation ceremonies'. For each objective, two or three performance measures were then identified, for example, 'How many academic staff currently attend?' and 'How many would you like to attend?' From here, 10–12 operational practice questions could be drawn up, such as 'Who invites them?' 'What incentives are there for attendance?' 'What difficulties prevent attendance?' Initial questions were suggested by SUMS, but active participation by consortium members was assured by assigning one person to act as 'sponsor' for a particular objective, reviewing and amending the list of questions as appropriate. Questions for each objective were also circulated to all group members, so that they could add their input. The final questionnaire was then sent to all participating institutions. After analysis by SUMS, the system is to send raw data for all institutions to each group member, enabling institutions to identify partners with whom to work more closely to improve their own practice. In the interim, each consortium member has conducted a self-assessment exercise with its own internal benchmarking team. The group will probably meet again to discuss the findings, although SUMS tries to avoid too directive an approach. The group also expressed interest in undertaking another study focused on registration.

For John Haywood (Managing Consultant at SUMS) the interest of this study lay partly in the fact of staff involvement at the academic secretary/ registrar level, ensuring that the project would be approached from an institutional viewpoint, rather than that of a particular interest group. He believes that senior management involvement, which brings an element of strategic leadership to the process, is essential for successful benchmarking.

The second SUMS study had a personnel focus: again, the aim was to examine the topic in an institutional context, as opposed to a personnel office-centred approach. Issues covered include communication and devolved management structures. Eleven institutions expressed interest in participating, but concerns about time and resources led to a more low-key approach than that taken for the graduation study. Data were collected via a straightforward and quickly completed questionnaire, and the emphasis was on resources, such as staffing levels.

Library and information services

Chapter 12 provides a detailed description of activities in this area so only a brief summary is presented here. Academic libraries were one of the first groups in UK HE to utilize benchmarking. The Royal Military College of Science (RMCS) library at Cranfield University launched a project in October 1993 drawing in part on Total Quality Management (TQM) methodology (use of critical success factors (CSFs) as a method of measurement). The exercise involved 20 other HEIs and focused on availability of up-to-date stock; staff development; ability and approachability; user experience, education and feedback; innovation; the learning environment. Planned scrutiny of unit costs was abandoned due to lack of data. Data collection, via a questionnaire, was followed by visits; institutions were then grouped in terms of 'better practice' in regard to four key processes:

1. User induction/education.
2. Information retrieval.
3. Information provision and delivery.
4. Facilities provision.

On-site measurement studies (availability; unobtrusive testing; subjective assessment gathered on a walk-through basis) enabled further identification of good practice. Participating libraries were then ranked in relation to the RMCS service, and received a written report summarizing the findings for their service. RMCS then developed and implemented plans to improve its performance to match that of its 'best practice' partners. Subsequently, RMCS took part in a research project led by Loughborough University to assess the relevance of benchmarking techniques to the library and information sector.

A project initiated by Surrey Institute of Art and Design is interesting for its inclusion, along with another art school and RMCS, of a commercial partner. It focused on the IT help desk service and the complete document and information delivery process. Each process was divided into sub-processes ('operating the student help desk', 'interlibrary loans', etc.) and each sub-process mapped. Data collection via a questionnaire and visits succeeded in achieving 'detailed quantitative comparisons' in all areas, including cost analysis. From this, the Institute was able to identify areas where each of its partners had achieved 'better practice' and to draw up an improvement programme.

The RMCS information service used benchmarking techniques again in 1998 for a 'conceptual review' focused on development of electronic library services and linked building requirements. Benchmarked processes were: provision of the physical learning environment; provision of electronic library services; provision of new methods of teaching and learning technology. Nine partners were chosen for the building strand and six (including two European institutions) for the electronic library element. Information on teaching and learning technology was collected on five UK instititions primarily from secondary sources. Methodology again utilized CSFs, developed with reference to HEFCE's framework for an effective academic library (HEFCE 1995b).

Autumn 1997 saw the start of work towards benchmarking pilot projects funded by the Standing Committee of National University Libraries (SCONUL). These aimed to 'give practical experience of benchmarking to a wide number of practitioners throughout the sector' and to develop a standard methodology for academic library benchmarking. The six pilot projects covered 'Advice Desks' (North and South), 'Information skills' (North and South), 'Counter services' and 'Library environment'. Membership ranged from two to five institutions; some institutions joined more than one project. Participants were asked to use Oakland's 15-point benchmarking plan (see Chapter 12). By November 1998, most pilots had completed the data collection and analysis stages. Reported benefits from the benchmarking process included the opportunity for reflection on service quality; development of improvement agendas by all institutions in one pilot; identification and adoption, during the pilot, of a partner's superior practice in the area of information skills. Challenges and lessons learned included the need for transparency with results; difficulties in producing comparative metrics, particularly relating to cost issues; the cost-effectiveness of benchmarking one particular process, possibly because too many benchmarks had been identified.

Facilities/estates management

In the area of estates/facilities management, the Conference of University Business Officers (CUBO) have for several years produced PIs with the specific aim of allowing its 60 members 'the opportunity of a comparison exercise' (CUBO 1997). Data is collected under six main headings:

- catered residences
- self-catering residences
- central catering
- general
- all-year-round centres
- conference marketing and training.

Within these categories, information is collected on a considerable range of activities: under catered residences, for example, there are 14 separate sections, including salaries and wages; fuel, power and water; maintenance of buildings; furniture and equipment; laundry and linen costs; food cost per student meal; student income; percentage occupancy (term and vacation); loan finance.

Institutions also use well-established databases maintained by the Association of University Directors of Estates (AUDE) and the Association of University Engineers (AUE) for comparative evaluation of performance (Chapter 13).

When it comes to benchmarking in its more collaborative sense, the Facilities Management Graduate Centre (FMGC) at Sheffield Hallam University is a major player. Its work is more fully described in Chapter 11, so a brief summary suffices here. FMGC has five years' benchmarking experience with public sector and commercial clients. HE work began in 1996 and has included maintenance expenditure and management, space management and development of key FM PIs. The core activity of FMGC is the understanding and dissemination of 'best' practice within the facilities management profession and its Director, Ilfryn Price, views benchmarking as an opportunity to work with and understand innovators in FM and to provide those innovators with a forum within which to learn from each other.

FMGC has developed a standard approach to benchmarking. An initial workshop introduces participants to the distinction between benchmarking (horizontal between peers) and audit (vertical stemming from funding/

government bodies). Participants then become involved in defining the numerical aspects of the process to be benchmarked; this tends to focus on costs of process delivery and resources used, but customer/user perceptions have also been included as comparators (though not yet in the HE environment). The data definition stage generates a wider range of questions and shows up inconsistencies of interpretation; these are reviewed at a second workshop, by which time participants have a 'numerical assessment of themselves' relating to various measures and set against those of peer organizations.

Quantitative analysis is translated into 'learning and action' via reciprocal one-day visits, typically within groups of four. The host organization can share, and be challenged on, its good practice, and at this stage operational staff can become involved in the learning process. FMGC staff attend the visits in order to capture the issues and 'cross-pollinate' ideas and information across groups and sectors.

FMGC's membership has included UK HEIs of all types. Given this diversity, absolute cost comparisons are considered almost meaningless, but benchmarking within peer groups has enabled FMGC to identify those institutions most committed to improvement. One factor leading to success, in terms of value for money and a modern and multi-skilled FM system, seems to be integration of facilities management in the hands of a member of the senior management team. Despite demands from HEIs and funding agencies for detailed statistical comparisons, FMGC has, interestingly, 'frequently seen the limitations of numbers, especially as they become more detailed'; this recalls one criticism of the benchmarking operation in the US by NACUBO (National Association of College and University Business Officers) (Chapter 14). In response, FMGC is testing the idea of a 'balanced scorecard' of FM indicators for HE, which normalizes total facilities cost against, for example, institutional income, staff/student numbers, m^2 teaching space. Other measures being tested include net space per staff member, complexity of the estate, utilization and capacity. This approach has some elements in common with the performance benchmarks suggested for development by HEFCE in its Building Repairs and Maintenance study (Chapter 13).

Finance

At the simpler end of the benchmarking spectrum, quantitative comparison of performance against published statistics looks set to increase with HESA's publication of its *Finance Plus* CD-ROM (HESA 1997). This includes detailed financial accounting data in hundreds of categories from all universities and CHEs, presented in a spreadsheet format so that data is easily comparable.

In 1996, a benchmark exercise run by the British Universities Finance Directors' Group (BUFDG) asked finance departments to supply quantitative data on their staffing (ratio of staff numbers to £100 million turnover and to 1000 FTE students). Staff were categorized, on the questionnaire, by specific function (financial accounting, payroll and pensions, accounts payable, etc.) to eliminate the possibility of omission or ambiguity. Data on volume of business and productivity was also requested (for example, number of employees dealt with per payroll staff member; how many thousand invoices are handled per staff member in accounts payable), plus average salary costs per FTE member of staff. Each participant received their own institution's figures, set against the overall survey results, expressed in terms of lower quartile, median and upper quartile.

The finance directors of eight London-based HEIs agreed in 1997 to meet, on a fairly informal basis, to benchmark their different approaches to financial accounting. Discussion also focused on the scope of the finance director's job; this apparently varied considerably, encompassing, in some institutions, areas such as management information systems (MIS), purchasing, and some estates work. One participant reported that just looking at differences between institutions in order to validate comparisons had proved time-consuming: for example, the extent to which finance offices handled projects internally or externally could lead to considerable variations in staffing costs. The exercise aimed to focus on the outcomes of activities, in the hope of producing a better representation of performance than had been achieved by previous studies that had only been concerned with 'inputs.' For example, one institution whose credit control operation might look comparatively 'expensive' in input terms, was more than able to justify this investment in terms of its results. The group is now working in sub-groups to concentrate on particular areas, such as credit control, but progress has apparently been fairly slow. One member was obliged to drop out because a major institutional project took precedence. This perhaps illustrates some of the difficulties that can affect informal benchmarking activities, and underlines the message (see also Chapters 13 and 16) that institutional commitment 'from top management' is crucial in determining the success of benchmarking operations.

Late in 1997, the Scottish Higher Education Funding Council (SHEFC) approved funding for a pilot benchmarking exercise focused on the finance office. The contract to act as facilitators was awarded to CHEMS, whose team comprised its Director, its Benchmark Club Manager, a respected former finance director within the Scottish HE system, and the author as researcher. A steering committee with members from Strathclyde and Glasgow universities directed the project. While CHEMS's international benchmarking work (Chapter 15) focuses on cross-institutional comparative analysis of *processes*, the SHEFC exercise had a narrower scope: the costs of some (but not all) functions within the finance office with a view to making efficiency gains. As such, the methodology combined the collection of information on financial processes, and how activities were undertaken, with a statistical/financial analysis.

Participation in the exercise was voluntary, so it was pleasing that initially 18 institutions, representing a good cross-section of the Scottish sector, expressed interest in joining the exercise. Two effectively dropped out halfway through, in one case due to an imminent merger with another benchmarking participant.

A first questionnaire aimed to identify the main contextual/background factors influencing finance departments' costs. For the purpose of the questionnaire, the finance office was divided into functional areas (payroll, pensions and benefits, cash and treasury, etc.). Participants were asked to supply both quantitative data (for example, the approximate number of payslips processed each month) and details of process (such as use of IT in invoice matching and authorization). Overall statistical data relating to the finance office and the institution as a whole was also requested, so that replies might be put into context. Following data analysis by CHEMS, a first workshop was held so that participants could agree upon the key factors.

Although the interim report delivered at that workshop was based on responses from just over half the institutions only, it had been possible to identify significant cost issues or 'benchmarks' to be investigated in the second stage. These included:

- cost difference between operating a 'finance-driven' and a 'personnel-driven' payroll
- the extent to which short-term contracts would affect the cost of servicing the payroll
- the difference in workload (or extent of outsourcing) involved in operating an in-house pension scheme as opposed to participating in a national scheme
- the extent to which devolved invoice processing would reduce duplication of effort between departments and the finance office
- the extent to which electronic payments (Bankers Automated Clearing System or Electronic Data Interchange) were used in accounts payable
- the extent to which increased use of IT in accounts receivable would improve efficiency
- organization of cash-handling within each institution and the extent to which treasury and cash management was a significant cost factor.

The second questionnaire, drafted by CHEMS and agreed to by workshop participants, aimed to explore differences in process with the goal of identifying the more cost-effective methods. Apart from a more detailed breakdown, by function, of finance office direct costs, institutions were asked to supply quantitative and qualitative information relating to the 'benchmarks' outlined above. The consultants' second report, based on responses from both questionnaires, was presented at a second workshop, which also featured talks from finance staff at institutions whose questionnaire responses had suggested evidence of particularly good practice. At this stage, several institutions wished to revise some aspects of their submitted data; a period was set aside for data validation and amendments were incorporated by CHEMS into the final report.

This report included a cost profile for each institution, which took into account the very wide variation in activities between the participants, and a comparison of finance office costs which indicated that the larger institutions benefited from an economy of scale. In relation to the seven benchmark areas, the more significant findings included:

- *Payroll*: the economy of scale expected at large HEIs was offset in institutions with a high level of fixed-term appointments and a high level of research/commercial activity, lifting them from a low to a middle-cost category.
- *Pensions*: while finance office costs varied widely, this did not seemingly relate, as expected, to the operation, or otherwise, of in-house schemes. One particular national scheme, surprisingly, was more expensive to administer than others cited, and a pensions working party was formed to explore this issue further.
- *Cash handling*: practice here was generally commended, with over 70 per cent of remittances being paid direct to bank accounts. Further comparison of practice between two institutions which seemingly exemplified good and less good practice was recommended.
- *Accounts payable*: the electronic remittance of 70 per cent of payments *to* Scottish HEIs was taken as a good practice standard achieved elsewhere in the public sector and outside it; while most participants used BACS for making payments or were converting suppliers to it, only five had achieved or exceeded this threshold.

From the consultants' viewpoint, the difficulties that attended this benchmarking exercise were fairly typical. Some institutions were unable to supply complete data to deadlines, which meant that analysis had, to some extent, 'to be done over'; data was sometimes inconsistent, both between partners and internally, and its meaning occasionally needed clarification. From the participants' point of view, although participation was voluntary, some were clearly more enthusiastic than others, suggesting perhaps that some felt constrained to join because of SHEFC's sponsorship of the project, or that in some cases senior management enthusiasm for the project was not shared by staff 'on the ground'. Another reason for disappointment was the unmet expectations of some participants who had hoped that, after all their hard work in gathering and analysing data, the consultants could have identified some clear-cut reasons for cost differences. Some of these problems can be attributed to the tight time constraints on the project (less than six months from design of the first questionnaire to the second workshop). In retrospect, CHEMS felt that the project would have benefited from a structure that permitted greater input by university staff following the consultants' aggregation of data, so that the final report could be a joint product. CHEMS also suggested that any future benchmarking work should follow processes and activities across all parts of the administration, rather than being confined to one section or unit, as this tends to set artificial limits on the examination of processes. A general conclusion from this study is that benchmarking based on quantitative or cost analysis is extremely difficult, even in activities that ostensibly might seem similar (such as accounts payable).

Human resource management: qualitative versus quantitative approaches to benchmarking

Discussion in Chapter 14 of HE benchmarking outside the UK suggests that comparative evaluation of performance sometimes founders due to the apprehension of participants about the use to which PIs, once generated, will be put. Evidence for similar concerns in the UK, and for certain tensions between opposed benchmarking 'lobbies,' comes from an account of a recent HRM pilot project. Arising from a Universities' Personnel Association conference in 1995 on continuous quality improvement, the project was, again, organized by an existing regional consortium. A questionnaire was developed, covering a broad range of activities and asking, first, whether these fell into the personnel remit, and then moving onto issues of quantity (for example, how many vacancies?), cost (how much) and time (how long). The aim was to use these issues to seek out best practice, share ideas, and inform further dialogue, in line with Camp's benchmarking philosophy (1989, 1995). As the work progressed, however, participants came to the conclusion that the 'quantitative issues' threw up few significant differences, and that the real issues related to the quality of processes and client satisfaction with the service, i.e. what level of service clients expect from the personnel function and how a particular personnel function matches up to that standard. The answers to such questions are essentially subjective and the view that a successful personnel function owes as much to client satisfaction in terms of 'advice, guidance, problem-solving and flexibility' as it does to provision of efficient processes required a qualitative process-based approach to benchmarking. This view found itself at odds with a 'widespread interest in hard facts' (e.g. personnel spend as a ratio of total income, etc.). Concerns that the project would be diverted from its focus on service quality into an 'unhelpful' cost-accounting exercise, whose results might then be used for ranking purposes, unfortunately led to the exercise being discontinued.

Conclusions

This chapter shows that UK universities have adopted a range of approaches to benchmarking administrative performance, from comparison against published statistics to full benchmarking action research-focused groups. The take-up of benchmarking within the sector is by no means uniform and barriers like lack of time or money or distrust as to the end purpose of benchmarking persist. The past two years have seen benchmarking endorsed by the Dearing Committee (Chapter 2), by QAA (Chapter 7) and HEFCE (Chapter 13). The growing prominence of benchmarking within HEFCE's VfM studies (Chapter 13) and the publication of 'official league tables' to facilitate comparison of institutional performance (Goddard 1999) should do much to promote the method. Hints of a growing trend towards consortium benchmarking, particularly within existing groups, suggest that universities are responding to calls for comparative evaluation of performance in ways that optimize their ownership of the process.

10

Benchmarking Student Recruitment: The UCAS Institutional Planning Service

Richard Coleman and Liz Viggars

Overview

Competition for applicants among UK higher education institutions makes the provision of benchmarking information vital for effective marketing and planning. The Universities and Colleges Admissions Service (UCAS) Institutional Planning Service (IPS) has been designed to address this need and to facilitate the analysis of applicant and applications data.[1] This chapter describes the available data; different methodologies for benchmarking; the importance of putting the analysis into context; and some of the more obvious pitfalls ready to trap the unsuspecting analyst.

Introduction

Recruitment to higher education is becoming increasingly competitive. Institutions spend millions of pounds annually on advertising and offer an ever-changing portfolio of programmes, carefully tailored to the anticipated requirements of their potential students. It is important that institutions use data available to them to assess who their potential students are, before launching marketing campaigns or introducing new courses. Benchmarking is therefore an important tool in the recruitment process.

The Universities and Colleges Admissions Service processes applications to full-time degree, diploma and Higher National Diploma (HND) courses at most of the HE institutions in the UK and some FE colleges. Currently this amounts to over 40,000 courses at 255 institutions. In doing so it holds and processes a wide range of data relating to applications and applicants. These data, which are complete from the 1994 year of entry, constitute a unique source of information relating to the demand for courses and the characteristics of those wishing to study in UK higher education.

Institutions have always received a wealth of data from UCAS in terms of their own students. Data is also published covering the national situation (e.g. UCAS 1998a and b). UCAS respects the wishes of institutions to keep most information about an individual institution's applications confidential and will therefore not release an institution's data without permission. With so many institutions spread across the country offering such a wide range of courses, top-level (national) data is often not sufficient for benchmarking purposes. It is probably not helpful, for example, for an institution that attracts predominantly local students to include data on institutions and applicants several hundred miles away. On the other hand, the provision of low-level (institutional) data is restricted by confidentiality regulations.

Clearly a middle ground is needed. The Institutional Planning Service is part of the Department of Research and Statistics at UCAS. Launched in September 1997, its remit is to provide data to institutions that is up to date, easy to manipulate and specific to each institution. Data sets are designed so that users can analyse data in the best way for them, instead of depending on pre-defined tables and charts, such as those published in the UCAS *Annual Reports.*

Initially two types of data sets were provided through the IPS – national and institutional. National data sets are available annually and cover applications and acceptances to all institutions while institutional data sets allow an institution to compare its own data with aggregate data for a relevant group of institutions. Both have their uses in benchmarking.

National data sets

Annual UCAS data may be downloaded from the UCAS website (http://www.ucas.ac.uk/higher/stats/ads/index.html). There are seven annual data sets for each of the years of entry 1996 to 1998. Each contains a range of demographic, qualification and operational information about applicants and accepted applicants such as ethnic origin, social class, main qualifications and grades and whether or not the applicant was accepted in 'clearing' (the process of placing students after the examination results are known). Two data sets contain institutional data and between them they provide comprehensive information on applications and accepted applicants by broad subject group, domicile, age and sex. The data sets are made up of various combinations of variables with different levels of detail to maximize the amount of information that can be extracted. For example, using the institution by subject data set, one can create a table showing applications and acceptances to medicine and dentistry. This can then be modified to restrict the analysis to applications made by men domiciled in the EU to institutions in the South East as shown in Table 10.1.

Interesting though the data may be, this is insufficient information on which to base significant planning and marketing decisions. UCAS is obliged to maintain individual institutions' confidentiality such that, apart from the above, little other information may be divulged regarding identified institutions. Although the data sets that are of immediate interest with respect to

Table 10.1 Example of the type of information that can be extracted from UCAS annual data sets

Institution region	H South East
Domicile	B EU
Subject group	A Medicine/Dentistry

Institution	Applications	Acceptances
Oxford University	59	3
University of Southampton	173	3
Grand total	232	6

Source: UCAS annual data sets – INSTSUBJ.XLS

benchmarking are those containing institution details, the others are just as important in putting benchmarking information into context, particularly in conjunction with the institutional data sets.

Institutional data sets

The institutional data sets are designed in much the same way as the (aggregated) annual data sets described above; they contain information about applications and acceptances by a range of demographic, qualification and operational variables. Typically they contain an institution's own data and aggregated data for a group of competitor, or comparator, institutions. Institutional data sets are tailor-made for each institution that requests them. There is, of course, no single definition of those institutions that should be considered as comparators. Five different models of data sets are available, each based on different themes. It is not anticipated that every model should be applicable to every institution, but between them they provide an insight into a range of issues that institutions may wish to address.

Selecting comparator institutions

Data for a minimum of six institutions are aggregated to create the comparator data. This ensures that individual institutions' confidentiality is maintained. This, however, should not pose users with any problems: in order to affect planning decisions, data about one or two institutions is not sufficient. It may be interesting and affect short-term decisions about small numbers of applicants, but does not provide the impetus for significant change. At the other end of the scale, aggregate information about too many institutions obscures the analysis. There is probably an optimum number of comparator institutions, somewhere between six and twenty, which depends on course provision, type of institution and a number of other factors. Four examples of ways in which comparators can be identified are shown below.

Institution region

Since 1994, there has been an increasing trend towards applicants choosing to study in their home region of domicile (UCAS 1998b). This is particularly true for mature applicants, applicants from ethnic minorities and partly skilled and unskilled social classes, although the trend is apparent among all types of applicants. It therefore makes sense for an institution with a strong local remit to consider the other institutions in their region as their comparators. By default, UCAS assigns each home applicant and institution to one of 13 Government Office Regions. For those institutions in particularly large regions or situated on the border of two regions, this classification is not necessarily the most useful. Institutions can therefore use the data sets to group local education authorities together to form more meaningful areas. This has the advantage that users can have more detailed information on their most profitable regions while aggregating others.

Applicants' other choices

Each applicant is permitted to make up to six applications through UCAS. An accurate indicator of an institution's competitors is the list of other institutions to which their applicants also apply. Generally, though not exclusively, an applicant's choices tend to be subject-based – i.e. the applicant is applying for a particular course or type of course. The choice of institution is based – depending on the type of course being pursued – on any combination of the availability of places/courses; preferred region of study; typical entry requirements; and the institution's perceived reputation. Most academic staff would be able to tell you a number of other institutions to which their applicants regularly apply. However, particularly at a subject level, the actual list can be somewhat different from the list of perceived competitors. By using an objective method of analysis, one can monitor the most popular alternative choices and whether these change as institutions develop new courses.

Subject mix

The analysis of subject of study is yet another way of determining comparator institutions. Again, it is a formalized way of establishing whether institutions thought to be comparators actually are, this time in terms of course provision. It is a particularly useful analysis for those institutions with a national catchment area. Comparator institutions for the subject data set

Table 10.2 Distribution of applicants accepted to institutions in the North by subject, 1997 entry

Institution	Science	Social studies	Arts	Combined	Sum of squared differences for Cleveland College
Cleveland College of Art and Design	0.00%	0.00%	100.00%	0.00%	
Cumbria College of Art and Design	0.00%	0.00%	94.22%	5.78%	0.007
University of Durham	39.48%	23.68%	30.15%	6.68%	0.704
University of Newcastle upon Tyne	58.59%	19.81%	14.38%	7.22%	1.121
Newcastle College	13.67%	23.62%	62.71%	0.00%	0.214
New College Durham	26.80%	73.20%	0.00%	0.00%	1.608
University of Northumbria at Newcastle	36.31%	37.30%	22.78%	3.61%	0.869
Northumberland College of Art and Technology	14.29%	0.00%	76.19%	9.52%	0.086
University of Sunderland	32.50%	23.96%	33.89%	9.65%	0.609
University of Teesside	33.98%	44.22%	15.83%	5.97%	1.023

Source: UCAS annual data sets, INSTSUBJ.XLS

are those who offer the same mix of subjects. At the simplest level, institutions with a similar subject profile to an art college will also be art colleges.

This list of comparator institutions is determined by comparing the distribution of accepted applicants at one institution with those for all other institutions. Calculating the sum of squared differences between one institution and each of the others across the subject groups generates a rank-ordered list of institutions. Those with the smallest sum of squared differences have the closest match to the subject institution.

The national data set showing institutions by subject is used to perform the analysis. Table 10.2 shows the distribution of accepted applicants across aggregated subject groups for institutions in the North for 1997 entry. The sums of squared differences have been calculated for Cleveland College of Art and Design. In this example, the closest matching institution to Cleveland College of Art and Design is Cumbria College of Art and Design followed by Northumberland College of Art and Technology. The majority of accepted applicants at both of these institutions were accepted to arts courses. New College Durham is the worst match – it accepted no applicants to arts courses. By taking a closer look at this summary data for just ten institutions, we begin to see several clusters of institutions with respect to subject provision. Four of the ten institutions accepted more than half of their applicants to arts courses while three others had a fairly even distribution across science, social studies and arts.

Figure 10.1   Subject analysis: University of Birmingham

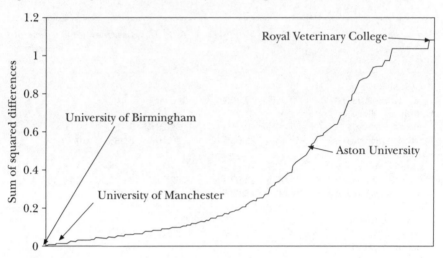

An indication of whether this method is appropriate to an institution can be obtained by producing a graph of the sums of squared differences. The analysis tends to produce an S-shaped graph. Figure 10.1 is the graph produced for the University of Birmingham. The institutions closest to the tail of the S are those with the closest match to the subject institution while those institutions that do not share any subjects in common are situated at the other end. If the S-curve is not particularly pronounced then this may indicate that there are no natural comparators in terms of subject mix.

Note that this method takes no account of the size or location of the institution or the breakdown of subjects within subject groups (the analysis is usually performed on 21 broad subject groups). The method can be refined to take some of these factors into account so that results can be tailored to specific needs. Examples include restricting the area of the institutions to include/exclude specified regions; having an upper or lower limit on the size of the institutions to be compared against; omitting specified subjects from the calculations or extracting others from subject groups. This analysis also goes some way to addressing different types of courses. For example, an institution offering mainly modular courses will have a high proportion of accepted applicants in the six 'combined' subject groups. This type of analysis is not restricted to subject. Similar techniques can also be applied to other variables, for example, the distribution of applicants across ethnic minority groups or age groups could be used. The final list is itself a guide. It may be appropriate to substitute some of the institutions at the top of the list with others further down and/or include more institutions. The main purpose is to build a foundation on which further – informed – decisions can be made.

Institutional profile

The 'best' method for selecting comparator institutions depends heavily on an institution's location, size, provision and market. We have shown several techniques to select comparators which take such issues into account. However, a range of other, diverse factors can affect applications and acceptances to individual institutions or groups of institutions. These may include:

- typical offers made to students
- Research Assessment Exercise ratings
- grades awarded through the Subject Quality Assessment process
- ratio of full-time students to part-time students
- availability of accommodation
- percentage of local school leavers with five or more 'good' GCSEs
- the price of a pint in the Students' Union.

Such data are available from a variety of sources, including UCAS, the Higher Education Statistics Agency, Funding Councils, Quality Assurance Agency and published higher education guides. The data can be used to assess and rank-order these factors to come up with a list of the closest comparators. Many institutions use a variety of factors to create their own lists of institutions against which they always compare their own data. UCAS is then able to produce a profile data set with this list of institutions as the comparators.

Benchmarking using the national and institutional data sets

Although the institutional data sets are of immediate interest with respect to benchmarking, national data sets are just as important when it comes to putting benchmarking information into context. Figure 10.2 brings together information from one of the national data sets and an institutional data set for a fictitious institution in Greater London (Institution X). From these two data sets, information can be extracted comparing Institution X with other institutions in Greater London and with all institutions.

Compared with all other institutions, it appears that Institution X accepted more than its fair share of applicants from ethnic minorities. But compared to other institutions in Greater London it does not attract as many students from ethnic minorities. However this does not necessarily mean that Institution X is doing anything wrong. It merely indicates that the issue of ethnic minority applications needs further consideration. The UCAS *Annual Reports* (UCAS 1999a, 1999b, 1999c) show that nearly half of accepted applicants from ethnic minorities study business and administrative studies, social studies or mathematical sciences and informatics. The next logical step is therefore to consider the mix of subjects offered by the institution. If Institution X does not offer many places on these courses

Figure 10.2 Distribution of accepted applicants by ethnic origin for selected institutions

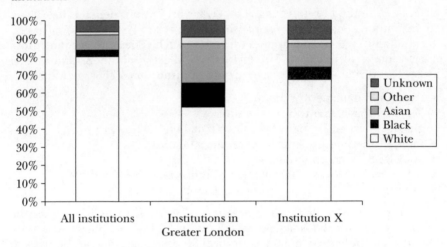

compared with other institutions in the region then the regional analysis with respect to ethnic origin is not helpful, and might even be considered detrimental as misleading 'evidence' could be generated. Such problems are typical when using too simplistic an approach to benchmarking. It is rarely acceptable to address an issue by analysing a single variable.

Available data

Each of the IPS data sets contains a range of variables. Different combinations of variables are used in different data sets to maximize the number of analyses that can be performed. Most of the data is obtained from the applicants' application forms and from the examination boards. Table 10.3 shows which variables are available in the data sets. Other data, covering not only higher education, are also important. External information about the general population is vital to put any analysis in context. For example, a fall in applications for 1998 cannot be simply attributed to the introduction of tuition fees: account also needs to be taken of demographic changes and possibly economic changes. When considering issues about widening access to higher education, it is probably more important to look at those people who do not apply than at those who do.

Employment of benchmarking methods in the recruitment process

Benchmarking is an important part of the assessment, planning and marketing of an institution's provision. Some of its more obvious applications include:

Table 10.3 Variables contained in IPS data sets

Category	Variables
Demographic	Age Sex Ethnic origin Social class Region of domicile Disability
Educational	School type (previous educational establishment) Qualifications – summarized results of A levels, Scottish Highers and GNVQs – summary records of other qualifications
Operational	Institutions' offers Applicants' decisions Clearing

- *Advertising*: benchmarking enables the institution to identify its current and target student markets and therefore focus its advertising more effectively.
- *Attracting additional funding*: to gain additional student numbers and funding, institutions need to demonstrate unmet demand. Benchmarking can be used to show gaps in provision, either locally or nationally for courses and/or types of applicants.
- *Monitoring initiatives*: benchmarking enables the monitoring of initiatives such as widening access to HE, taking factors such as course provision and the potential student base into account.
- *Adjusting course provision*: before making changes to courses, or introducing new courses, it is important to assess trends in supply and demand. A fall in demand for an individual institution's course should not be viewed in isolation, but in comparison with other courses at the institution and similar courses at other institutions.

Conclusions

Benchmarking, in its simplest form, involves the comparison and evaluation of one set of data with another. When a range of data are available, the key to benchmarking using data sets such as those described above is in selecting an appropriate mix and subset of the available data against which to make comparisons. It is possible to apply multivariate techniques to such data sets to obtain single-figure 'performance indicators'. While this is a perfectly acceptable statistical technique, it is not easily understood by non-statisticians who need to be convinced that the information they are being shown reflects the true 'state of play'. The conclusion that can be drawn from this is that the benchmarking techniques outlined in this chapter are best used to *describe*, *illustrate* and *summarize* the wide range of data relating to a particular aspect of an institution's performance (e.g. performance in recruiting students). In order to engage in this type of benchmarking an institution will need to pose questions like:

- What *information* is required and why?
- What *data* is required to illustrate this information?
- What *factors* could affect the analysis?
- How can this information be best illustrated?

It is crucial that conclusions are put into context. A detailed understanding of the construction of the data and any discontinuities is vital. To inform recruitment strategies, benchmarking should not be restricted to simple, single-variable analyses of UCAS data. No factors affecting applications to HE should be considered in isolation – students and institutions are not one-dimensional and therefore should not be analysed as such. The inclusion of external factors not directly related to admissions, such as regional, national and international demographics, local and national economies and government policies, help to complete the picture.

Note

1. Further information on the Institutional Planning Service can be found at the UCAS website at: http://www.ucas.ac.uk/higher/stats/index.html or email IPS@ucas.ac.uk

11

Benchmarking UK Higher Education and Public Sector Facilities and Estates Management

Ilfryn Price

Overview

This chapter describes the use of process benchmarking in facilities and estates management within UK HE institutions. Comments are offered on the spread of benchmarking in higher education and on comparative studies in other UK public sector groups. Finally, arguments are advanced concerning the effective integration of facilities management in the educational offerings of different forms of university.

Introduction

Benchmarking is generally acknowledged as having been formally introduced to western managerial practice by Rank Xerox in the early 1980s. It has since become one of the two or three most widely used managerial techniques in private sector management in both the UK and North America. In recent years it has also increasingly crossed the divide between the public and private sectors and is now formally encouraged as an instrument of 'best-value' management (e.g. DETR 1998). In the process, as testified, for example, by the range of contributions in this volume, the term has come to hold a variety of subsets of meaning and practice. While most reflect the original, in the Rank Xerox sense, philosophy of looking outside an organization or organizational unit for examples of better work processes, some reflect, to this author at least, a worrying sense of denoting, as 'a benchmark', an imposed standard with which an organization is expected to comply. The trend is not surprising. A parallel diversification of meanings can be found in other managerial tools or fads (Price and Shaw 1996, 1998). Unfortunately it is confusing to the user.

Over the previous five years the Sheffield Hallam University Facilities Management Graduate Centre (FMGC) has treated benchmarking as a process of action research and active learning among those involved. Our philosophy is that benchmarking is a process through which groups of 'competitive' organizations share information on the performance and management of key business processes so as to learn from each other. Our working definition (Price 1994) is: 'Benchmarking is the open and collaborative evaluation of services and processes with the aim of emulating or improving best available practice.'

Our benchmarking projects are undertaken within the context of Research and Application Forums, ongoing 'learning clubs' of facilities managers from participating institutions who support a series of linked developmental workshops and research projects over the course of a year. In practice most members continue year-on-year so that projects may have a longer life. While benchmarking, strictly speaking, may constitute only one project at any time within a given forum, in a wider sense a forum is an ongoing arena for collaborative enquiry between competing institutions, albeit competitors who share a common sectoral heritage.

Data set

This chapter summarizes our benchmarking experience, drawing especially on work within higher education institutions (HEIs) but informed also by work with the NHS, local authorities, Single Regeneration Budget partnerships (SRBs) and commercial clients. The FMGC benchmarking data set (excluding confidential consultancy projects) is shown in Table 11.1.

Table 11.1 Benchmarking projects facilitated by FMGC

Sector	Project	Year
NHS	Benchmarking of the catering process between 18 trusts	1995/6
	Portering services (cost, user's satisfaction and management)	1996
	Space utilization and management	1997/8
	Overall FM spending and performance	1998
HE	Maintenance expenditure and management	1996/7
	Space management	1997/8
	Assessment (a pilot study in collaboration with Robert Gordon University Teaching and Learning Institute and QAA)	1997
	Key FM performance indicators	1998
Local government	Office space management and user's perceptions Comparisons with private sector	1998/9
SRBs	Management structures and processes including board member, staff, and project manager's perceptions	1998/9

It will be seen that, as forums develop over time and their membership become more familiar with benchmarking, so the complexity, and strategic impact, of the processes benchmarked increases. The table illustrates what we would term complete benchmarking projects, i.e. projects which followed the complete process outlined below. Parallel collaborative research projects have investigated management structures in FM (Rees 1997, 1998) and managerial practices (Price and Akhlaghi 1999 and references therein). We would not normally term such studies benchmarking because they are conducted by researchers investigating others' practices, rather than being arranged as a process through which those involved directly compare themselves with, and learn from, similar institutions.

Benchmarking's history and the FMGC benchmarking process

Benchmarking, as the managerial activity of openly contrasting the performance of one's own organization with that of others, probably predates its 'invention' by Rank Xerox. Covert comparison, legitimate or not, certainly does so. What Rank Xerox achieved was to give the process a name, one which enabled others to describe their similar activity in the same way, and one which enabled the emergence of the profession or activity of benchmarking agents, whether they operated as internal members of organizations or as consultants. The author was an early recipient of the term's passage across the Atlantic, being introduced to the formal concept in 1987 (during the course of the acquisition by British Petroleum (BP) of full control of Standard Oil of Ohio). The term enjoyed an explosive growth in the early 1990s with the appearance, in the space of two years, of several books/guides on the topic (e.g. Codling 1992; Spendolini 1992; Zairi 1992; Bendall *et al.* 1993; Karlöff and Ostblom 1993; Liebfried and McNair 1994; Price 1994 – no claim is made that the list is exhaustive). The 'benchmarking explosion' can be illustrated by the publication frequency of such books. Figure 11.1, drawn from a search of the Amazon.com database, reflects the typical boom and decay dynamic found in many managerial fads (Pascale 1991).

In the course of such an explosion it is small wonder that the term came to take on many meanings. Other successful 'fads' show the same tendency. Price and Shaw (1996) develop the theme as an example of the epidemiology of ideas. Some promoters of 'benchmarking' would apply the term to the mere provision of numerical comparators to subscribers while others, including the author, insist that true benchmarking includes a comparison of work processes. The most dramatic proponents of the process see the biggest benefits in so-called 'generic benchmarking': the search for inspiration outside one's own sector.

Other meanings have also emerged. It is common to hear managers describing themselves as 'benchmarking' when, in fact, they are comparing

Figure 11.1 Benchmarking books published per year

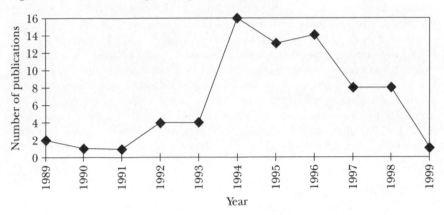

themselves to others without the exercise being reciprocated. It is also common to hear those charged with maintaining standards or judging investments to describe as 'benchmarking' a process perceived, by the recipients at least, as scrutiny, audit, or performance measurement. We observe this latter trend to be particularly prevalent in the UK public sector at the present time (see below).

Facilities management (FM) is another term of the late 1980s and 1990s which has seemingly enjoyed an exponential spread (research in progress) with consequent diversification of meaning. As used here it embraces the full management of the built and serviced environment in which an institution carries out its perceived core business, resulting in the product its customers pay for. FMGC, as an academic centre of excellence in FM, sees the understanding and dissemination of 'best' practice in the profession as its own core activity. A strong caveat must be placed around the word 'best' in this context. Its use frequently carries an implicit, and unchallenged, assumption of there being a single best way of organizing a particular activity – an assumption strongly rooted in the prevailing paradigm of managerial thinking (e.g. Morgan 1986). Price and Akhlaghi (1999) review applications of that pattern in FM and argue that best results are not in fact delivered from a 'Taylorist' managerial approach. Best practice is not found by seeking a single 'best' way.

We have viewed benchmarking as a simultaneous opportunity for us as researchers, to work with, and understand, innovators in the field of FM, and to provide those innovators with a forum within which they can learn from each other. A primary need in such a forum is a sense of trust between participants; trust which in practice takes time to develop. The importation of 'competition', 'market testing' and compulsory competitive tendering (CCT) has introduced to public sector institutions a perception of overt rivalry (in some cases for survival and employment) which was not there, say, ten years ago. These pressures have frequently fallen more heavily on

Figure 11.2 The FMGC benchmarking road map

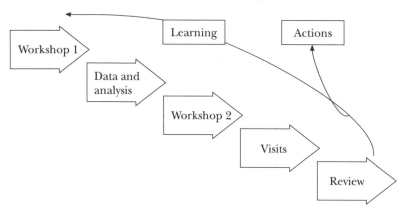

perceived 'support services' where outsourcing seems a viable option, cost pressures are intense and appreciation – by senior managers – of the value added to their core services is often tenuous. In these circumstances the building of trust can be a laborious process.

Our design of a benchmarking project has become standardized (Figure 11.2) to try and allay those fears. We always start with a project workshop in which prospective participants are first introduced to the distinction between benchmarking, as a horizontal process between peers, and 'audit' as a vertical process stemming from funding bodies and various government agencies. Indeed techniques for coping with such 'top-down' processes frequently become a matter for considerable informal benchmarking!

Participants are then involved in the definition of the numerical aspects of the process selected for benchmarking. Inevitably, given that we are benchmarking services that are part of the internal processes of not-for-profit organizations, the numerical data available tend to focus on the costs of delivering a particular process, and the resources used. We do, wherever possible, also include comparators of the perceived service received by customers/users. Hence, for example, our catering benchmarking tested perceptions of clinical staff and patients with the food served, using the *Patient's Charter* as a framework. Our current local government project seeks feedback from users of local authority buildings; users being both staff who work in the buildings and members of the public who visit them. To date a similar comparison in higher education has not been seen as feasible. The lack of research into user perceptions of how educational environments impact on the learning process seems to be a general feature of the sector (Fleming and Storr 1999). In practice we find that the data definition stage tends to generate a wider range of questions than is later proved relevant. It also reveals inconsistencies of interpretation in respect of definitions. Occasionally participants choose data that present them in a particularly favourable light, or do not reveal full costs (for example, where a department's overheads are shared with another directorate in a local authority). The second workshop is an opportunity to review such inconsistencies. At that stage all participants have is a numerical assessment of themselves, on a variety of measures, against a comparable set of organizations.

The next stage of the process seeks to convert quantitative analysis into learning and action. We arrange a series of reciprocal visits, typically with a group of four participants each hosting the rest of their group for a day's visit. That visit is a chance for members of the hosting organization to share their good practices, ask questions of an external group, and be challenged concerning how they do things. For participants who treat the process proactively it is also an opportunity to engage operational staff in the learning process. Some host organizations have, for example, found the day an opportunity to present, to a peer group, a particular problem for discussion. Others have involved first-line supervisory staff in a visit to another institution. FMGC researchers/facilitators with a variety of specialist backgrounds attend the visit days, both to capture the issues raised and to cross-pollinate ideas and information between groups and sectors. The visits begin to enable what we take to be true benchmarking, i.e. an exercise in which people not only compare themselves but also take action as a result.

Such willingness to take action is itself a function of wider issues of organizational culture. Resistance to change is a well-documented feature of all forms of organization and several surveys of senior managers reveal 60 to 80 per cent dissatisfaction with the results of any 'change' initiative (e.g. Schaffer and Thompson 1992; Scott-Morgan 1994). Benchmarking, as a tool for continuous improvement, will only produce results when it is deployed by organizations committed to such improvement. The phenomenon is not by any means restricted to public sector organizations. The phrase 'industrial tourism' is frequently used as an accurate summary of many a private sector benchmarking exercise.

Recent government policy in respect of 'best value' is emphasizing continual and regular benchmarking, accompanied by concrete evidence of continued improvement, as an alternative to reliance purely on CCT in the search for improved value and reduced cost of a range of services. The approach demands a culture that is not always found in practice. In many cases the reaction of managers involved in benchmarking is one of defence: the search for statistics to justify current performance levels, or to escape the imposition of reforms by various national regulatory agencies. We do, however, believe that our series of studies have revealed generic issues for the management of facilities services both in HE and the wider public sector.

Key messages for HE

The prime beneficiaries of a benchmarking project should be the organizations that undertake it. We have not found specific standards or targets that can be set for the sector, or for particular aspects of FM within it. We have evolved a database of examples of good practices and key questions for facilities/estates managers to use in aspects of their work. These conclusions are the intellectual property of the subscribing membership and are not available for open publication. We can, however, draw some key messages, for HE and more generally for benchmarking of public sector support services in the UK.

The HE estate

The UK higher education estate has an insurance value of £18 billion (HEFCE 1998e). The general challenges facing the sector in terms of increasing diversity, increasing student numbers, diminishing funding per student, technological changes and changing student expectations are documented virtually weekly in, for example, the *Times Higher Education Supplement*. Price and Kennie (1997) used Porter's (1980) classical five frameworks model to suggest a sector displaying all the hallmarks of a major equilibrium shift – one that was anticipated at least 25 years ago (Schön 1973). Individual universities are having to position themselves on a strategic possibility space defined broadly by the ranges of options available in 'education' and 'research' (Figure 11.3).

It is worth noting that this model derives from an earlier exercise conducted within the FMGC HE Forum, namely the construction of a series of mini-scenarios using standard scenario planning approaches (e.g. Schwartz 1992). However radical the resulting mini-scenarios (Matzdorf *et al.* 1997) we find forum members report 'pilots' or 'items under discussion' exploring

Figure 11.3 Strategic dispersal in UK HE

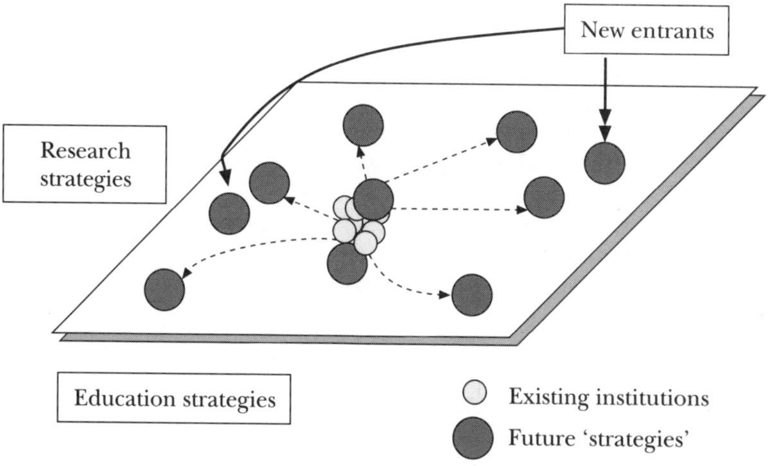

Source: Matzdorf *et al.* 1997; Price and Kennie 1997.

a given option. The sector does not lack creative ideas. In practice, however, the nature and geographical location of a particular institution's fixed estate severely constrains its medium-term strategic options. Institutional traditions and buildings are deeply interrelated.

'Estates' versus FM

Institutional orientation, size, wealth and expenditure on the fixed estate varies widely. Our forum embraces virtually the full range of the sector from elite, research-led establishments to institutions that do not have full HE status. Absolute comparisons of facilities costs per student, per member of staff, or per m^2 of the fixed estate are well-nigh meaningless.[1] The data set is, however, sufficiently large to compare like with like. Further, by repeating benchmarking, and by examining data in the peer groups established in visits, we are able to gauge individual institutions' commitment to, and delivery of, year-on-year improvement. The single largest common factor established among the better performing institutions seems to be the degree to which an integrated responsibility for facilities management (whether or not the name is used) is held by a manager who is a member of an institution's senior management team.

Traditional academic management has tended to delegate responsibilities for the upkeep and procurement of buildings to an estates department, a tendency reinforced by the language of the funding process for buildings. Some institutions have placed within an estates directorate all responsibility for the delivery of various services (e.g. cleaning, portering, catering, conference management, security). Some have termed the equivalent department a facilities directorate while others have incorporated responsibility for the full range of facilities services within the remit of a bursar or finance director. Such integrated directorates seem to be the ones which deliver best value for money. A number of factors may contribute. The integrated directorate commands a greater visibility in the decision-making process and offers opportunities for multi-skilling and modern facilities management systems. It provides ancillary staff with a sense of their own identity within an institution and perhaps signals vice-chancellorial commitment to the total management of an institution.

We have observed parallel trends in the NHS (Rees 1997, 1998) and recently in local authorities (work in progress). Organizations that grant FM, in name or fact, a voice at the top managerial table achieve a better performance.

Statistical detail versus key indicators

HEIs and the agencies that fund them are particularly prone to a desire for detailed statistical comparisons. Given the size, diversity and complexity of the HE estate and the arrangements for servicing it, the phenomenon is perhaps not surprising, nor is it unique to the sector. In the course of two years of sector-specific benchmarking discussions we have frequently seen the limitations of numbers especially as they become more detailed. We have also discussed the desirability of a 'balanced scorecard' of FM indicators for HE. The current programme is testing a prototype scorecard comprising the total facilities costs (rent/depreciation, maintenance and all services) normalized against:

- institutional income
- 'core academic income'
- staff numbers
- m^2 professional space
- m^2 teaching space
- student numbers.

We are also testing other measures, namely:

- net space per staff member
- management to academic space ration
- complexity of the estate
- net space per student
- utilization and capacity
- balance of space-intensive activity.

This list is currently being tested as a basic balanced scorecard for institution-level benchmarking.

As a matter of good practice for the future we have also seen institutions beginning to compare space utilization at a departmental level. An example is provided by two chemistry departments with identical research assessment scores, similar student numbers and similar subject quality assessment scores (see Chapter 2 for explanation of these ratings). One occupies $12,000m^2$, the other $4000m^2$. There may of course be significant differences in teaching methods and in the type of research being carried out. Nonetheless, we believe such comparisons must form part of the more effective management of institutions in the future. At the very least they pose a legitimate question concerning the effective return an institution is achieving on its investments in its buildings.

Space management – to charge or not?

As the example just used could show, amount or cost of space may not be the only criteria on which to judge an institution's, or department's, managerial performance. A strong body of opinion, including the National Audit Office (1996), advocates space charging as the best way of delivering effective space utilization. We would not challenge their conclusion concerning the benefits of more effective use of space; however, it is not clear from our

Figure 11.4   Conversations on space in HE institutions

benchmarking that space charging automatically leads to better use of fixed assets. Some institutions with alternative approaches to allocation have succeeded in achieving equal or greater gains in efficiency. Some have found the cost of charging to outweigh the benefits whereas others report considerable success.

Various stakeholders have very different perspectives on an institution's space. Estates professionals, 'central' management, and academic users have not only different priorities but also completely different mental models regarding space. Figure 11.4 displays a model we have used to capture the differences.

Effective space management systems must seek a balance between these different perspectives. Space charging is often seen as a vehicle to deliver such a balance. From the business and estates management perspectives, it is seen as increasing user awareness of the cost of the space they occupy, and encouraging a greater participation in moves to reduce it. Many variants of charging are practised by our member institutions. To date at least, there is no evidence of any *one* model of space charging producing superior outcomes.[2] There is not even any proof that space charging *per se* automatically promotes in practice a greater drive for efficient or effective usage; a point also made by Shove (1993).

The challenge faced by any organization (Duffy 1997) is the provision of space that is both more effective (i.e. facilitates enhanced performance) and more efficient (i.e. achieves greater density of occupation per m^2 or £). However, in academia as much as elsewhere, users tend towards a conservative perception of space as a 'free good', status symbol or even bargaining chip, although an awareness of space as a valuable asset and as a (scarce) work resource is beginning to grow, especially in institutions that are 'short of space'. What is needed is a space management process that encourages a search for both economy and effectiveness. We have tentatively identified four different 'charging' options from our benchmarking of space management systems:

1. The formula approach uses a space allocation model by department. Those models that have gained wide workability appear to require academic credibility (i.e. credibility with academics), achieved through a real or imaginary numerical rigour. Some institutions have found that involvement of suitably numerate academics in the development of the model has lent such credibility.
2. The landlord approach imposes a rent on departments, either directly or through some form of income distribution model. The rent normally incorporates other service costs attributed on the basis of occupied useable area. Departments, as cost centres, have some freedom to exchange 'space' for other budget items.
3. The balance sheet approach views departments more as profit centres and incorporates space and other premises charges into an overall year-on-year account. Strategic decisions on 'excessive' investment in particular areas might be justified in terms of desired future returns (which can take various forms).
4. The mutualist approach has some form of space management group, and enables open exchange of data on space quality/usage. It is through peer negotiations or dialogue that the institution enhances its return on space.

In an unpublished report to forum members (Price and Matzdorf 1998) we have suggested a correlation between the four styles and the managerial culture of a particular institution. Best space management seems to be achieved when the two match. This proposition is currently being examined.

Facilities management in the UK public sector

In the minds of many the term facilities management is synonymous with 'outsourcing' and the previous ten years have seen an explosive growth of the market for outsourced facilities services. This has been fuelled in part by the general service productivity challenge facing any white-collar business (Akhlaghi and Tranfield 1995) but also by the particular reliance, prior to the 1997 election, on 'market testing' to deliver better value for money. We have not seen, in any of the studies referred to here, evidence of outsourcing always in fact delivering better value, but nor have we seen automatic evidence to the contrary. Genuine partnerships across the private/public provider divide are still rare but are capable of yielding innovative improvements.

The approach taken to the management of support service workers, and to innovation in general, seems more important than the specific managerial structure. Price and Akhlaghi (1999) contrasted the 'learning' approach to a variety of aspects of FM with an approach steeped in 'control', whether expressed as overtly 'Taylorist' or disguised as modern human resource management (HRM). The more successful innovations we have seen have come from organizations applying the 'learning' approach. An unfortunate side effect of the previous government's approach to compulsory competitive tendering (CCT) appears to have been the wholesale importation, into areas of service delivery in the public sector, of managerial paradigms of control; paradigms which had already failed in the world of commercial organizations (e.g. Pascale 1991; Price and Shaw 1998).

Karlôff and Ostblom (1993) make the theoretical case for benchmarking as an alternative to pure reliance on free markets to secure innovation and improvement. Practised as part of an open approach to scanning the world outside an organization, benchmarking can yield signs of under-competitiveness before the market does. That possibility is now recognized in the more flexible, albeit equally determined, policies on best value which are starting to emerge as current government policy. If benchmarking, in the sense conveyed above of not only looking at other organizations but also acting on what is learnt, can become more widespread, we perceive significant opportunities for enhanced value from FM, in HE as much as other public sectors. The challenge may require shifts of perception concerning FM, not just on the part of those who manage facilities departments but also those who use their services.

Notes

1. Comparisons using as a norm the ratio of estates expenditure to total income are currently being researched.
2. Subject to the caveat that we have not attempted a year-on-year historical analysis nor an examination of facilities costs per unit of income earned.

12

Benchmarking the Learning Infrastructure: Library and Information Services Case Studies

Stephen Town

Overview

This chapter reviews the development of benchmarking in UK HE libraries and information services (L&IS) since 1993, including an initial analysis of the Standing Committee of National University Libraries (SCONUL) benchmarking pilot projects. Earlier projects are described in terms of rationale, characteristics, scope and breadth of participation, methodologies and metrics, results and actions, issues raised and lessons learnt. The SCONUL pilots were designed to build on this experience and the extent to which they confirm previous assumptions is assessed. The chapter also attempts to set these benchmarking activities within the context of HE information services and their concerns in the late 1990s.

Introduction

It is worth noting that cooperative approaches to problem solving, development of services, and quality improvement are frequently part of the academic library culture; librarians tend to be open to learning from others' experience. This helps to explain the wide take-up of benchmarking in the sector, with well over 50 UK HE libraries involved in some way. It is likely too that any new management trends will have at least a few librarians on board. Their intimate association with the literature of any subject means that new developments are often picked up immediately. Camp's monograph (1989) marks the start of benchmarking as an academic publishing phenomenon; in 1992 four further titles appeared. In April 1993 benchmarking was tabled at an academic librarians' training meeting (Cheetham 1993), and by October a full-scale HE benchmarking exercise was under way (Town 1996).

Benchmarking in academic libraries grew naturally at the conjunction of two related issues: performance measurement and quality management. Performance measurement has featured strongly in academic library discourse for a considerable time (see Cullen 1998). SCONUL has collected detailed standardized statistical measurements of academic library activity in support of performance measurement since 1987 (SCONUL Annual) and has an advisory committee devoted to this subject. A recent research project defined a small number of PIs (now designated management statistics) for the HE library sector (Barton and Blagden 1998), and there has been overlap and synergy between this and the SCONUL benchmarking pilots; both may ultimately influence SCONUL's statistical collection methods.

Quality management is well established as a way of improving academic library performance; the range of quality techniques used in libraries is summarized by Brophy and Coulling (1996). Benchmarking was one of four recommended 'highly proactive' methods of understanding customers included in Tenner and DeToro's matrix (1992; the same authors' TQM 'road map' also influenced the design of the RMCS project described below). Of the other three, the 'mystery shopper technique' has a long history within librarianship (Blagden and Harrington 1990), while designed surveys and focus groups also came into use by academic libraries in the early or mid-1990s (Bell 1995; Hart 1995). Four case studies will serve to illustrate various approaches to benchmarking within HE academic information services (see also Town 1998a). In each case there is an attempt to define the type of benchmarking being undertaken according to Oakland's categorization (1993).

Cranfield University RMCS library benchmarking project

The library of the Royal Military College of Science (RMCS) is operated by Cranfield University for the Ministry of Defence under an overall contract for academic activity on the Shrivenham site. As part of the university's quality policy for this campus, the library initiated a TQM programme in 1993. The appearance of benchmarking on the TQM road map forced library staff to consider how they could claim to be seeking continuous improvement without using what industry apparently considered to be one of the simplest but most effective tools available. Funding for a benchmark project was successfully sought from the Principal, demonstrating the organization's strong commitment to quality. Support for the initiative may also have been connected with an imminent new competition for the academic contract. In this sense, the benchmarking exercise was 'competitive', but it was also 'generic' in trying to compare all processes against best practice. In addition, the contemporaneous decision to bring together library and computing services on the Shrivenham campus provided a focus for benchmarking the process of convergence within the exercise (Town 1996).

Sixty potential benchmarking partners were approached, with the aim of shortlisting about 20. These included: libraries in technological universities; small academic libraries; those with some claim to excellence; libraries involved in quality initiatives or active in performance measurement; special libraries, including some which had received quality awards; academic libraries with whom RMCS already had some relationship. Thirty agreed to participate and 20 were selected, based on ability to accommodate visits during the data collection period (October to December 1993), relevance, and geography. In the event, 17 institutions (10 'old' or pre-1992 universities and seven 'new' or post-1992 universities) were visited; another three completed questionnaires. Other libraries were also generous in providing relevant information or advice.

Critical success factors (CSFs) are a standard measurement method in TQM. CSFs developed for the library were as follows:

- we must provide current, accessible information resources which match user needs
- we must provide cost-effective services which match contract requirements
- we must have well-trained, motivated and approachable staff
- we must have effective communication with users
- we must respond positively to change
- we must provide the right environment for learning.

From this list it was possible to develop potential areas to measure for the benchmarking exercise:

- availability of up-to-date stock
- unit costs
- staff development, ability and approachability
- user experience, education and feedback
- innovation
- learning environment.

Due to the short timescale and the fact that this exercise represented both research into benchmarking and an attempt to benchmark, external consultants were employed. Involvement of staff at all levels was, however, seen as essential to ensure their ownership of the final product, and to facilitate long-term links with the target organizations. It was also important to maintain the connection between the benchmarking exercise and the TQM initiative.

Preliminary data was gathered through a questionnaire, followed up by site visits. As the questionnaire returns revealed a lack of availability of unit costs it was decided not to pursue this aspect further. The degree of honesty and openness in completing the questionnaire, and indeed throughout the process, was marked, reflecting the partners' enthusiasm for using the exercise as an opportunity for learning and sharing experience and data.

The follow-up visit was designed to elaborate the questionnaire responses, to discuss with staff general issues of quality, benchmarking and convergence, and to conduct three separate measurement studies. As a result, shortlists of those libraries which might be considered 'best-in-class' for a particular process were drawn up. These were grouped around four key processes, based on the CSFs:

• user induction and education
• information retrieval
• information provision and delivery
• facilities provision.

The measurement studies were:

• availability
• unobtrusive testing (carried out in 16 institutions)
• subjective assessment gathered on a walk-through basis.

These aimed to quantify user-related measures so that comparisons could be made across all participating libraries. Use of the results to rank participating libraries, in this case in relation to RMCS, would also provide a more rigorous and reproducible basis for identifying best-in-class performance. On completion of the exercise each participant received a written report summarizing the findings for their library.

RMCS then developed plans for improving performance to match that of those considered best at a particular process, and to implement a number of improvements. The project demonstrated the applicability of the basic benchmarking methodology to libraries and the general willingness of libraries to act as partners. An early decision was taken not to try and involve completely different industries.

Lessons learned included the need to focus benchmarking at the sub-process level, i.e. a more 'functional' approach. Staff involvement was critical. The use of consultants was necessary in order to meet the timetable and added a great deal of useful theoretical knowledge of both libraries and quality management, but the project was not, in consequence, as strongly owned by staff, which might have inhibited take-up of learning and individual commitment to continuing the process through follow-up visits. The issue of choosing who is 'best' remains; unit costs were a problematic area of measurement. Libraries probably needed to map their processes before embarking on benchmarking, and knowing what users consider a 'capable' process required more investigation.

Towards library excellence: best practice benchmarking

This project, led by Loughborough University, demonstrates early recognition of the importance and significance of the application of benchmarking in libraries, and the need for research to assist in its successful development. It is described fully by Garrod and Kinnell (1997) and Brockman

(1997). Though primarily a research project, it did involve benchmarking as action research within the overall exercise. The objective was 'to assess the relevance of benchmarking techniques to the library and information sector, and to evaluate levels of activity in, and current attitudes to, quality methods'. As such, it was not limited to academic libraries, but the RMCS library acted as one of the 'demonstrator' projects.

The exercise was funded by the British Library as one of a range of projects focusing on quality management. In the action research element, the approach was described as 'generic', but it might equally be called 'functional' in the sense that one process was identified for benchmarking purposes. The chosen process for RMCS as demonstrator was interlibrary loans (ILL), and the standard CSFs and process mapping (by flowcharting) approach was taken. The process map alone suggested several immediate improvements. One month's worth of quantitative data was collected and some analysis of reasons for delays undertaken. No comparison took place with other demonstrators as they chose different processes.

Two of the conclusions drawn were that benchmarking could be time-consuming; and that selection of partners is difficult and would require a critical mass of involved libraries before it became simpler. Confidentiality concerns were expressed by some participants. The development of a suitable methodology for HE libraries which fitted the culture was considered desirable, and the need for appropriate staff training was highlighted.

Surrey Institute of Art and Design benchmarking project

At Surrey Institute of Art and Design, academic services are converged, with the library, IT services, reprography, staff and educational development under a single head. The rationale for engaging in benchmarking came from the institute directorate, aiming to improve quality, provide an incentive for improvement through 'peer' comparison, and undertake an objective evaluation of activities and services. It was hoped that benchmarking would improve staff understanding of processes and their impact on the institute's customers, and would challenge complacency and align staff behind corporate goals. The directorate sought a department to act as a pilot for testing these assumptions and academic services responded.

This exercise can be characterized in part as 'functional', in that two processes only were selected for benchmarking, though one of these was very broad, involving many sub-processes. It can also be seen as 'competitive' since partners in similar specializations were sought and the overall aim was to make the institution more competitive in its niche. For this reason, the institute sought partners who could reasonably be said to have 'better practice'; prior involvement in quality initiatives, or publication of work on quality management and benchmarking was one means of identification.

The methodology chosen followed the familiar pattern of:

• establish team
• decide what and how to benchmark
• identify partners
• collect data
• analyse data
• action planning.

The team included the Head of Academic Services, the IT Manager and the Librarian, plus staff specifically involved with the processes selected. In choosing what to benchmark, a CSF approach was again employed, but this time CSFs were largely based on input from customer surveys. Once again, benchmarking overlaps with active efforts of the service to understand its customers at a deeper level. Processes were selected which would support the achievement of the CSFs and which had previously experienced quality problems. Other criteria included:

• high value for users
• affecting a large number of users
• measurable in a way that allows the evaluation of the quality of the process
• covering more than one area of the department.

Processes thus selected were:

• 'providing an effective technical and user support service' (the IT help desk service)
• 'making relevant information available in a timely manner' (the complete process chain of document and information delivery in the library).

Process mapping was then undertaken of seven relevant sub-processes, which included operating the staff/student help desk, selecting library stock, cataloguing and classification, interlibrary loans. Metrics and data were again collected via a questionnaire and follow-up visits. This exercise involved a thorough and detailed attempt to elicit relevant information and succeeded well in areas in which earlier projects had not. Cost analysis was undertaken, and detailed quantitative comparisons in all the areas were achieved. Partners included RMCS Information Services, another HE School of Art library and, for the help desk side only, the treasury services of a building society.

The great strength of this benchmarking exercise was the work done to translate the mass of data collected into clear and cogent statements about which of the partners had the better practice based on the evidence of the metrics, and to identify performance gaps between the institute and the other partners. For example, better practices at Partner A included the human response to telephone requests to the help desk and its automated reservations; Partner B's strengths included the motivational skills of the Deputy Librarian and its supplier response times. Superior practice at

Partner C included use of highly skilled staff and the systematic reporting and publishing of performance measures.

These examples show that the exercise had gone beyond the surface metrics to identify some of the root causes of good performance. Best practice may result, for example, from the quality of the library automated system, from the skills of an individual staff member, or from quality systems that the organization has been foresighted enough to put in place. Performance gaps could thus be identified and the results fed into an improvement programme at Surrey Institute of Art and Design involving an action plan and target setting.

This project showed that the planning stages were crucial to a successful benchmark exercise. Choice of processes, their subsequent mapping, and the measures chosen were critical in achieving a useful outcome. The metrics again proved problematic, as the partners counted, accounted for, and assessed their service in different ways, and a great deal of effort was required to normalize them. Published figures such as SCONUL statistics provided no help. As in previous exercises, selection of partners was difficult; the Head of Academic Services favoured the formation of a benchmarking club to provide prepared and willing partners. Once again, the exercise entailed a heavy burden of effort for participants, and analysis of results took some time. Finally, a mechanism for change management needs to be in place before embarking on a benchmarking exercise so that lessons learnt can be implemented.

Cranfield University RMCS library 'conceptual review'

Watson (1993) suggests that benchmarking should play a role not just in improving processes but at the strategic planning level. Senior management should guide benchmarking efforts so that they remain focused on key business processes, thus obtaining maximum return on investment. Strategic issues which benchmarking might address are: building core competencies; targeting specific shifts in strategy, for example, entering new markets, developing new products/lines of business; creating an organization more capable of learning.

In the RMCS annual review of information strategy, the Director of Information Services presents a policy statement to the Principal and the College Commandant. In 1997, these senior managers asked what the library's strategy was regarding future building requirements in an increasingly digital information environment. This challenge encompassed precisely the kind of strategic issues identified by Watson. It entailed assessment of a shift in library strategy towards the development of electronic information services; whether this would mean doing business in a radically different way, particularly with respect to physical building requirements; and whether this also opened up possibilities in relation to new teaching and learning technologies. There was also the implicit question of whether staff (and users) would have the competencies to cope with these changes.

It was decided to meet this challenge via a strategic benchmarking exercise aimed at developing a concept of the future RMCS library. Three processes ('strands') were selected:

- provision of the physical environment for learning
- provision of electronic library services
- provision of new methods of teaching and learning technology (T&LT).

In this sense the benchmarking was 'functional'. In another, it was clearly 'competitive'; the terms of reference demanded 'a position paper which assesses the RMCS Library against its competitors in Higher Education, taking into account the Post-Follett investment in HE Libraries'. Due to funding provided after the Follett Review (HEFCE 1993c), many new libraries and learning resource centres had been built and many electronic library projects undertaken. There was no shortage of potential partners; the issue was to select the excellent and the relevant. In all strands, relevant international developments were also taken into account. In the event, nine building exemplars (three 'old' and six 'new' universities) agreed to participate. Partners for the electronic library strand were sought from institutions which had been involved in the eLib programme (eLib 1998) or were to be involved in its hybrid libraries element (referring to access to digital and non-digital resources within a common information framework): six 'old' UK universities and two European institutions were chosen.

For the T&LT strand, information from five institutions (four 'old' universities, one 'new' one) was collected solely from websites and published information. This represented the choice of the staff member responsible for this strand, but it did serve as a test of whether benchmarking can be conducted in this way. Some institutions were subsequently contacted to follow up specific issues. There was also an attempt to benchmark various published visions for the future of library services, learning resources and indeed HE itself against currently held visions within the college.

Much effort again went into the metrics. The terms of reference suggested that library performance improvements arising from physical and electronic developments should be quantified if possible. CSFs were developed around the 'effective academic library' framework (HEFCE 1995b), and metrics developed which formed the framework of the data collection instruments. During the exercise it was necessary to refocus attention on the measurement aspects, as these tended to become secondary to the efforts to develop a strategic synthesis.

This exercise proved that Watson's application of benchmarking to strategic planning was transferable from an industrial context to HE information services. Compared to earlier exercises, difficulties with metrics did not hinder the process, and the choice of partners was much simpler, as it was obvious from various sources which universities had invested successfully in new buildings and electronic library developments. It also proved relatively simple to bind the strands together in a way which clarified the strategic choices open to RMCS. The final report (Town 1998b) contained both a clear competitive position statement and a choice of strategies.

The outcome reconfirmed the existing strategy, but expanded the concept of what a new RMCS Information Services Centre might provide in addition to traditional library services. The exercise also helped raise the profile of parallel essential developments, such as network infrastructure and T&LT provision. It was concluded that a key element in a successful *strategic* benchmarking exercise is an institutional learning style which permits open comparison with external competitors and a willingness to learn from them.

SCONUL benchmarking pilot projects: introduction

Within UK HE, the obvious agency for taking library benchmarking forward, and for creating benchmarking clubs or partnerships, was SCONUL. A benchmarking seminar at the 1996 Annual Conference was followed by the formation of a small working party to plan a way forward. In November 1997, SCONUL's advisory sub-committee on PIs (ACPI) sponsored another seminar, attended by staff from 12 institutions. This included presentations on previous experience and the development of an action plan and position statement, as follows:

- benchmarking could be a useful technique for improving performance
- SCONUL was committed to encouraging use of benchmarking
- the focus for benchmarking would be provided by ACPI
- a core group of institutions would be invited to engage in pilots
- a larger group of interested institutions would be invited to engage in follow-up testing
- the need for a benchmarking clearing house was identified
- a number of SCONUL Pilot Projects would be supported, and a co-ordinator appointed.

In the event, both the core group and the larger group of institutions were invited to form pilots, and the author was asked to coordinate the venture.

The intention of the pilots was to give practical benchmarking experience to a wider number of HE practitioners. For the library community, and SCONUL members particularly, the aim was to produce a standard methodology for academic library benchmarking. Subsequently this aim crystallized into the key deliverable of a benchmarking manual, which would include examples of standard metrics, so that difficulties in deciding on, collecting and normalizing measurement data could be avoided. The manual, combined with collections of data from benchmarking exercises, and staff skills developed through participation in the pilots, would comprise a resource for facilitating further exercises.

Seven pilots were originally agreed upon. Leaders were able to decide how many partners they wanted, what sort of partners (some wanted universities of the same type), and how much input they needed from the coordinator. The aim was to respond to expressed needs, especially for training or facilitation in the early stages. Three pilots took up this offer and three did not. In the event, the exercise took longer than originally envisaged, due in part to the serious and thorough approach taken by all; some pilots had not completed all stages by December 1998 and one failed to start for local reasons. However, to get six pilots active was far beyond expectations. The make-up of each pilot is described below. All participants were asked to attempt to follow Oakland's (1993) 15-point plan for benchmarking.

Planning stages
- select process groups
- identify best competitor (effectively settled by the make-up of each pilot)
- identify benchmarks
- bring together team
- decide information and data-collection methodology
- prepare for visits and interact with target organizations
- use data-collection methodology.

Action stages
- compare using data
- catalogue information
- understand 'enabling processes'
- set new objectives/standards
- develop action plans
- implement actions and integrate
- monitor results and improvements
- review measures and relationship.

Results and findings from the pilot projects

These are largely based on reports delivered at a general pilots' meeting in November 1998.

Advice desks (North)
Despite the involvement of five institutions (one 'old' and four 'new' universities), this pilot achieved a quick start and had run two tests of its data collection methodologies. The group had committed itself to repeating the process to check improvements in 1999, and to benchmark another area when the current exercise is complete. This project apparently had little difficulty with the methodology and involved a wide range of data collection methods, due in part to its leader's previous experience and activity in the field of customer understanding. These included an information desk query form; a 'smiley face' questionnaire for instant feedback; mystery shopper; a behavioural study; and exit interviews.

As well as specific lessons about the various data collection methodologies, the group learnt that:

- cooperation is possible, but there is a need to be transparent with results
- benchmarking requires good project management and training of the staff involved
- the constraints of running busy services meant that short bursts of testing were preferable to continuous assessment.

In terms of services provided, the exercise confirmed views about the location of enquiry desk services, and provided ammunition for various changes. It clarified that the partners were similar, but also highlighted different levels and quality of services provided within the group. It confirmed that advice desks are appreciated by students, and that they were generally satisfied; but one result of the exercise was to leave participants wondering if that satisfaction was warranted. One of the main benefits of benchmarking over the collection of statistical information was felt to be the opportunity for reflection on service quality for everyone involved.

Advice desks (South)
This group (two 'old' universities and one 'new' one) had completed its data collection and analysis phases, with few problems in moving through the CSFs exercise to a range of data collection methodologies. These included a self-assessment form for each institution; a user questionnaire; a logging form; and structured interviews with both librarian and user after an enquiry. It was accepted that the process of providing advice was being benchmarked rather than the quality of the outcome.

So far, participants had achieved very positive results relating to accessibility, availability and staff helpfulness. Areas for improvement had been identified, and all sites felt it worthwhile to review signing, supporting guides and documentation, and database support for remote users. Each institution also developed and implemented its own improvement agenda.

Information skills (North)
Although this involved two similar ('old') institutions, the contrasting organization of the libraries affected the chosen process significantly. Partner A provides training through subject librarians (diffuse); Partner B uses a functional team whose work includes training and documentation (centralized with formal aims, objectives and review mechanisms). One of the aims for B, therefore, was to identify gaps in its management information; for A the goal was to provide more of an organizational framework.

Both participants found the exercise a good opportunity for thought about the service; and the honesty on both sides was felt to be impressive. Though the measures were, again, the hardest part, the partners' efforts to get to grips with cost issues will probably result in profound changes. Realization of the comparative costs of staff teaching against independent learning packages will certainly change practice in one institution.

Information skills (South)
Initial challenges for this pilot, comprising one 'new' and one 'old' institution, were how to compare different approaches to library skills training and how to identify best practice. The leader of this pilot was not comfortable with the CSFs approach; instead a process review and peer review approach was adopted. Data collection via evaluation forms and other feedback methods is still in progress at the time of writing. The partners wanted to focus strongly on the training's effectiveness rather than collecting yet more management information; but it was recognized that this meant measuring real outcomes in trainees. The project therefore concentrated on comparing like processes; skills training for the MBA Course at Partner A was compared directly with that provided for a specialized MBA-type course at Partner B.

During the benchmarking process, it was recognized that Partner A had achieved a very high degree of integration of the school's library staff with the course, and that this involvement had a highly developed theoretical basis. This was a much more solid model than existed at Partner B, and during the pilot, practice at B began to move towards a similar model and use of A's methods. This might not have been anticipated at the outset given the differences in the parent institutions.

Counter services
This pilot, involving one 'old' and two 'new' institutions, began by defining areas for inclusion as all aspects of loans services, personal and telephone enquiries, queue management and general customer services. An end product was defined using a CSFs approach, processes required to deliver this product were identified and approximately 98 benchmarks chosen. Data was collected by questionnaire and visit.

Some initial conclusions emerged through the comparison: some benchmarks were dependent on the type of library automated system used; there were a number of overlap areas with other processes; because the libraries served different types of customer groups, and because staffing levels and work patterns varied greatly between partners, a best practice model which all could follow was difficult to decide upon and to achieve. The methodology was judged to be useful and transferable and positive achievements included recognition of the benefits of systematically analysing counter services from the customer's viewpoint for the first time, and of exchanging experience with other institutions. Improvements have resulted from the exercise.

Issues of concern included: the cost-effectiveness of benchmarking in this way, given the possibility of improving customer service with less time and effort; the identification of too many benchmarks; the difficulty of measuring the more intangible elements of the quality of a counter service.

Library environment
This pilot, involving two 'old' and two 'new' universities, commenced with a scoping exercise to define the 'library environment', and ensure that

elements covered by other pilots were excluded. On this basis, it was decided to benchmark two areas:

- library physical space (appropriateness; accessibility; organization; reader places)
- atmosphere and ambience (environmental control; quality of appearance; staff approachability; security and safety issues).

This was a conscious attempt to include both the tangible physical space aspects of the environment and the more intangible 'soft' environment experienced by users. The 'virtual' environment was excluded.

The methodologies chosen were customer surveys, library questionnaires, and visits by staff to assess other libraries. CSFs were developed for both main areas; the exercise then identified processes and developed benchmarks (44 different measures) and data collection methods, leading to a detailed questionnaire. Because partners were geographically widespread, much of the early work was carried out by email, but this proved no barrier to a successful conclusion. As with other pilots, the participants had found the opportunity to think deeply about their chosen aspect very stimulating. They also found that the library environment is a very subjective thing, which makes measurement difficult. Early conclusions include the need for institutional backing for benchmarking; more research theory input to give the process greater academic rigour; provision of more training in benchmarking methodology, to include those undergoing initial training in library schools.

Conclusions

There has been substantial benchmarking activity in the L&IS sector since 1993 and there is a coordinated national effort to understand and implement this tool for the wider benefit of the UK HE community. The UK HE context is now, paradoxically, not only highly competitive but also, due to recent government policy, likely to encompass strong pressure for increasing collaboration. Benchmarking fits this context precisely; it springs from the competitive environment, but provides the mechanism for increased competitiveness through collaborative comparison. It also fits current demands from different groups of stakeholders for different measures of performance. Benchmarking can focus on service users who are interested in qualitative performance; it can encompass the financial measures required by paymasters and senior managers, and demonstrate the true competitive position through comparison; it also provides the deeper insight into process performance differences required by information professionals and managers to generate positive change and development. Benchmarking can also contribute to the strategic planning process, and in particular to the development of an institution's information strategy, now a Funding Council requirement.

In the area of information services, benchmarking has provided a significant insight into measurement of aspects not previously assessed by other methods. The failure of quantitative approaches to measurement to illuminate the quality of a service was recognized in the first RMCS exercise. Within the SCONUL pilot projects, many participants wanted to address the more intangible, personal and subjective elements of providing a service, which experience suggests is critically important to library users. Performance measurement in these areas required new metrics and data collection methods, or at least the transfer of methods not previously employed within the academic L&IS context. The pilots have apparently succeeded in developing some new approaches to this problem. Some areas of quantitative measurement also required development, particularly the analysis of service costs. Benchmarking has provided some impetus here to a relatively dormant area of library performance measurement.

Standard benchmarking methodologies have been used successfully in the L&IS sector. Problems have related mainly to measurement and choosing partners. It is not easy to identify who is best at a particular service/process, and the best is often discovered in unexpected places. Published measures are of limited use, although rudimentary benchmarking can be done through them. An alternative popular method is the use of email discussion lists to share a problem, seek data or solutions, and ethically share the findings. Benchmarking can be time-consuming and therefore expensive, but the full-scale type involving visits and deeper interaction with partners seems to be the most fulfilling and successful, and the staff development dimension should not be forgotten. Library and information services have proved willing to act as benchmarking partners, and ethical or confidentiality problems have arisen only occasionally within the academic sector to date.

The future challenge for benchmarking as a technique in the L&IS area is whether it will gain widespread acceptance. The benchmarking approach is as much a state of mind as a tool; it requires curiosity, readiness to copy, and a collaborative mentality. These qualities already exist in many academic libraries. SCONUL's future task is to provide suitable guidance and support to encourage the use of benchmarking by those who wish to do so, and the proposed manual will condense the experience of the pilots into a simple procedure with a choice of metrics available.

Acknowledgements

The author acknowledges the help of all participating institutions, their libraries and staff and the many others who have offered advice and support over the last five years, in particular, Elizabeth Marsh, Janet McLeish and Aravind Vasu, who worked on the first RMCS project; Marion Wilks for providing details of the Surrey Institute of Art and Design exercise; leaders and members of the SCONUL pilots; SCONUL and its ACPI, whose members have provided resources and support of all kinds.

13

HEFCE's Value for Money Studies

Helen Lund

Overview

This chapter examines the contribution made by the Funding Councils' Value for Money (VfM) studies to the development of benchmarking within UK HE. It is based on an interview with John Rushforth, Chief Auditor at the Higher Education Funding Council for England (HEFCE) and the studies themselves. The background to VfM and the study methodology are discussed. HEFCE's experience of running VfM is briefly reviewed, with a look at benefits accrued, problems encountered and future plans. It is argued that VfM's connection with benchmarking is threefold. First, the VfM methodology has elements in common with benchmarking exercises. Performance within a group of 'peer' institutions is analysed in order to identify good practice and findings are disseminated, both to participants and more widely, by means of published reports and handbooks, and via regional seminars. These 'enable the discussion of findings and alternatives by practitioners in an active way and lead to the creation of new networks and communities of practice' (J. Rushforth, personal communication). Second, the VfM management review guides or handbooks are powerful tools, enabling institutions to 'benchmark' their existing practice against a recommended set of checks and guidelines, and to develop an action plan for improvement, if necessary. Third, as the studies have progressed, benchmarking is increasingly prominent among the methods recommended for use by HEIs in measuring and enhancing their performance (see Figure 13.1).

Background to VfM studies

The concept of 'value for money' as fundamental to the 'mission' of UK HEIs goes back to its appearance, in the late 1980s, in the financial Memorandum drawn up between institutions and the Universities' Funding Council (UFC). Provision for specific 'studies to improve economy, efficiency and effectiveness in the management or operations' of HEIs was made in the Education Reform Act of 1988 (DES 1989) and reiterated in the Further and Higher Education Act of 1992 (DfE 1992). Previously, HE efficiency studies were undertaken by the Audit Commission for Local Authorities in England and Wales, but the 1992 legislation also gave powers to the new Higher Education Funding Council for England (HEFCE) and its counterparts for Scotland and Wales to carry out such work. The duty to ensure and promote value for money was also expressed in HEFCE's own Audit Code of Practice (HEFCE 1993a).

Establishing VfM studies

Government-led scrutiny of managerial efficiency and cost-effectiveness within local government and the NHS, via audit studies, had been a feature of the late 1980s. Studies by the Audit Commission (established 1983) included procurement, environmental health, the care of the mentally ill, road construction, and human resources functions. In 1992, the National Audit Office (also established in 1983) turned its attention to HE, with a VfM study on purchasing practice (NAO 1992). The launch of VfM studies by HEFCE in 1993 can be seen as a response to these political imperatives.

The challenge, as HEFCE perceived it, was to ensure that demands from external stakeholders for greater accountability and cost-effectiveness were met in a way that the institutions it funded found both acceptable and useful (J. Rushforth, personal communication). Clearly it made no sense for HEFCE to reinvent the wheel. John Rushforth, appointed as Chief Auditor at HEFCE in 1993, brought with him ten years' experience of work at the Audit Commission (AC). Accordingly, the methodology adopted by the Funding Councils for VfM drew on the Audit Commission model. Constitutionally, however, there was one crucial difference between the AC and HEFCE. Whereas the former was legally *required and obliged* to carry out audit exercises, the latter had no such power to impose VfM studies on HEIs. The initial premise, therefore, behind VfM was that the studies must be carried out in cooperation with the sector. It was also decided that audit studies should be conducted across the UK, i.e. with the Scottish and Welsh Funding Councils (SHEFC and HEFCW) and the Department of Education for Northern Ireland (DENI).

An initial workshop, attended by 15 or so senior managers from UK institutions, discussed three main options:

- the Audit Commission approach to special studies on specific topics
- a national benchmarking club
- the development of a model (probably using management consultants) as to what made an effective HEI.

The reaction was mixed, with resistance mainly focused on the need for such an initiative, together with suspicion as to how results might be used.

This workshop confirmed for HEFCE that if VfM was to succeed, it was crucial 'to establish ownership of VfM by the HEIs themselves' (J. Rushforth, personal communication). A steering group, comprised entirely of representatives from institutions, was set up, and a consultation paper (HEFCE 1993b) offered a range of options as to how the studies might be undertaken; again, these included a formal benchmarking club or quality exchange.

The response to the consultation document was also mixed. Although most of the respondents favoured the idea of VfM studies, some felt that they should be undertaken by the universities' own Committee of Vice-Chancellors and Principals (CVCP), rather than the Funding Councils. A small group took the view that audit work of this sort was inappropriate within HE, representing a threat to institutional autonomy. Some feared that cost savings identified by VfM studies would be deducted from the institution's grant. The Chair of the Steering Group issued a statement reassuring institutions that this would not happen and established the guiding principle that the VfM initiative was 'by the sector for the sector'.

VfM study methodology

The formation of a project group for each study, composed entirely of university personnel, has ensured active involvement by representatives from HEIs in monitoring the progress of each study and in developing the study products. The precise methodology for each study varies, but typically might comprise:

- initial discussions with a representative group
- a research phase, involving data collection within each institution
- detailed visits to interview a range of staff at 15–20 pilot institutions
- development of performance indicators
- publication of national reports and review guides
- training/implementation seminars
- evaluation of impact.

A small-scale feasibility study has preceded most exercises, leading to the development of detailed terms of reference.

Basic research and institutional visits are conducted by HEFCE staff and/or external consultants. Typically, consultants on one study will comprise an auditor and a professional with subject expertise (e.g. IT management). Usually at least one of these has experience of HE. For its VfM work, HEFCE tends to use consultants working independently or for small companies, rather than the large management consultancy firms. HEFCE's VfM studies involve use of quantitative and qualitative data, and have from the outset concerned themselves with 'processes' as well as input and/or outcome measures. The cost to the Funding Councils of mounting one study has been estimated at between £50,000 and £100,000 (Lund 1998a) and

Figure 13.1 Summary of main VfM studies showing the progressive influence of benchmarking and some of the important outcomes from the studies

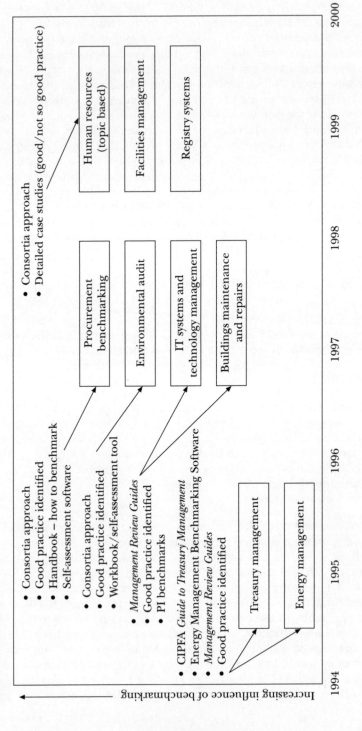

approximate direct costs for the four studies completed so far amount to £380,000 (J. Rushforth, personal communication). Considering the scale of UK public funding for HE (£7 billion per annum) and the real and potential savings arising from VfM study findings, this is a relatively small investment. Participating institutions do not pay a fee, but involvement will 'cost' approximately four person days' input from staff.

VfM studies 1994–6

Since 'everyone wants to save money and get cheaper energy' (J. Rushforth, personal communication), the first VfM studies focused on treasury management and energy management.

Treasury management

Fifteen institutions piloted this study which covered: overall treasury management arrangements; cash flow management; banking arrangements; management and investment of short-term funds; endowments and long-term investments; financing arrangements. Data was collected for each element via two questionnaires. 'Good' practice identified by the study (HEFCE 1996b) included preparation and monitoring of cash flow forecasts, to maximize funds for investment; market testing of banking services, leading to significantly reduced bank charges; a proactive approach to treasury management to ensure the best returns on short-term investment of surplus funds.

In this initial study, benchmarking plays a fairly minor role in terms of action recommended to HEIs. Institutions are advised, in respect of endowments and long-term investment, to establish 'a robust system of monitoring and reviewing', which will include consideration of benchmarks against which performance is measured (e.g. the FTSE Index); a regular review of the performance of investment managers should include comparison of performance against 'benchmarks' since the last review. HEIs are also advised to consult a recent guide to HE treasury management by the Chartered Institute of Public Finance and Accountancy (CIPFA 1995). This contains a 'model' treasury management policy statement and constitutes a good 'benchmark' against which to measure existing policies (HEFCE 1996c). The study's *Management Review Guide* itself (HEFCE 1996c) constitutes a type of benchmarking tool, offering, for each topic area, a review objective and recommended areas for consideration. Institutions are encouraged to assess their existing practice against these guidelines. Self-assessment is an important feature of all the VfM studies and, for institutions, it is 'the regimen of fitting existing processes into the self-assessment model that gives VfM its power' (J. Rushforth, personal communication).

Energy management

Nineteen institutions piloted this project, which also drew on good practice within public and private sector organizations outside HE. An initial set-back was the discovery that, unlike other public sector organizations whose energy use had been scrutinized by the Audit Commission, essential data on energy use was simply not available within many HEIs. The council overcame this by hiring 200 portable energy consumption monitors.

The study's main findings (HEFCE 1996d) were that energy savings of 10–20 per cent of utilities spend could be achieved over a period, but only with senior management commitment and sufficient funding for staffing. Recommended good practice included more effective utility purchasing, installation of energy-saving equipment, use of energy awareness programmes. The study's products included Energy Management Benchmarking Software, designed to provide HEIs with the means to produce regular management information relating to energy performance. The software compares the energy performance of each building against set benchmarks; poor performers can then be made a priority in any action plan. The need for such tools within the HE sector is borne out by the high level of take-up for the product (70 per cent of HEIs) and subsequent requests for an update of the software (J. Rushforth, personal communication).

VfM studies late 1996 to 1997

The two major studies focused on Building Repairs and Maintenance (BRM) and on Information Systems and Technology Management (IS/IT). The Funding Councils also conducted smaller scale studies on Environmental Audit and Procurement Benchmarking. The second round of VfM studies is notable for an increased emphasis on benchmarking, either as the focus of the study itself (procurement), or as a recommended 'next step' for HEIs arising from the findings of the study. The environmental audit study marks the start of HEFCE's experimentation with a new approach to 'efficiency measurement': consortium benchmarking.

Building repairs and maintenance

This study arose from the view that 'an appropriate and well-maintained estate . . . is critical to the delivery of the institution's core business objectives in a cost-effective way' as 'it supports the delivery of teaching and research and . . . provides a stimulating and supportive environment for students and staff' (HEFCE 1998e: 7). The total spend on BRM in UK HE in 1997 has been estimated at £200 million, i.e. 1 per cent of the insurance value of UK HE's combined estate.

Three HEIs took part in a feasibility study and 12 institutions acted as pilot sites. A key aim of the project was to develop performance benchmarks for

HEIs on managing their building maintenance arrangements, which would cover standards, investment, planning and staff. In order to incorporate into the study the views of a wider constituency, HEFCE also invited other HEIs to provide examples of their buildings maintenance arrangements, and still others to provide feedback on issues raised by the study. In addition, a buildings maintenance questionnaire sent to all UK HEIs was returned by 60 per cent of institutions. Recommended practice (HEFCE 1998e) included development of a maintenance strategy; use of condition surveys to inform planning processes and enable prioritization of funding; use of agreed customer service standards; review of procurement arrangements for buildings maintenance; use of quality reviews and benchmarking of service standards.

One difficulty for HEIs wishing to compare their performance with that of peers is often the lack of available data to serve as benchmarks. In the BRM field, this problem is alleviated by the existence of two long-standing databases, established by the Association of University Directors of Estates (AUDE) and the Association of University Engineers (AUE), with a primary aim of improving institutions' understanding of their performance relative to that of other HEIs. HEFCE's commitment to benchmarking as a means to improve practice in the area of BRM is underlined in its recommendation that UK HEIs which currently did not contribute information to these databases should do so (HEFCE 1998e).

The *Management Review Guide* for this study (HEFCE 1998f) also provides practical help in the form of a checklist illustrating how specific performance benchmarks could be developed. These are listed under four main areas: standards; investment; planning; and staff. Typical benchmarks include ratio of statutory work spend to total maintenance spend; investment per student/staff member; ratio of planned maintenance spend to reactive maintenance spend; ratio of maintenance spend on in-house staff to spend on external contractors. The Funding Councils also commissioned an estates management statistics study, involving 38 pilot institutions, in order to facilitate performance benchmarking in this functional area. The first report from this study was published in 1999 (HEFCE 1999a) followed by consultation with HEIs regarding the extension of this work to the whole sector (HEFCE 1999b).

Information systems and technology management

Investment by UK HEIs in IS/IT is big business, currently standing at around £500 million per annum, or 4.5 per cent of annual sector income. This represents a higher than average investment compared to HE sectors in other countries (HEFCE 1998g), reflecting the desire of the UK sector to stay at 'the cutting edge' in the development and delivery of IT services. Consequently, the need for 'appropriate management arrangements . . . to ensure that this investment provides value for money' is 'essential' (HEFCE

1998g: 4). This was a more sensitive topic than those covered in earlier VfM studies, as assessment of the IT function would also involve scrutiny of its impact on academic delivery. Furthermore, there were no established methodologies for assessing the impact and effectiveness of an IT system.

The two-year project began with a feasibility study involving three institutions; eight institutions piloted the main study. Another 20 HEIs agreed to complete a questionnaire. Six HEIs (three of them pilot sites) took part in a user satisfaction survey, and visits were made to another six. In all, the opinions of 4–5000 staff and students were canvassed. Recommended good practice (HEFCE 1998g) included quantification of total investment in IT; strategies driven by information needs and integrated into the institutional mission; senior management responsibility for IT; standardized use and procurement of IT equipment; formal monitoring of key activities. Encouragingly, the report concluded that most improvements needed 'relatively little specialist IT knowledge' and most could be effected by the use of 'conventional recognized management practices'. The study also recommended to HEIs the use of 'key benchmarks' (HEFCE 1998g, 1998h) for help in quantifying their total investment in IS/IT and measuring the effectiveness of their operational management. Four financial benchmarks were suggested:

- total IS/IT expenditure per FTE student
- total IS/IT expenditure per FTE staff member
- total IS/IT expenditure per workstation
- total IS/IT expenditure in relation to total institutional recurrent expenditure.

Eleven operational benchmarks were also developed:

- number of students and of staff (total, academic and administrative) to a workstation
- hours of availability of open access workstations per student
- number of workstations per IS/IT staff member
- number of workstations and of software applications supported by the central IS/IT department (CITD) per member of CITD staff
- number of hours of introductory IT skills training provided to students by the CITD, per student
- number of hours of user support provided to students/staff by the CITD, per student/staff member.

These 'study benchmarks' are derived from data supplied by the 20 HEIs that completed the questionnaire, and are expressed in terms of lower, median and upper quartiles. For example, total IS/IT expenditure ranged from 4.21 per cent of total institutional expenditure to 5.48 per cent, with a median of 5.06 per cent. The total number of FTE staff per workstation ranged from 0.9 to 1.4 with a median of 1.1. Institutions are encouraged to do their own calculations and to compare their performance against these study benchmarks. The council recognizes that these benchmarks may not be relevant for all institutions and is keen for them to 'develop further benchmarks that are more pertinent to their own circumstances' (HEFCE 1998h: 44). Performance which equates to the lower quartile of the study benchmarks is not necessarily a cause for alarm; HEIs should evaluate these benchmarks in terms of their own institutional objectives. Further development of these benchmarks on behalf of the sector has been entrusted to the Universities and Colleges Information Systems Association (UCISA).

Environmental audit

Six HEIs were involved in this study, which was prompted in part by the Toyne Report (DfE and Welsh Office 1993) and facilitated by the University of Sunderland's environmental consultancy and training unit, ESAS. An important aim was to benchmark current environmental performance against best practice, including that in private sector organizations. Participating institutions were more involved in shaping this study than in previous VfM exercises, though the methodology fell short of full collaborative benchmarking, since there were no meetings to share findings formally from individual visits. Although diversity within the group, in terms of size, operations, culture, attitude and priorities meant that on some occasions it was initially difficult to establish a 'group view' on the issues up for analysis (J. Rushforth, personal communication), the report (HEFCE 1998i) did identify a number of examples of existing good practice, including the drawing up of an environmental grounds policy with detailed objectives, and an environmental training programme for staff.

The other major product of this study was a workbook (HEFCE 1998j) to help institutions review their environmental performance. This included a comprehensive set of detailed self-assessment questions, giving institutions the opportunity to benchmark their own practice against the ideal. When asked, for example, 'Do you have an environmental policy?' or 'Is good environmental performance by individuals recognized?', institutions must say whether the question is applicable, and if so, whether their current practice is fully/partly/not satisfactory. They then detail what action (if any) is required and what priority that action has. There is also the opportunity to cite examples of practice or comment on action required.

Procurement benchmarking

Bought-in goods and services now represent as much as 40 per cent of costs for UK HEIs, making it 'critically important ... to maximize the value secured through the whole procurement process' (HEFCE 1997e: 4). This study, therefore, aimed to develop 'a methodology for the improvement of procurement practice'. Seven institutions participated in the exercise, which divided the procurement function, for benchmarking purposes, into 25 or so processes. These included strategy development; purchasing horizons; purchasing procedures; customer service; supply chain integration; price management; cost management; supplier relationships; risk management. The end product was not a study report, with conclusions and recommendations, but a 'handbook', with accompanying software, designed 'to provide senior and line managers . . . with a powerful set of tools which they can use to assess their current strengths and weaknesses and to develop those aspects of procurement management which do not currently meet their aspirations' (HEFCE 1997e).

Procurement is clearly an area where HE can benefit from benchmarking with other industries ('out of the box'). Informal evidence from HEIs suggested that the average cost of processing purchasing orders is between £50 and £100 *per item* (multiplied by 50,000+ orders per annum) as compared with 'good practice' benchmarks of £20 to £25 *per order* outside the sector. A medium-sized HEI could potentially save £1 million a year. The council believes that it makes sense for most institutions to benchmark their actual levels of performance against realistic management aspirations, rather than against world class standards which may not be cost-effective or feasible. Accordingly, a *Management Aspiration Workbook* (HEFCE 1997e) provides guidelines on how to 'reach agreement on the most appropriate level of management aspiration once a commodity or service to be benchmarked has been selected' via a workshop involving all 'key stakeholders' in the procurement process.

The *Observation Workbook* (HEFCE 1997e) then enables participants to map their actual practice. Faced with more than 150 statements, such as, 'We include customer service in our training programme for buyers', institutions indicate their standpoint from six options (don't know; strongly disagree; disagree; neither; strongly agree; agree). Ideally, this is done at the end of the Aspirations workshop, as this 'encourages a level of discussion about actual practices, which helps to promote better quality information'. The accompanying software includes a programme that analyses data gathered from the first two stages and presents it as a radar chart. Each aspect of the procurement process (e.g. stock management, customer services) is graded on a scale from 0 to 4 in terms of (a) aspirations and (b) actual practice. The difference between the target set for a desired level of performance and the actual performance, the 'aspiration gap', is presented graphically via the radar chart. Institutions then consider the likely benefits, and costs, of closing each gap; they are advised 'only to close gaps which deliver a business benefit'. The chart also enables benchmarking participants to see clearly the areas of the procurement process in which they are already achieving 'good practice'.

This manual and software seems to offer HE procurement practitioners a helpful steer through the benchmarking process. HEFCE itself saw the development of this package as a test exercise 'to assess whether the general techniques of benchmarking would benefit institutions'. In launching the study's products, Brian Fender, HEFCE's Chief Executive, declared himself 'convinced that benchmarking does offer significant advantages' and announced that he 'would be looking to support other benchmarking exercises in the future' (HEFCE 1997e). Reaction from the sector, so far, however, has been mixed, with some institutions expressing reservations about the very time-consuming nature of the proposed benchmarking work (J. Rushforth, personal communication).

VfM studies from 1998

Three topics were chosen by the sector in response to a consultation document issued by HEFCE at the end of 1996 (HEFCE 1996e). A facilities management study will build, in part, on work undertaken for the further education sector (FEFC 1997). All VfM studies so far have included 'cameos' (mini-case studies) of good practice, but more detailed case studies will be included in this report, illustrating both good and less successful practice.

The second topic, human resources, is the most sensitive, and therefore the most controversial tackled so far. The sector's willingness to see this function set under the VfM microscope is perhaps a measure of its growing confidence in the council's work so far in this area, and the perceived value of its outcomes. The HR function will be broken into manageable 'chunks' and covered over a number of years. The first study will cover sickness and stress, using AC methodology and building on (unpublished) survey work by the University of Birmingham. The associations of university personnel and safety officers will be actively involved. Other possible topics are Investors in People (a national quality standard which sets a level of good practice for improving an organization's performance through its people); the strategic aspects of human resources management (HRM), possibly modelled on studies done by the Institute of Personnel Development (IPD); systems for reward and for appraisal. It is hoped that the end products of these studies will comprise a mixture of 'good ideas, practical exercises and some numbers' and that these will serve as building blocks to support a larger strategic study on HRM (J. Rushforth, personal communication).

The third study will look at registry systems. Probable topics are the IT and service aspects of the registry function: the time taken for student registration; and the right balance between self-registration and staff-based registration.

Commentary

In terms of challenges presented by VfM and lessons learned, lack of performance management data within HEIs has been a persistent problem (J. Rushforth, personal communication). With the BRM project, this difficulty was addressed by looking at the 'cameos' of good practice emerging from the study and via the estates statistics project discussed above. Lack of data relating to IT management was addressed by sending out a questionnaire to 20 institutions.

It has proved possible to apply models from other sectors to HE, but they needed to be tailored accordingly. At the start of the VfM initiative, the dispatch of sector-wide questionnaires was considered, but the council has learnt that it is more effective to work with a group of around 20 institutions in order to obtain consistent data and enable thorough testing of proposed benchmarks.

HEFCE also needs to ensure that 'the tremendous diversity' of the sector is reflected fully in the studies. The council has found 'that nearly everyone does something well, but hardly anyone does everything right'. HEFCE's task is 'to stitch these bits together' (J. Rushforth, personal communication). VfM studies thus fulfil an important role in helping to bridge some of the existing communications gaps within the sector, since institutions have tended to interact mainly with members of a peer group. The VfM studies so far completed have managed to capture the experience of a broad and representative cross-section of the sector. While a handful of institutions are clearly 'enthusiasts', having participated in two or more projects, there is no sense that voluntary participation has led to the studies being dominated by a small and unrepresentative group. HEFCE has also taken care to prevent the possible 'capture' of a study by one 'interest group' within institutions, by ensuring that project groups always include a senior management representative (e.g. a vice-chancellor or finance director). In this way, the topic can be looked at from a broad *institutional* perspective.

At the developmental stage, it has not always been easy for the council to get consistent messages on the perceived quality of products where there are a number of diverse stakeholders. However, where a view is identified that an element of a study is seen as unhelpful, it is fully explored. If no consensus is reached, then the UK Steering Group will consider the issue at a formal level. Inevitably, this desire for consensus adds significantly to the development time.

Once the VfM study is completed, institutions may be keen to act upon the findings but encounter difficulties doing so, particularly at departmental level within a system of devolved budgets. This is likely to be due, in part, to the tension that still exists within some HEIs between professional managers and academic staff. Even at senior management level, negative feelings persist within some institutions on the issue of performance audit. The views of the audit or value for money committee may be construed by the chief executive as constituting criticism or interference, while among governors and other laypersons with a stake in the institution, VfM is often perceived solely as a cost-cutting exercise. The focus on improvement of process is thus overlooked. In attempting to overcome such misconceptions, the regional seminars that HEFCE hosts at the close of each study play a major role in raising the broader contexts and implications. These seminars are generally well attended, with as many as 100 institutions represented, and serve as an important vehicle for evaluation and information exchange.

Findings for all VfM studies so far have included the statement that senior management commitment is essential for successful performance evaluation, leading to improved practice. An analysis of attendance at the post-study workshops for energy management and BRM found, however, that 'the challenge remains to secure a real level of support for these events by members of institutions' senior management teams' (HEFCE 1998k). One option to improve this situation is to consider the possibility of providing funding incentives, possibly along parallel lines to HEFCE's Fund for Development of Teaching and Learning (FDTL). Another is to look at how the sector responds to the Dearing Report's recommendation (NCIHE 1997) that institutions should research and report on their own effectiveness. At the time of writing, consideration of these options was at a very early stage (J. Rushforth, personal communication).

Future plans

For the next five years, HEFCE's VfM work is likely to concentrate on the two main areas where cost savings can be achieved: staffing and the estate. After that, the IT study will probably be repeated since this is a fast-changing area. So far, VfM work has focused on the infrastructure underlying academic activity in higher education, but the next step may well be the application of VfM to areas such as teaching and learning and the management of research (J. Rushforth, personal communication).

Dissemination of the good practice identified by the studies is a central feature of VfM. All HEIs receive the national reports and management review guides, with copies also provided to the Further Education Funding Council (FEFC), the Department for Education and Employment (DfEE) and the National Audit Office (NAO). The World Wide Web (WWW) is likely to become increasingly important for disseminating VfM products both to UK HEIs and abroad. HEFCE has established with other HE agencies, an HE Estates website. When fully developed it will include good practice guides, examples of good practice provided by HEIs, statistics, relevant legislation and product information (http://www.heestates.ac.uk). If successful, the idea could be extended to other VfM topics.

It is likely too that any comparative studies of performance within HE will in future need, increasingly, to take account of international practice (see Chapters 14 and 15 and Appendix B). HEFCE has already drawn on the experience of HEIs abroad for VfM studies; for example, the universities of Dortmund in Germany and Utrecht in the Netherlands provided input into the IT study. As a spin-off from the facilities management study, HEFCE staff have met with Australian FM officers, and there is the possibility of HEFCE undertaking collaborative work on estates management with institutions in Australia and the US. So far there has not been any sustained attempt to monitor the impact of the VfM studies on HE practitioners abroad, but hits on the VfM website and email from countries including Finland, Canada, India and Argentina do reflect a degree of overseas interest.

From audit-based VfM to consortium benchmarking?

The preceding narrative shows that audit and benchmarking have been combined creatively in the VfM studies so far undertaken, but the balance has progressively shifted towards the latter. With its publication of the pilot procurement study, HEFCE (1997e) endorsed the usefulness of benchmarking as a performance improvement tool for HEIs. In the same period, the council demonstrated interest in the concept of consortium benchmarking, with an invitation to small groups of institutions to apply for funding to conduct VfM studies on a topic of their choice. One of the most successful of these projects, facilitated by external consultants, involved a group of small and medium-sized CHEs, and focused on learning resource centres. As this was a topic not yet covered by the Audit Commission, it provided a useful test bed for HEFCE in developing a methodology that could be applied to a larger scale study. Another outcome of this initiative was the environmental audit study discussed above. HEFCE has also provided financial support to the Midlands Consortium, whose VfM studies, facilitated by KPMG, have included IT and procurement. Again, this provided access to methodologies with potential application to larger scale projects.

The shape of things to come?

In 1998, the council gained first-hand experience of consortium benchmarking through its involvement in a knowledge management project facilitated by the European Foundation for Quality Management (EFQM). The methodology used by EFQM is highly participative: representatives from different organizations work within 'consortia' to identify 'best practice' both within the group and in other 'peer' organizations, using a mix of workshops, questionnaires, group analysis and visits, ending in a knowledge-sharing session. HEFCE staff found this approach beneficial, both in terms of seeing first-hand 'that things worked', as opposed to being instructed by an 'expert', and in regard to the group dynamic and peer exchange. This consortium-based approach was also found to be cost-effective: it would have cost HEFCE between two and four times the EFQM participation fee to commission a study on knowledge management from one of the major consultancy firms (J. Rushforth, personal communication). Is the application of this approach to evaluating and improving performance within groups of peer HEIs the next logical step?

Conclusions

Over the last five years, VfM studies have focused on those functions which the sector itself has identified as areas of need, and where external research confirms that considerable gains can be made, both in terms of financial savings and streamlining of operations. During this period, benchmarking techniques have played an increasingly important part in the Funding Councils' VfM work. The management review guides, handbooks and software produced from the studies serve as tools that enable institutions to assess their own processes and performance, identify areas for improvement, and take action to implement better practice. Some studies (IT and BRM) have led to the creation of benchmarks against which performance can be measured. The development of a benchmarking model for the procurement function, based on 'realistic management aspirations', confirmed for HEFCE the relevance and utility of benchmarking techniques for HE. HEFCE's own experience of consortium benchmarking with EFQM, together with small-scale trials conducted in the sector, suggest that the council may adopt this approach for the next stage of VfM studies.

The studies themselves have revealed a wealth of existing 'good practice', which can be adopted or adapted by other HEIs, while informal evaluation has already identified examples of impressive cost savings and more efficient management at institutions piloting the studies. Savings of £150,000 per annum, for example, were achieved by one institution participating in the energy management study, while one of the institutions piloting the treasury management project benefited from an annual saving of £10,000 through reduced bank charges. In December 1998, a formal evaluation of the first VfM study on energy management was discussed by the UK Steering Group (HEFCE 1998l). Subsequently, an electronic survey was conducted. This was designed to identify 'key beneficial changes' achieved by HEIs in managing energy costs and consumption, and to assess the contribution made by VfM national products in raising awareness of energy management issues and helping HEIs to achieve energy cost savings. The survey included questions on institutions' use of the energy management benchmarking software that was a product of the study and the development of institution-specific benchmarks. Similar evaluations of the other VfM studies over the next few years should reveal the full impact of VfM, and the benefits arising from this form of benchmarking.

Acknowledgement

The author is most grateful to John Rushforth, Chief Auditor at HEFCE, who gave generously of his time to contribute to this chapter, in the form of an interview, the supply of unpublished materials relating to VfM and a critical review of the draft chapter.

Part 3

Benchmarking in Other HE Systems and Transnational Benchmarking

14

Benchmarking in Other HE Systems

Helen Lund and Norman Jackson

Overview

This chapter reviews some approaches to HE benchmarking in use outside the UK. So far, activity has been primarily geared towards business/administrative practice rather than educational processes, with the US and Australia being most active in the field. As in the UK, benchmarking activities cover a spectrum that ranges from development of management statistics and performance indicators to inform managerial decisions to more dynamic approaches in which partners actively discuss issues and contexts with the aim of identifying 'best' practice and adopting or adapting it to improve performance. Benchmarking of physics education in Europe provides an example of transnational subject-based benchmarking, while a subject-based model developed in Australia strongly influenced the strategic steer from the Dearing Committee to develop benchmarking for regulatory purposes in UK HE. Some of the approaches now being applied in other countries might usefully be applied in the UK.

Introduction

Increasing globalization of HE, and the consequent extension of 'competition' beyond regional and even national boundaries, makes it incumbent on UK policy makers at both sectoral and institutional levels to look to practice in other countries to inform their decisions. The area of performance evaluation is no exception: already, for example, the highest grades awarded to UK HEIs in regard to research performance designate 'international excellence' and researchers overseas play a part in confirming that award (see Chapter 2).

The examples of different approaches to benchmarking discussed in this chapter provide a broader context for benchmarking in the UK and serve as a foundation for the accounts of two international benchmarking initiatives that follow. An important source of information on activity in the administrative and management fields was the review of international benchmarking produced by the Commonwealth Higher Education Management Service (CHEMS) for UNESCO (Schofield 1998).

United States

Given the original development of industrial/commercial benchmarking in the US, it is not surprising that US HEIs were among the first to become involved in benchmarking. The National Association of College and University Business Officers (NACUBO) initiative (established in 1991) originally covered 40 functional areas, with performance evaluated via 600 different benchmarks (Alstete 1995; Farquhar 1998). Subsequently, this was amended to five core functions, with the option of up to 35 additional areas. From 1997/8, a revised model offers institutions six basic modules (overall indicators; accounts payable; facilities; purchasing; financial aid; student accounts receivable) with add-on blocks of five modules up to the maximum of 40. Depending on the number of modules chosen, the participation fee is between $3500 and $9500. This includes pre- and post-data collection workshops and training on data collection and electronic entry. Participants receive a report which compares their performance of a particular process with mean scores based on the performance of all other participants and of appropriate cohort groups (Farquhar 1998; NACUBO 1998). While the NACUBO project pointed the way to a quantitative performance indicator-based approach to benchmarking in HE, criticisms from participants have included too high a level of data aggregation and of detail in results; lack of any mechanism to encourage institutions' implementation of findings; failure to look for best practice outside HE (Alstete 1995). Declining membership (from 150 in 1991 to around 100 in 1997) may also reflect dissatisfaction with the methodology, although some participants have reported improved practice. For Farquhar (1998: 24), the NACUBO programme 'provides information for benchmarks', but will not 'necessarily result in benchmarking' in its fullest sense of shared discussion and evaluation with the aim of identifying and implementing 'good' or 'best' practice. Projects run by the Association for Continuing Higher Education and the American Assembly of Collegiate Schools of Business, through its consulting company Educational Benchmarking Inc., are likewise judged to be 'services that provide data from which an institution can establish benchmarks' rather than 'operations that perform true benchmarking'.

Where US institutions have engaged in 'full' benchmarking, it has apparently been done on an independent basis. For example, Oregon State University benchmarked with seven 'peers' and one 'aspirant' university in order to assess the efficiency of its administrative and support services. The University of Central Florida benchmarked its employee performance evaluation against practice within a major commercial corporation and a schools system within Florida. Harvard Business School benchmarked its MBA programmes against more than 20 business schools in the US and overseas as well as corporate training programmes (Alstete 1995; Farquhar 1998).

Two initiatives are now furthering benchmarking in a more collaborative sense. The first is the development and piloting of an educational version of the Malcolm Baldridge Quality Awards, which have identified and rewarded best management practice within commercial organizations since 1987. The Baldridge Award for Education requires institutions to undertake an extensive self-assessment exercise and includes benchmarking as a specific factor for evaluation in determining the winners (Fisher 1995; Farquhar 1998; Chapter 15, this volume). Seymour *et al.* (1996), investigating the experience of seven HEIs competing for the Baldridge awards, singled out the University of Northwest Missouri State as an institution where benchmarking is central to the institutional mission and has resulted in positive change. Of the other competitors, those with the highest scores translated their performance data into stated goals, but in some cases benchmarked 'only metrics rather than practices', and it was not always clear how performance had improved.

The second initiative involved the establishment of an Institute for Education Best Practices by the American Productivity Quality Center (APQC). The Institute encourages educational institutions to benchmark not only with other HEIs, but also with business, health care and government. It applies to HE the consortium approach to benchmarking developed previously by APQC's International Benchmarking Clearinghouse (IBC). Ten to twenty institutions participate; each provides at least two representatives who meet initially to decide on the study's scope, identify criteria for selection of best practice, and nominate organizations considered exemplary in the process to be benchmarked. The institute collects data from these organizations and sends it (unidentified) to participants, who choose, on this basis, five or six organizations for site visits, and work on drawing up a visit questionnaire. Following these visits, accompanied by institute staff, consortium members meet for a final sharing session attended also by representatives from the 'best practice' organizations. Site visit reports and key findings are presented at this meeting and up to six staff from the benchmarking institutions can attend. By mid-1997, two studies on institutional budgeting and the creation of electronic student services had been completed, with a third, on measuring institutional performance outcomes, in progress. Between them, these studies attracted more than 50 institutions, all of them new to 'systematic benchmarking'. Plans for further work included studies on a wide range of topics relating both to academic practice and administrative functions (Grayson 1998; Farquhar 1998).

Canada

While APQC's arrival on the US scene is likely to result in more sustained and concentrated US benchmarking activity (Farquhar 1998), the Canadian situation is very different: 'Canadian institutions of higher education remain largely stalled at the performance indicator stage' (1998: 28). Even the progression from collecting and distributing management information to the development of PIs has been somewhat troubled. As in the UK (Chapter 2), pressure to generate PIs came from outside. It took two forms: media interest in presenting consumers with university rankings and the desire of provincial government to obtain information on university 'performance' in a context of shrinking funding for HE. The first set of rankings produced by *Maclean's* magazine in 1991 from data supplied by the universities were widely condemned by university CEOs on the basis of methodology. Though relations between *Maclean's* and the sector have subsequently improved, this experience, together with concern as to how government would use PIs given an agenda of funding cuts, left a 'nervousness among the institutions about performance indicators' (Farquhar 1998: 28). Subsequent national and regional efforts by the Association of Universities and Colleges of Canada (AUCC) and the Council of Ontario Universities (COU) to take ownership of developing PIs have fallen foul of continuing mistrust of the concept. There has also been disagreement 'on what should be measured, how calculations should be done, and which interpretation of results should be reported' (Farquhar 1998: 29).

While PIs are being generated by some individual institutions, and a new reporting system in Alberta has ensured, at least, comparative publication of university management information, the relative lack of PIs has not encouraged benchmarking activity. In the mid-1990s, the Canadian Association of University Business Officers (CAUBO) engaged consultants to collect data with the aim of identifying best practice relating to payroll, purchasing and mail services, but the general failure of institutions to act on the findings effectively brought the project to an end. CAUBO staff now seem sceptical about the value of benchmarking in HE, at least on a national level, because of different interpretations by HEIs of what constitutes 'best' practice, and problems in collecting contextual information in enough detail to understand properly another's 'practice' (Farquhar 1998).

Though benchmarking projects brokered by national and provincial HE agencies have so far been frustrated, there is evidence of some activity within individual institutions, and regionally, between officers working in specific functional areas. Since 1994, the University of Toronto has used core indicators originally developed by COU as its framework for management reporting to the Board of Governors. The university also benchmarks its performance in selected functions against that of 'peer' institutions that are fellow members of the Association of American Universities, through its American Universities Data Exchange (AUDE). Identification of superior practice in a peer has sometimes led to site visits and subsequent adaptation of this 'best practice' to the Toronto context. This benchmarking work at Toronto, using US data, has prompted some other large Canadian universities to compare their performance with that of Toronto and its US peers (Farquhar 1998).

Within Ontario, human resource professionals have conducted for several years a 'well-received' benchmark survey on salaries, as it was found that many university jobs did not conform to standard benchmarks in purchased surveys. In 1997, six Ontario universities formed a group to develop benchmarks relating to HR measures and organizational health indicators: this was driven partly by external demands for 'meaningful and measurable information', and partly by the desire to learn from each other's expertise in a 'systematic way' (Lund 1998b).

Australia

Judging from Massaro's review (1998) and other sources, there is substantial interest in benchmarking within the Australian HE system. An early form of systematic review, which contains elements of benchmarking, resulted from the work of Academic Standards Panels (ASPs) established by the Australian Vice-Chancellors' Committee (AVCC 1987). This approach to benchmarking academic standards was an important influence on the policy proposals made by the Dearing Committee for subject benchmarking (NCIHE 1997). The ASPs conducted a 10-year rolling programme of subject reviews based on institutional visits by the panels and evaluation of extensive statistical data relating to provision in each subject and degree outcomes. The published report (e.g. ASHE 1993) contained a wealth of quantitative and qualitative contextualized information on such matters as admissions criteria; student enrolments, progression and outcomes; graduate destinations; common and distinctive course objectives; curriculum content and structures (all courses identified by institution); delivery modes and assessment; options and specialisms. Given the current focus in UK policy development (Chapter 7), it is worth noting that information was also included on particular skills and qualities developed in students through study in the subject. Issues that affected teaching, learning and outcome standards were discussed and guidance to help improve practice was provided. These included examples of perceived good practice in documentation such as supervisors' reports; assignment assessment sheets; thesis examination reports; examination essay marking schemes. This was perhaps the first attempt to use the idea of benchmarking for regulatory purposes, that is to improve the HE system's capacity to regulate standards.

Benchmarking surveys

By 1996, 36 institutions in Australia and New Zealand were taking part in an annual facilities and services survey run by the Australasian Association of Higher Education Facilities Officers (AAPPA). Care is taken to ensure that institutional information is truly comparable through precise definition of terms used in the data collection. The survey covers nine areas: maintenance costs; refurbishments; backlog maintenance and other outstanding/deferred works; cleaning; energy consumption; grounds maintenance; security; parking; telephones. Statistics are collected on costs of staffing, materials, contracts, consultants, energy consumption plus data such as total areas cleaned/patrolled/maintained. Contextual or general statistical data is also gathered. Data is tabulated by topic area, while two performance indicator tables present the topic data in terms of aggregated averages, for example, m^2 per student, cost of maintenance per m^2, maintenance cost as a percentage of capital replacement value.

Massaro (1998) makes the point, however, that since *functions and processes* are not described and data are not interpreted in terms of operational efficiency or effectiveness, the survey has its limitations as a tool for benchmarking in its fullest sense. While the data enable institutions to identify problem areas and to make comparative assessments, which may lead to further scrutiny of process and change in practice, the survey as it stands does not comprise benchmarks, as the information is reported 'without attempting to make any value judgements about it' (Massaro 1998: 41).

The results of a benchmarking survey of international offices, for use in measuring and increasing international competitiveness and enhancing quality of service, were published by the Australian International Education Foundation in 1998 (AIEF 1998). Instigated by the universities themselves, the survey's primary focus was the efficiency of internal operations, together with scrutiny of some aspects of 'customer value adding' and financial performance. A questionnaire with several hundred questions was completed by over half the sector. Survey findings for each area investigated (for example, office facilities, service and quality management, financial management) are presented in terms of 'key indicators'. These consist of statements such as 'over 80 per cent of International Offices surveyed clients' or 'International Office budgets . . . ranged from 6–20 per cent of the total university fee income from international students, with the majority managing on less than 10 per cent'. The survey report also highlights recommended areas of 'best practice', such as use of country-specific marketing plans and operational plans; use of staff and customer surveys for evaluation purposes; greater use of IT for handling applications/queries and marketing. Subsequent phases of the project will focus on seeking international comparisons and on developing indicators for 'soft' areas, such as innovation and client responsiveness (AIEF 1998).

The survey does, however, have some limitations, such as the absence of contextualizing information (for example, nature, mission and priorities of the institution) and a tendency to suggest that if most offices do a certain thing, e.g. produce an international student newsletter, then the others should follow suit. Without evidence to link a particular practice to success in attracting and retaining international students, it cannot be assumed that it is necessarily 'good'.

Benchmarking exercises

Since 1995, Australian institutions have also been invited to join the NACUBO project (see United States) but take-up so far has been disappointing (benchmark topic areas proffered for 1997 attracted between seven and 10 institutions). Variation in membership from year to year and universities' choosing different functions for benchmarking from each other has limited the prospect of gaining 'the benefits of local comparison' (Massaro 1998: 36). Other disincentives seem to have been the time and staff commitment required, problems caused by a failure to adapt the material to the Australian context, and the need to 'recreate institutions in the image generated by NACUBO to ensure reliable results' (Massaro 1998: 38).

In 1996, the consultancy firm Ernst and Young ran a project for seven institutions focused on student administration (examinations, enrolment, results processing and graduation). The aim was to identify 'best practice' and opportunities for improvement within participating institutions; identify appropriate key PIs; facilitate understanding of the cost base for each process; and ensure adequate transfer of benchmarking skills to participants. A baseline for each process was established based on current practice at one institution; this was then used to define key sub-processes, the boundaries of each process and key PIs for that process. After recommendations for improvements had been made, a follow-up meeting was held to report on progress (Massaro 1998).

This study highlights some of the difficulties arising from a typical benchmarking exercise. There were problems in ensuring that data, in terms of costs and the definition of processes, were truly comparable: some institutions extrapolated global information from data provided on a faculty basis; others provided actual costs from an institutional perspective. A common survey instrument to gauge student satisfaction relating to enrolment worked well, but one institution conducted its own survey instead. The facilitators tended to equate 'best practice' with lowest unit cost, rather than in terms of customer satisfaction. Nevertheless, the project did lead to 'the identification or formulation of questions which then enabled the relevant administrative area to examine its activities and to improve them where necessary', while the very detailed analysis of sub-processes and their impact on processes together with the recommended improvements 'provided managers with a clear pathway for problem solving' (Massaro 1998: 39).

In the area of library and information services, benchmarking played a part in efforts at Northern Territory University (NTU) to achieve continuous quality improvement in the delivery of research information services. A set of processes common to all libraries was chosen and NTU practice compared with that at eight other Australian libraries; a study was also made of comparative US practice, which led to changes in process at NTU. Future benchmarking in this area should be facilitated through work by the Council of Australian University Librarians (CAUL) to develop key PIs in six broad categories (general library use and facilities; collection quality;

catalogue quality; availability of items; reference service; user satisfaction) (Massaro 1998).

An approach to international benchmarking regarded by Massaro (1998: 43) as 'very effective' was undertaken by the University of Melbourne's Counselling Service, which compared its practice with US and Canadian counterparts, drawing on two long-established and extensive databases. Melbourne was able to establish, for example, that it served a larger number of clients with less staff than its international 'peers', but also that this was managed through a less frequent appointment system and more extensive referral to other centres. The focus of this exercise was, however, on diagnosis of process, rather than precise comparison of specific outcomes, and the identification of issues for further investigation arising from scrutiny of international practice. Massaro praises this project for being 'relatively inexpensive, while providing significant levels of comparative information to guide management decision-making' (1998: 43), but concedes that it had 'the advantage of being focused on a very precise set of processes' so that instances of lack of comparability were relatively few.

Government interest in promoting comparative performance assessment in HE manifested itself in two ways in 1998. In November, the Department of Education, Training and Youth Affairs (DETYA) published its third attempt to produce sector-wide PIs (DEET 1994, 1996; DETYA 1998). *Characteristics and Performance of Higher Education Institutions* comprised 37 indicators, covering staff, finances, student outcomes and the broad higher education context, and drew on DETYA's own statistics on students, staff and finance, plus data from the universities themselves and the Graduate Careers Council of Australia. Though not 'league tables' as such, this publication met with a negative response similar to that which greeted commercially produced university rankings in Canada and the UK (see above and Chapter 2). Indeed, the Australian Vice-Chancellors' Committee (AVCC) called for the establishment of an independent body to compile university statistics (*Australian*, 18 November 1998).

DETYA also commissioned a project 'to develop and trial benchmarking criteria', run by the consultancy firm McKinnon Walker in partnership with IDP Education Australia. Fourteen key areas were identified for benchmarking: planning; external reputation; management efficiency and effectiveness; student progression; student support and facilities; teaching and learning; staff recruitment and development; library and information services; equity; internationalization; research; commercialization; financial management; space and equipment. These are being addressed progressively by six working parties, whose membership includes both senior university managers (Vice-Chancellor, Pro-Vice-Chancellor, etc.) and people with specific expertise (McKinnon Walker/IDP 1998a). By December 1998, the consultants were able to report that 32 of the 36 public universities had agreed to participate, and to identify the challenge of the project as 'to define more relevant benchmarks, to define these precisely so that any comparisons are of like-with-like, and to use the resulting benchmarks both to improve universities and to inform the public' (McKinnon Walker/IDP 1998b). The first plenary meeting had decided that 'criterion referenced qualitative indicators were as important as numerical comparisons' and debate had, therefore, included 'reconsideration of important areas often thought incapable of comparison or measurement', at least beyond the confines of 'small sets of self-chosen peer universities'.

It was acknowledged that one difficulty facing the project and slowing its progress was suspicion within the sector about 'the motives of government authorities and the possible misuse of statistical and other benchmarking material'. It was necessary, therefore, to reassure participants that the aim was 'the production of objective indicators rather than inappropriate rankings of universities'. By this time, each working party had identified a number of 'key features' and/or possible processes for benchmarking, but would be continuing to review the fundamentals of each area. Significant (though partial) results were expected by the end of 1999.

Europe

By 1990, a fair amount of work had been done within continental Europe (Austria, Denmark, Finland, France, Germany, the Netherlands, Norway, and Sweden) on the development of management statistics and perform- ance indicators (Dochy *et al.* 1990; Kells 1990). During the 1990s, German work in this area included statistics on staff and student numbers collected at state and federal level, and an annual survey of graduate completion rates by the *Wissenschraftsrat* (Science Council). The methodology of the latter's comparative study on the costs of academic training in different universities was heavily criticized, but did lead to work by universities and the council in piloting the collection and publication of cost comparison data at institutional and departmental level. A regional exercise in Lower Saxony, managed by a body somewhat similar to HESA, which collected data and created PIs for areas including courses offered, expenditure, SSRs and space available, seems to have been influential (Schreiterer 1998).

Extension of this work into full benchmarking has, however, been limited as yet. Schreiterer (1998: 65) puts this down to the fact of state ownership and operation of nearly all European HE systems, with a limited private sector. In consequence, 'procedures to govern and run universities and colleges . . . are those prescribed and practised by the respective states, and there has been little, if any, room for self-governance and management'. By the late 1990s, however, a shift in the HE funding system towards lump-sum budgets or block grants together with formula-based resource allocation was occurring in many European countries. Like their UK counterparts a decade earlier (Chapter 2), European universities faced calls for greater account- ability and better academic and managerial performance in the context of shrinking or frozen public funds. In this context, Schreiterer predicts a growth in benchmarking and other performance evaluation and improvement activity.

In the area of academic practice, benchmarking techniques have been succesfully used at the University of Kaiserslauten to compare engineering courses at eight 'peer' institutions with the aim of reducing duration of study. Factors leading to over-lengthy study were identified as the number of courses and the formal organization of final exams; the university therefore changed its practice on both fronts (Schreiterer 1998).

In Denmark, Copenhagen Business School ran a benchmark analysis focused on undergraduate management studies. Data was collected from 12 European HEIs on 16 areas including costs per student; subject fields; QA; undergraduate programmes; teaching staff; business links; teaching and examination methods. Student feedback, relating to two institutions, was also utilized. The survey results, however, proved disappointing, in part because the meaning of terms like 'cost per student' or 'lecture', which varied according to country, had not been clearly enough defined; and partly because data were incomplete or inaccurate. Also, because there had been no attempt to select key elements which would allow identification of 'best practice', there could be no 'benchmarks' for self-improvement (CBS 1995; Schreiterer 1998).

The only 'full' benchmarking exercise identified by Schreiterer was the German Benchmarking Club of Technical Universities (BMC) set up in 1996. This exercise was notable for its 'strong inclination towards a process orientation', and by collection and exchange of data according to 'commonly defined' needs. The first two topics covered the *procedures* used to distribute and allocate financial resources, and a comparison of data, internal organization and PIs for three major academic fields (chemistry, engineering and physics) with the aim of assessing and possibly readjusting staffing and resource levels. Expectations of completing the first round in nine months proved optimistic, due to problems in generating truly comparative data and then its interpretation, but solving these prompted communication about practice between members, with the club operating as a 'non-hierarchical learning circle'.

A Brussels-based organization which has run benchmarking projects involving commercial and public sector clients is the European Foundation for Quality Management (EFQM). Its highly participative consortium benchmarking methodology is likely to have at least an indirect effect on UK HEIs, following the enthusiastic participation by staff at the Higher Education Funding Council for England in an exercise focused on knowledge management (Chapter 13). It will be interesting to see whether EFQM will come to involve itself more directly in European HE benchmarking, in a move parallel to that taken by APQC in the US.

Transnational benchmarking

A number of the studies described above have incorporated an element of transnational benchmarking. Chapter 15 and Appendix B will describe the approaches taken by two international benchmarking 'clubs'.[1] Two other contemporary approaches to transnational benchmarking are described below.

The Conference of Rectors of European Universities (CRE) have described their own Institutional Quality Management Reviews, run since the mid-1990s, as 'implicit benchmarking'. Focused on a specific issue each year, these involve peer reviews and mutual visits; participation is voluntary. As yet, however, procedures for collecting, comparing and assessing the data are not sufficiently strict to make this a proper benchmarking exercise (Schreiterer 1998). CRE is trying to promote the use of benchmarking and has invited consultants to address its membership on the topic, but like its counterparts in Canada, is trying to overcome universities' apprehensions regarding the development of PIs and their subsequent use.

The application of benchmarking to the international comparison of quality and standards of education is still in its infancy, but its potential is illustrated by the work of the European Physics Education Network (EUPEN), established in 1996 and embracing over 100 physics departments in 15 European countries. Benchmarking of physics education has been conducted through surveys of practice organized by five working groups covering: the student experience; curricula structure and development; organization of physics studies; career aspects; research in physics teaching. The findings were brought together, discussed and published in a EUPEN General Forum (Ferdinande and Petit 1997). The report does not attempt to identify best practice (this would be inappropriate given the enormous contextual differences between national systems), but it provides information on the range (norms and extremes) of practice which enable participants to position their own practice. Working group reports offer important perspectives on issues such as student workloads (e.g. undergraduate contact hours ranging from 350 to 870 hours over four years); approaches to teaching and learning (e.g. hours spent in laboratories or problem-solving classes); expectations of private study; curriculum content; gender participation; average teaching costs per student; use of student questionnaires to assess quality. EUPEN has also constructed a glossary of terms and definitions that can be applied to benchmarking exercises, providing a common vocabulary and conceptual language that transcends national barriers.

Conclusions

This review suggests that outside the UK, the USA and Australia are the countries in which benchmarking has been most actively used as an aid to improvement within HE systems. Published information suggests that so far benchmarking has primarily focused on business/administrative functions rather than educational processes. The EUPEN model, however, provides a good example of transnational collaboration within a discipline to compare and understand educational provision. Australia's early subject benchmarking was an important influence on the Dearing Committee's recommendation that benchmarking should be developed for regulatory purposes in UK HE, providing an illustration of international 'policy transfer' of benchmarking. While there has been a tendency, as in the UK, for benchmarking activity to develop from the generation of management statistics and PIs towards a more dynamic, collaborative way of identifying and implementing 'best practice', several recent initiatives are still confining themselves to a survey approach. It is clear that there have been tensions where exercises have been initiated by national or provincial government to inform funding decisions or to produce rankings of performance as a form of public information. Examples of international benchmarking are relatively rare, but two initiatives that do transcend national borders are described in Chapter 15 and Appendix B.

Note

1. One of these organizations, the Commonwealth Higher Education Management Service (CHEMS), is launching a European benchmarking club in 2000 in partnership with the European Centre for Strategic Management of Universities (ESMU).

15

CHEMS International Benchmarking Club

John Fielden and Michael Carr

Overview

This chapter describes a pioneering approach to benchmarking the management of universities internationally. John Fielden describes how the process benchmarking methodology used by the CHEMS Club has evolved, in response to its members' needs, from a model closely based on the US Baldridge assessment method to one incorporating self-assessment, peer evaluation and a high level of ownership by club members. The chapter concludes with a 'personal reflection' by Michael Carr of the University of Liverpool on the experience of benchmarking with the CHEMS Club.

Origins and design options

The Commonwealth Higher Education Management Service (CHEMS) has two core functions: identifying and publishing information about good practice in managing universities and providing management consultancy help to HEIs. The origins of the CHEMS International Benchmarking Club on University Management owe much to this rationale. Judging that a benchmarking operation for Commonwealth universities would be an excellent way of identifying good management practice and helping universities to adopt it, John Fielden, Director of CHEMS, began, soon after CHEMS's establishment in November 1993, to investigate its feasibility. There were five design questions to be answered:

- What would be the conceptual basis for agreeing good practice?
- What would be benchmarked – inputs, outputs or processes?
- How would the problem of distance be overcome?
- Who would decide what good practice is and how?
- Would any form of ranking or scoring be adopted?

At the time, the only example of international HE benchmarking was that run by NACUBO, the US-based National Association of College and

University Business Officers, involving universities in America, Canada and later Australia. This annual study adopted a very quantitative approach, collecting comparative information from participating institutions about the costs and operational efficiency of detailed administrative activities. In return, institutions received statistical reports showing how they compared with others. While membership had once been as high as 300, it was steadily falling and there were signs in 1994 that some members felt that the statistical and analytical effort needed was not repaid by the information gained.

Since there was no existing university model that CHEMS could adopt, the search had to be focused on the commercial/industrial world. Helped by the London office of Price Waterhouse consultants, CHEMS began to explore the relevance to HE of the well-proven Baldridge Award principles (Baldridge 1992). In this model a framework had been developed for assessing the effectiveness of commercial organizations in setting strategy, managing all categories of resource and satisfying customer needs. It was organized under seven headings, each with between two and six sub-categories:

- leadership
- information and analysis
- strategic quality planning
- human resource development and management
- management of process quality
- quality and operational results
- customer focus and satisfaction.

This framework had been refined and used very successfully as the basis for an annual award to the best-managed US commercial company. Price Waterhouse had recently successfully adapted it for a European Quality Award scheme (Loveday 1993) identifying the company with the best record in customer satisfaction. This proved that the principles could be adjusted to comparing organizations in different countries, since the mechanics of the exercise were free from using costs or quantitative ratios.

The Baldridge model came with a tested conceptual framework. A classification had been developed to cover all aspects of managing a business and, for each element in that classification, the organization was asked to describe how its processes worked. These were then assessed in three ways: to judge the approach itself; how far it had been successfully implemented; and the degree to which evaluation and feedback operated effectively in continually reforming the approach. Businesses that entered the Baldridge Award scheme were assessed on all their activities each year and given marks on each element in the classification. The sum of these marks aimed to show their overall management performance. The highest scoring business won the award, i.e. following the principle of 'best in class', but against a scoring system which implied that 100/100 would be a 'gold standard' of performance.

Unknown to both CHEMS and Price Waterhouse, parallel attempts were being made in the US to adapt the Baldridge principles to higher education institutions (Seymour *et al.* 1996). These led to the publication of draft frameworks that have recently been refined and approved by Congress as applicable to universities.

The decision to adopt the Baldridge approach, suitably adapted both to HE and a non-US environment, thus answered the first design question, and the second: by adopting Baldridge, CHEMS was rejecting an approach based on comparing costs or ratios (earlier CHEMS work had shown this to be almost impossible across the Commonwealth) in favour of one based on comparing processes. All universities have similar functions and organize themselves to undertake similar processes; comparisons of how universities perform these processes can be made quite independently of costs or quantitative data, but can reveal the reasons for wide discrepancies in cost as well as identifying ideas or processes which might be innovative or worth repeating.

The third design question relates to the geographical spread of club members and the consequent high costs of any meetings. Operations would have to be based principally on the exchange of information rather than face-to-face contacts or visits. It would, however, be unwise to remove personal contact altogether, since it brings networking benefits which are crucial to getting value from the follow-up stages of any benchmarking exercise, i.e. in the exchange and transfer of good practice between members.

The fourth question relates to the role of the consultants vis-à-vis the club members. If the Baldridge approach was to be used as the basis for judgements in the first instance, who would make those judgements and what kind of assessment or validation would be required? In the club's first year, the consultants played the major role in drafting the report that identified good practice, with limited external validation. Over the next three years, the consultants' work was supplemented by a more participative and transparent exercise involving respected professional assessors and a final stage of self-assessment.

The final design issue was the scoring system. Is it necessary in benchmarking to award marks? Can good practice be quantified in this way when institutions have such different purposes and there are so many other qualitative variables explaining performance differences? Initially, CHEMS followed the Baldridge approach, but later found it necessary to amend it in response to member concerns.

Approach

CHEMS launched the club at the end of 1995, inviting selected institutions to join. A process of 11 stages followed:

- the development of draft 'frameworks' of questions for each agreed topic
- a meeting of advisers to review and amend the frameworks
- despatching a handbook to members, which described the methodology, and included the final version of the frameworks plus questions to be answered; responses were requested within an eight-week period

- marking of submissions by the CHEMS Director and a consultant appointed as Club Manager (CM)
- identification of good practices in each institution's submission (CM)
- identification of areas of relative weakness in each submission (CM)
- production of a composite statement of good practice for each topic drawing on the findings from individual submissions
- despatch to members of an individual report showing their strengths and weaknesses, plus the composite statement of good practice
- a workshop for members in which each topic was discussed and amendments made to the draft composite statement of good practice. A presentation was also given for each topic by an institution with a high-ranking performance in that area
- review of the methodology and agreement on next year's process and topics
- production of a final report for the year incorporating the final agreed statement of good practice and a workshop report.

At the end of the process it was hoped that members would contact each other, where they felt they had something to learn, in order to improve their own performance in the topic areas. Members paid a management fee of £4000 to CHEMS to cover the costs of the staff time involved. They were also expected to meet their own costs in attending the final workshop.

The club's objective was to achieve Commonwealth-wide coverage in the membership without too large a representation in any one country. Recruiting proved harder than anticipated: CHEMS was still relatively unknown and the concepts and benefits of benchmarking were poorly understood. Extracting a decision involving a new cash commitment from institutions under continual financial pressure proved an added hurdle. Members were recruited using the Director's contacts and networks; as a result four of the first year's members were former clients of CHEMS or the Director himself. The membership tally for the first year was 10, smaller than hoped for, but nonetheless giving a good coverage of six countries (Australia, Canada, Hong Kong, New Zealand, South Africa and the UK – Table 15.1).

Evolution and development

The club is an evolving experiment and responds to ideas for change which emerge at the closing workshop each year. In this way, members have significantly influenced the process followed and the content of each year's final report. The changes are summarized in Table 15.2.

The design of the frameworks is now a joint effort between members (who usually prepare the first drafts), CHEMS staff and assessors who add comments in their specialist fields. Although this has drawbacks in that there may not always be a consistent approach to the structure or style of questions in the topics, it ensures greater ownership of the resulting framework.

Table 15.1 CHEMS Club membership 1996–9

	Australia	Canada	Hong Kong	New Zealand	South Africa	UK
1996	U. of Queensland RMIT Sydney Victoria UT	Waterloo	U. of Hong Kong	Auckland	Cape Town Natal	Liverpool
1997	U. of Queensland Queensland UT Victoria UT	Calgary	U. of Hong Kong	Victoria U. of Wellington	Natal	Durham Liverpool Leeds Metropolitan Nottingham UMIST
1998	U. of Queensland RMIT Swinburne Victoria UT	Calgary Memorial U. of Newfoundland York	U. of Hong Kong	–	Natal	Leeds Metropolitan Liverpool UMIST
1999	U. of Queensland Queensland UT Victoria UT Swinburne UT	Calgary Memorial U. of Newfoundland York	U. of Hong Kong	–	Natal	Leeds Metropolitan Liverpool

Table 15.2 The changing process

	1996	1997	1998
Framework design	CHEMS only	Members, CHEMS and assessors	Members, CHEMS and assessors
Marking and assessing	CHEMS only	CHEMS followed by assessors	Assessors followed by self-assessment
First draft report	One per institution and a draft composite of good practice	Only one report with a draft composite of good practice. Report also contains contextual indicators	As for 1997
Scoring systems	Marks out of 100	Three grades: excellent; up to benchmark; below benchmark	Scores of 1 to 5 for each topic
Use of assessors	None	Attend workshop and provide commentary	As for 1997
Final report	Includes composite good practice statements and a report on the workshop	Assessors' reports and self-assessment ranking are added	As for 1997
Self-assessment against composite good practice	None	Members do this after workshop and their rankings are included in the report	As for 1997

The marking or ranking of members' submissions is a lengthy exercise as it involves reading a large amount of material. The arrangement in 1997 and 1998 has been that the Club Manager reviews everything and then sends assessors all the material related to their topic together with a first draft of the good practice statements. Assessors then give their initial ranking of each submission; this is included in the draft report sent to members before the workshop.

The scoring method has been the most regularly discussed part of the process, although the basic judgmental criteria adopted by the Baldridge Award have continued to form the basis of rankings and assessments. These are wholly adaptable to the fitness for purpose philosophy that is at the root of the club's comparative judgements (see below).

It was clear, however, at the first workshop that members did not like the Baldridge system of giving every topic and sub-topic scores which, when weighted and totalled, allowed an overall score of 100. This was thought to be far too specific and precise for what was a difficult art. It also made little sense to create a total from only four management processes, when the whole Baldridge exercise included seven different activities. In consequence, a much simpler ranking was adopted in Year 2: * for a ranking above average; + for an average result; a blank for a response that was less good. In the event, each assessor adopted different criteria for scoring each topic with some more generous than others. This was not a problem, however, since no aggregation of overall performance on all four topics was desired. In the third year, the ranking was extended slightly by allowing assessors to give five marks to each sub-topic. Unfortunately, they used different methods of averaging these to arrive at totals for each topic and yet again scores between subjects were not consistent.

The use of specialist assessors in each topic area was one of the major changes to the initial design and has proved to be valuable. Assessors must be professionals in the discipline or activity area under review, ideally with international experience, and of a stature that will earn the participants' respect for their judgements. In return for a fee, they are expected to devote up to three days to the ranking exercise and, where their topic is a major one, to attend the workshop and present a brief report.

The self-assessment scoring element was added in 1997. Members are sent the good practice statements in the draft final report and asked to return their own scores (1–5) against each statement within four weeks. Although this adds another stage to the process, it is a very valuable tool for participants to use internally with their colleagues and also offers (if members are honest) a useful guide to other club members as to where they can turn for information on good practice. The practice has continued in 1998, although one member abstained in 1997 and continues to have reservations.

The format of reports prepared by CHEMS for members has changed dramatically. In 1996 members received two reports; one unique to each institution, recording individual strengths and weaknesses, and one composite statement of good practice. The first was sent in the middle of the process, while the second went first in draft form, and then as a final report after the workshop. For 1997 and 1998, there was an interim report for the workshop; this was common to all and contained the assessors' reports, draft good practice statements and tables giving the assessors' scores for each of the sub-topics. After the workshop and self-assessment phases, a final report was produced containing revised good practice statements with self-assessments against each one and a report on the workshop.

One new component of the report followed discussions at the first workshop. It was decided to include key statistical data on member institutions, e.g. student numbers, staff categorized by research and teaching, overall expenditure split into teaching and research, and income, showing sums generated externally from non-government sources, etc. These 'contextual

Figure 15.1 University management model 1996

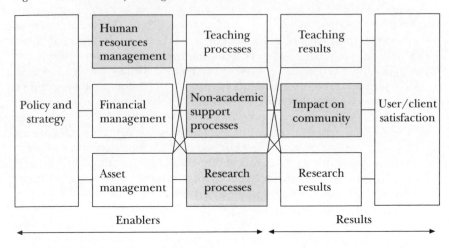

Note: Management processes in the shaded boxes were included in that year's assessment.

indicators' allow readers to interpret the relative scores or rankings for each topic. If, for example, a university with a very low research activity scores highly in the way it manages that research, it may not become the first source of advice for a highly research-intensive institution wishing to improve its performance.

The choice of topics is left entirely to members to decide, although CHEMS puts forward ideas for consideration each year. The initial Price Waterhouse concept was to adapt the Baldridge framework and plan a programme which covered all university activities within a five-year period (Figure 15.1). However, the classification was not thought to be wholly appropriate as it omitted several key areas of university activity and several emerging cross-cutting concerns such as internationalization, or the use of IT in teaching. The notion of a cycle has remained and in 1999 the club is revisiting two of the topics studied in Year 1.

The spread of topics over the four-year period is shown in Table 15.3.

Membership numbers have risen from 10 in 1996 to peak at 12 in 1998 with an additional three associate members. Five of the founder members were still members in 1999. At least five countries have been represented each year and members have included long-established research universities (Liverpool, University of Manchester Institute of Science and Technology, Queensland, Hong Kong), comprehensive universities like Calgary and Natal, as well as the newer technological institutions (Royal Melbourne Institute of Technology and Victoria University of Technology). This strengthens the importance of the contextual indicators in helping members to interpret their respective rankings. Table 15.1 gives details of membership by year.

Table 15.3 Topics reviewed in each year

1996	1997	1998	1999
Management of human resources	Financial strategy	Internationalization	IT in teaching and learning
Management of research	Management information systems	Library and information services	Commercialization
Student support services	Management of teaching and learning	Management of estates and buildings	Management of human resources including staff development
Strategic planning	Resource allocation	Student administration	Management of research
External community relationships			

Lessons from the three years

The main lesson from the exercise has been the importance of interpreting the core concepts of Baldridge sensitively in an academic environment. It was not possible to transfer either the total framework or the scoring system from the commercial environment and new approaches had to be adopted in both cases. The conceptualized adaptation of the Baldridge topics developed by Price Waterhouse (see Figure 15.1) was good in theory, but it was not close enough to the real concerns of senior managers who wished to select other topics for comparison. The main trend of the changes in the club's processes has been to bring them closer to the peer evaluation model, so familiar in the academic environment, but to retain some of the disciplines of Baldridge. Thus, CHEMS's judgements were gradually replaced with those of professional assessors, and self-assessment rankings were added to those from external sources.

One of the biggest issues for debate among members has been the criteria for agreeing good practice. Is there one universal best management practice that all universities can aspire to? Can the club identify a set of best management practices that can fit all cultures? Or should a judgement be made using the fitness for purpose criterion? If the latter is selected, how can a group with disparate purposes and goals find a common ground?

Early in its life the club dismissed the idea of a 'gold standard' approach. It is clearly unrealistic, even in the same national environment, to suggest that the same activities and processes are the best in all circumstances. Instead, the concept of fitness for purpose was adopted; universities with one strategy will not necessarily find applicable to them an activity or management approach in which another institution with a different strategy excels. Members are free, therefore, to reject those good practice statements that do not match their circumstances or philosophy. An example of this, identified very early on, is the issue of decentralization or centralization. The club agreed that it would be quite wrong to imply that a decentralized approach, although widely considered effective in getting good decisions and encouraging initiatives, was necessarily good practice in all circumstances. Statements of good practice relating to this area should therefore be neutral.

As we have seen, the Baldridge conceptual framework assesses management activities in three ways: the existence of a clearly defined and agreed strategy; how well that strategy has been applied; and how the agreed process is evaluated and continuously improved. Fortunately, there is no conflict in applying this three-level approach to an environment in which fitness for purpose rules.

Feedback from members

The end purpose of benchmarking is to improve performance and to identify transferable lessons or practices; the Benchmark Club's reports are not the end of the story. In 1998 a survey of members at the final workshop asked what benefits had accrued from the exercise, how they had used the club's final report and what had happened as a result. Answers naturally varied, but the main points that emerged were as follows.

- Some members found that the exercise of compiling their answers to the framework was valuable. It provided some difficult questions and forced managers to think about how they did things. It also enabled the senior administrator (who was usually the person coordinating the answers) to learn more about how the university operated.
- Most members circulated the final Benchmark Report to their senior management team (SMT). In some institutions, the sections of the report were split up and distributed to the relevant senior administrator for review; in others, this process was formalized by asking senior managers to report back to the SMT on the changes they intended to make as a result; in one university these responses were reviewed by the Registrar in person with the relevant manager.
- There was less interaction between members after the workshops than had been expected. A few members had visited their club colleagues when in the country concerned, building on the personal rapport established in the workshops; one university had contacted a colleague which had self-assessed itself as Grade 5 (the highest ranking) only to find that the assessment was extremely generous. This anomaly might have arisen due to poor vetting of the self-assessment rankings by the senior person concerned.
- There was very little self-audit of the initial returns. When Price Waterhouse designed the original process, there was the expectation that members

might decide to audit their returns themselves or even get together within a country to check each other's responses for accuracy. In the event, the more academic model of trusting each other's professionalism took over. Also the softening of the outcomes in terms of scoring may have lessened the need to ensure that responses were accurate. Had a more public ranking resulted, along league table lines, there might have been more call for auditable results. Since the club's consensus was to frown on institutions publicizing their success, this pressure never emerged.

One lesson that members have learned is that further work is required if full benefit is to be gained from membership. It is not enough to circulate the report with the message that it may contain good ideas that can be adopted. The document has to have the backing of the senior management team who should use it as a basis for a follow-up report on whether the ideas are applicable or not. If transferable good practice is found, management may need to encourage and fund contact with the universities shown to be particularly good in that activity.

Future challenges

One of the club's strengths is that it is small enough to develop good personal links between members and to have effective discussions in the annual workshops. These have usually led to changes in the process being agreed, although as time goes on the scale of the changes is becoming smaller. This responsiveness may be one of the reasons why five of the original 10 members have remained with the club.

There are three challenges to this happy state: the threat (or opportunity) of growth in numbers; current decisions on how to revisit topics the second time around; and the challenge for CHEMS of giving members continued value for money in this situation.

Growth in numbers has not been a worry to date (see Table 15.1), but this may not be the case for long. Worldwide interest in benchmarking continues to grow and the CHEMS Club, although small, remains the only international grouping with a methodology to which its members are committed. Universitas 21, the grouping of research institutions managed by the University of Melbourne, committed itself in 1997 to designing a benchmarking process but work is still in its early stages (Appendix B). The present CHEMS process has a limit of about 15–20 members before its staffing load (one set of assessors and one manager) will have to be revised. If members were presented with this option, the most likely scenario would be a decision to peg the numbers and limit new applicants, rather than change the approach.

Another solution to growth in numbers would be to have two clusters or groupings of members with different characteristics; an obvious basis for this grouping might be research strength. However, as the club has seen, attempts to make this distinction explicit arouse great sensitivities and members invited to join a league of less research-intensive institutions might be mortally offended, particularly if they were on the borderline between a good comprehensive institution and a strong research one.

The second challenge is less emotive and relates to the process. In 1999, two of the topics studied revisited those looked at in 1996. For some members it was a useful chance to see how they had progressed and this might have suggested that the framework of questions used should be the same as that in 1996. However, the peers who compared themselves in 1999 were not all the same and the club has advanced in its thinking and in the way it frames its questions. This suggested that no attempt should be made to devise a process closely linked to that in 1996. In the event a new set of questions was devised.

The final challenge is common to all recurring benchmarking or self-auditing processes and may be unanswerable. How does one retain interest after several cycles of self-analysis and enquiry? Will an institution inevitably feel that no more progress can be made and that a fresh line of enquiry is needed? Experience in similar international exercises would suggest this is the case. The NACUBO benchmarking operation found that it retained very few members for more than two, or at the most three, years. However, a recurring membership presents very little risk to a club such as CHEMS with a small number of members and merely highlights the need to continue adding a few new institutions each year.

In conclusion, what can be said about the CHEMS experiment? It has shown a way of making international comparisons with which members are happy. It has not cracked the tyranny of distance but has found a way of exchanging ideas between continents. The resulting annual reports present helpful ideas, but there are indications that the reports could be better used by members to achieve improvement in performance. Even if the good practice statements in the reports are at a relatively high level of generalization, they have been found useful in prompting questions about change at a senior level.

University of Liverpool case study

Perspective

As an old civic university with a broad subject base and a high proportion of 'professional' programmes the University of Liverpool had, by the mid-1990s, considerable and varied experience of comparing its performance and processes with other HEIs, using many of the evaluative mechanisms discussed in Chapter 2: national quality assessment of teaching and research; accreditation by professional bodies; systems of external examining, audit or value for money; subject and organizational reviews involving external peer analysis; use of nationally and internationally generated PIs covering academic and non-academic activities.

Why international benchmarking?

In the mid-1990s, the university decided to extend its experience to international benchmarking. The reasons were as follows:

- Almost since its inception, Liverpool had benefited in the widest sense from the enrolment of large numbers of overseas students; it had always worked to international standards in research. The university needed to compete internationally and the process of globalization was making that competition more difficult and yet more important than ever to its long-term health and vigour.
- Although some of the existing UK arrangements for comparability and benchmarking had international perspective, this dimension tended to be measured solely in terms of output, rather than input and process. Yet it is only though close analysis of input and process that performance improvement can really be directed and delivered.
- Any organization operating in the international arena should want to be able to demonstrate that its processes and systems of organization and management are up to the task and reflect best international practice. Liverpool was looking for a group of like-minded and broadly comparable institutions with which to compare and contrast processes and practices at a sufficiently detailed level to allow meaningful change and improvement to be identified through processes of mutual- and self-help.

Why CHEMS?

By 1995/6, the university was looking for a suitable vehicle to meet its international benchmarking requirements. The initiative from CHEMS was welcomed as especially appropriate because:

- the planned emphasis was on input and process, rather than simply on measuring output
- the proposed benchmarking process combined self-assessment in the compilation of the submission with formal evaluation by expert consultants followed by direct collective comparative analysis of the outcome
- topics for analysis were to be determined by club members rather than according to some assumed orthodoxy
- membership would be drawn from institutions with sufficient common elements of heritage and structure to facilitate comparability, despite geographical distance, while a common language would facilitate the necessary depth of understanding.

Evaluation of the CHEMS benchmarking process

This is best done in terms of three principal elements: selection of topics; the self-assessment process; and the identification of best practice.

The 15 substantive topics benchmarked between 1996 and 1999 are listed in Table 15.3. The process of choosing these topics and the number to be covered in any one year has not been entirely straightforward, due to competing pressures between the desire to cover a sufficient range of functions over a reasonable timespan and the wish to have sufficient depth of discussion of those subjects at the annual members' forum. Furthermore, the priority of interests between, for example, universities funded for teaching and research, and those primarily funded for teaching and community purposes does not always coincide. In some cases, topics have perhaps been cast on too broad a canvas to permit analysis at a truly useful scale; this experience is guiding future choice of topics. Nevertheless, the university feels that a sufficient range of functions was covered in the first three years to enable the process to have a comprehensive input on its consideration of its organizational and managerial arrangements.

For each selected topic, benchmarking commences with a self-assessment statement by each club member. This is primarily a descriptive process, aided by the 'frameworks' discussed above. Initial apprehension that this element might be essentially unproductive, a chore that had to be completed in order to commence the substantive work, has proved to be unfounded. Provided the process is undertaken rigorously and objectively, with a genuine questioning of why activities are conducted in a particular way and to what purpose and effect, self-assessment has shown itself to be a useful tool for self-improvement. Of particular value has been the emphasis, in this initial submission, on an analysis of how the university monitors, evaluates, and responds to feedback on the outcome and effectiveness of its particular organizational and managerial arrangements.

Collective identification of best practice is, of course, the most important aspect of the club's work and one that brings to the fore the international dimension. It has also proved the most difficult stage to arrange optimally. Without a tight framework to guide discussion from the outset, the benefits of collective review can easily be lost in a series of discursive statements that merely describe the different practices in the different institutions. It has taken time to develop a process that encourages a deeper analysis that can withstand detailed differences and focus upon what seem to be the essential elements of good practice. This comprises the use of independent assessors, the preparation of a draft best practice statement and its subsequent refinement towards a composite model of best practice described above.

This final statement of best practice has proved a useful template against which to review practices at Liverpool. Out of that review have come some genuine improvements, though not all of these are necessarily immediately visible to the institution at large, because they may involve management processes rather than administrative or organizational procedure. Some of the recent changes which benchmarking with CHEMS has helped to pro-mote include:

- *Academic planning*: the importance of annual planning statements from budget centres in support of the institutional planning process has been reinforced; the format of these statements has been revised extensively.
- *Personnel*: the need to provide clear role definitions for personnel staff and to support these with a directed Management Development Pro-gramme has been recognized.
- *Estates*: the importance of developing a 'service agreement' with depart-ments and users, to set out more clearly the standards which should obtain, has been acknowledged; an agreement is being developed.
- *Finance*: in recognition of the need to improve costing and pricing proced-ures for external work, and to ensure that all costs are covered and that there is a proper return, revised procedures are being introduced and are being developed further to permit greater sophistication.

Conclusions

Liverpool intends to review as a matter of good practice whether it wishes to continue with international benchmarking in the form promoted by CHEMS, or whether it should investigate alternative arrangements. These might in-clude benchmarking more closely with a smaller group of HEIs selected for their comparability in type and scale, or developing a looser arrangement of benchmarking with individual institutions known for excellence in iden-tified areas. However, the university's experience to date suggests that the CHEMS model is proving sound and has shown itself capable of improve-ment through adaptation. Above all, perhaps, members have recognized that any benchmarking process will only be as good as the effort that they themselves are willing to put into it. Apart from the organization and broker-age offered by the CHEMS team itself, the club has worked in part because its members have enjoyed working together and have been willing to devote to the exercise the time and energies of some of their most senior staff.

Conclusions

16

Benchmarking for Higher Education: Taking Stock

Norman Jackson and Helen Lund

Overview

Benchmarking processes are conceived as lying along the continuum: metric benchmarking – diagnostic benchmarking – process benchmarking. Four benchmarking practice models are proposed. The conceptual framework underlying these models discriminates between benchmarking processes that are essentially dialogical (involve active discussion between collaborating partners) and those which are essentially bureaucratic (primarily based on databases or other information and not necessarily involving partnerships). Factors that influence the potential take-up of benchmarking in national HE systems are considered. Benchmarking is likely to prosper in political systems that embrace the 'new public management' and which promote the 'evaluative state'. The chapter concludes by reviewing some of the themes and issues that have emerged through this compilation and synthesis.

Conception

Our conception of benchmarking as a process is that it contains four main activities:

- comparing or referencing one thing with another
- creating and using criteria, quantitative measures or other sorts of information to evaluate differences between one thing and another: and through this process recognizing what is better or ideal practice
- using insights derived from such activities to identify the directions and targets for change
- changing practice in line with the new insights gained.

Figure 16.1   Continuum of benchmarking processes

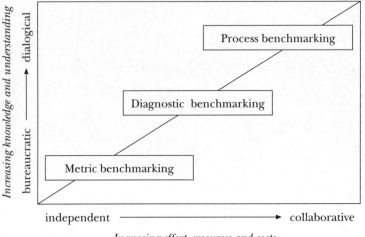

Source: Adapted from Appleby (1999)

The benchmarking continuum

Different approaches to benchmarking can be conceived as occupying a continuum of activities and practice (Appleby 1999 and Figure 16.1). In its simplest form benchmarking might be based on comparison of own practice or results with a data set, specification or other information base (the metric benchmarking of Appelby). This type of benchmarking can be used to identify differences/gaps in practice and performance; it can also be used in a regulatory sense to help ensure conformance to certain minimum input, process or output standards. Examples of this type of benchmarking can be found in Chapters 2, 3, 5 (in part), 7, 8, 9, 10, and Appendix B.

The continuum of practice might then progress into applications where self-evaluation is guided by performance criteria and/or is facilitated by the perspectives and insights of one or more well-informed individuals. Such individuals may control a database enabling them to construct comparators and recognize what appear to be best practices (the diagnostic benchmarking of Appleby). Examples of this type of benchmarking can be found in Chapters 5 (in part), 13, 15 and Appendix A.

The continuum of practice progresses into more collaborative exercises involving partnerships, clubs and consortia, the sharing and collective evaluation of information and the identification of good practice internal and external to an organization and between different types of organization (the process benchmarking of Appleby). Examples of this type of benchmarking can be found in Chapters 4, 5 (in part), 6 (in part), 11, 12, 13 (in part) and 15.

Practice models

Four different practice models can be recognized from the case study materials and review chapters.

Collaborative, group action research model

This model treats 'benchmarking as a process of action research and active learning amongst those involved' (e.g. Price 1994: Ch. 11). The dynamic is created through a club, forum or consortium composed of people who are committed to the process of learning more about themselves through learning about others. Such benchmarking activities may be organized by members of the group or by an independent facilitator. The process begins by establishing the main research topics and develops through elaboration of the key research questions and the construction of data-gathering instruments. Information is collected and synthesized in feedback reports which provide the basis for discussion and further enquiry targeted at identifying benchmarks or good/effective practice and understanding the reasons for this. The process often, but not invariably, involves site visits to view facilities or operations. Participants set new goals and adjust practice using the knowledge and insights gained. The products of benchmarking (information and learning) may be kept within the benchmarking group (particularly if it is a commercially motivated exercise) but they may also be shared with the system as a whole, through conferences, published reports and information placed on the internet. This is normally the case with state-sponsored activity (e.g. Chapter 13, this volume; QAA 1998a). Examples of this model approach can be found in Chapters 3, 5, 6, 9, 11, 12, 14, 15 and Appendix B.

A variation on the model outlined above is provided by the CHEMS approach (Chapter 15) which also incorporates a criterion-referenced scoring system to facilitate the self-assessment of management processes.

Collaborative one-to-one partnership model

In this practice model one institution creates a partnership with another and systematically gathers information in line with its own developmental agenda, normally on the understanding that the sharing of information will be a two-way process and the dialogue will be of benefit to both participants. Information is gathered using survey instruments by telephone, mail/email, visits and interviews. Information is synthesized by the lead institution and shared with the partner. An institution may conduct a number of one-to-one exercises, effectively building its own information base, but no attempt is made to engage the participants in group discussion. Example: Chapter 4.

Specification- or criterion-referencing model

This approach to benchmarking may involve collaboration but it is not necessary to do so. The defining characteristic is a referencing process against a predetermined process model, specification or code of practice which may also contain within it criteria to guide self-evaluation of different levels of performance.

1. The simplest scenario is where participants with a common interest come together to compare and codify existing good practice and create a specification, guideline or code of practice based on agreed 'good/ acknowledged best/ideal' practice. The specification (perhaps accompanied by illustrative material) is then used to provide reference points to facilitate self-evaluation and, where appropriate, to provide the prompt for improvement. The EPC quality management project (Chapter 5) is a good example of this and several examples are given in Chapter 13.
2. An added sophistication is to include performance criteria within the model. This approach constructs a model process relating to a particular function (e.g. recruitment within the human resource management function). Performance criteria are created for each element of the process by management consultant or group of expert practitioners, enabling an institution, or part of an institution, to evaluate the extent to which it meets the ideal practice. The approach might also incorporate a scoring system which facilitates comparative evaluation, and external expert panels to provide an independent evaluation of the evidence of performance. This is the approach used by CHEMS (Chapter 15), by APQC in the US and by the benchmarking projects run by EFQM in Europe (Chapter 14 this volume; EFQM 1999 – http://www.efqm.org).
3. At the regulatory end of the spectrum a specification of a process or outcome can be constructed by an expert team of peers (or a regulatory/ awarding body) that can then be used by institutions as reference points against which their own processes and performance criteria can be compared. This is the approach being used in outcomes-based subject benchmarking (Chapter 7) and some institutional approaches to incorporating national key skills standards in the HE curriculum (Chapter 8).

Brokered models

This approach to benchmarking may involve the use of data sets constructed by an agency or consultant that are then used to compare performance without the involvement of active partners.

Figure 16.2 A conceptual framework for representing the benchmarking practice models described in this volume

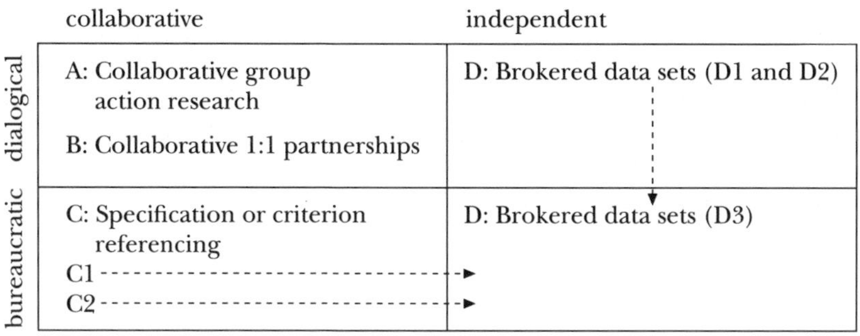

	collaborative	independent
dialogical	A: Collaborative group action research B: Collaborative 1:1 partnerships	D: Brokered data sets (D1 and D2)
bureaucratic	C: Specification or criterion referencing C1 - ► C2 - ►	D: Brokered data sets (D3)

1. In this practice model a consultant creates a survey instrument and progressively constructs a database of performance statistics. The database grows as the client base expands and consultant(s) work one-to-one with individual providers, facilitating evaluation of provider performance data against the performance of peers or competitors in the database. Example: Appendix A.
2. A variant of this practice model is where a benchmarking forum is established but the data gathering and synthesizing exercise is controlled by an independent facilitator. The facilitator/consultant acts as a type of benchmarking agent but participants do not actually meet as a group to discuss and evaluate findings. Examples of this approach can be found in Chapter 5 (in part) and Chapter 13.
3. Another variant on this theme is where an agency or function-specific group (like librarians) has constructed a national database that can then be made available interactively to contributors. Users can then use the information to compare/evaluate their own practice and performance using comparators that they define. Examples can be found in Chapters 9, 10, 11 and 12.

If these practice models represent the spectrum of approaches that can be legitimately described as benchmarking then it is possible to represent them in a conceptual framework (Figure 16.2) that distinguishes whether the process is essentially **dialogical** (i.e. involves discussion between participants in the process) or **bureaucratic** (i.e. comparison is based on referencing against a variety of information sources and does not require participants to meet).

Benchmarking and the 'evaluative state'

Benchmarking is fundamentally an approach to self-evaluation that is based on the idea of learning from others. Outside HE, self-improvement in business processes can be defined in terms of seeking to improve profitability and gain competitive advantage. In educational contexts (at least in the UK), in addition to the notion of improvement applied in business processes, there is also a strong interest in benchmarking as a means of maintaining the collective reputation of HE providers and the capacity of the system as a whole to regulate itself. For this reason, it is argued that the definitions of benchmarking used in business environments do not adequately reflect the range of purposes to which benchmarking is put in the educational environment.

The two fundamental purposes of any method of self-evaluation in HE are:

• to facilitate improvement – development – change and
• to satisfy expectations and requirements for professional accountability (Kells 1992 and 1995).

Self-evaluation processes in UK HE satisfy, to varying degrees, both of these purposes and effective self-regulation is dependent on achieving a healthy balance in addressing both purposes (Jackson 1997a, 1997b, 1998g). While there is a considerable investment of resources in the UK in self-evaluation, until recently, benchmarking-type activities were comparatively rare. The case studies described in this volume demonstrate the speed with which a whole new field of intellectual and applied endeavour can be created (i.e. within about four or five years).

Effective self-evaluation is crucial to a healthy self-regulating HE system; a framework of four approaches is shown in Table 16.1. The first two approaches use internally determined criteria and reference points to evaluate results and functions, but it is the third and fourth approaches, that connect with externally determined criteria and reference points, that relate to benchmarking. The strength of benchmarking as a method for self-evaluation is that it has the potential to be used for both accountability/regulatory purposes (the third approach) and as an aid to self-determined development (the fourth approach).

HE institutions and functional or subject communities will not participate in resource-intensive self-evaluation activities like benchmarking unless they are required to, or see distinct advantages in doing so. The application of benchmarking in any national system will therefore reflect closely the policy drivers, funding and market incentives/or disincentives. In the case of the UK, history has shown (Chapter 2) that the HE system has been driven, since the 1980s, by both policy and funding mechanisms to engage in systematic self-evaluation. This strategy (mirrored, more recently, in other European countries) has been integral to a shift in public policy management in which central control of inputs is being progressively displaced by centralized strategic control that focuses on performance and outcomes (Maassen 1997). The idea of the 'evaluative state', in which a variety of funding mechanisms and policy levers are used to promote the assessment of teaching, research, management and administration in order to evaluate the extent to which performance contracts are being delivered, is central to

Table 16.1 Four approaches to self-evaluation in higher education

---

1. *Measurement of the achievement of stated intentions* – evaluation is based on demonstrating and assessing the extent to which stated intentions (purposes, values, objectives, goals, targets) have been met. The approach is internally focused and evaluation focuses on the clarity of intentions and the extent to which they are achieved.

2. *Measurement of the adequacy of functions or processes* – evaluation is internally focused. It is concerned with matters of process within the particular environment in which the individual, unit or subject functions. The approach is internally focused and evaluation poses questions of the type: What are we trying to do? Why are we doing it? How are we doing it? Why are we doing it this way? How do we know it works? Can we improve it?

3. *Measurement of the extent of compliance with externally set standards* – evaluation is focused on comparing internal processes or performance against externally defined criteria, specifications, codes of practice or performance standards.

4. *Measurement of the extent to which practice matches up to acknowledged 'best' practice* – evaluation is concerned with comparing activities and performance against acknowledged best practice. The process is concerned to identify and understand the characteristics of best practice and the conditions that lead to such practices in order to emulate it.

Source: Based on Kells 1992, 1995; Jackson 1997b

this strategy (Henkel 1991; Dill 1998). The conditions for benchmarking in a higher education system are likely to be influenced greatly by political environments in which public policy management requires the existence of an 'evaluative state'.

Systemic factors that encourage/inhibit benchmarking

Our intention has been to provide a flavour of the way benchmarking is being used in different HE systems rather than to map the extent of application and diversity of approach. Nevertheless, our perusal of the accessible literature suggests that there is considerable variation in the extent to which benchmarking is being promoted and taken up in different HE systems. The reasons for this are complex but they are likely to reflect such inter-related factors as:

1. The size of the system: the larger and more diverse a system is, the more difficult it is to promote benchmarking as a systematic activity on a national scale; conversely, benchmarking might also be inhibited in small competitive systems.

2. The extent to which a system is differentiated (there might not be the same need for some benchmarking activities, e.g. those linked to academic standards in differentiated systems like Japan).
3. The extent to which organizations, functional communities (e.g. registrars, estates managers, librarians), regional groupings and subject communities are networked: the existence of good organizational and communication structures can facilitate benchmarking.
4. The extent to which collegiate attitudes and behaviour are a feature of an HE system: it is easier to promote benchmarking where there are already cultures that are predisposed to collaborative working.
5. The extent to which a culture of self-evaluation pervades the system: it is easier to promote benchmarking where there exists a culture of self-critical evaluation of performance.
6. The extent of state control over inputs (e.g. staff appointment); functions (such as administration); process (such as curriculum and teaching): it is difficult to promote benchmarking in tightly regulated and prescribed systems.
7. The degree of competition for national and international student markets: small, extremely competitive market-based systems will militate against benchmarking.
8. The extent to which a society embraces the 'new public management' (Kettl 1997; Dill 1998) or 'managerialism' (Pollitt 1993): government policy drivers and funding mechanisms will promote benchmarking as a means of implementing public management policy (see below).

The interdependence of the factors noted above is self-evident. For example, a small to medium-sized, publicly funded, well-networked HE system that is not tightly regulated by the state, which has a well-developed culture of collaboration, is likely to be receptive to the idea of benchmarking. This is because there is both a collective advantage in maintaining the reputation of the system and an individual advantage in demonstrating membership of certain peer groups and gaining competitive advantage over others in the peer group. Large, competitive market-based systems (e.g. North America) may also be receptive to benchmarking. On the other hand the conditions for benchmarking are unlikely to be fostered in small, highly competitive market-based systems and in systems where there is a tight state control on financial management, administration, curricula and teaching.

Of particular interest is the idea that benchmarking will prosper in social/political environments that embrace the 'new public management' (Kettl 1997; Dill 1998). In many countries the application of this approach to public policy in higher education has resulted in reforms in which 'governments act as monopsonistic purchasers, developing explicit performance contracts with HE institutions for teaching and research' (Dill 1998: 363). The idea of the 'evaluative state' is central to this strategy (Henkel 1991; Dill 1998) and the state needs information on which to judge whether performance contracts are being delivered. This approach to the management of public policy may also be coupled to the funding and contractual policies that promote competition in the public service environment as a way of improving value for money and returns on the public investment. Thus, the assessment of performance through self-appraisal or external review becomes integral to the application of the new public management (Dill 1998). The progressive emphasis on performance measurement (through PIs), the growth in external review and institutional self-evaluation and now the expansion of benchmarking in UK HE is a direct response to this approach to the management of public policy and the creation of the evaluative state. By analogy, benchmarking tends to flourish in national systems that also embrace the new public management (Australia being perhaps the closest analogy).

Some observations, themes and issues

The contributions to this volume have emphasized the many positive benefits of benchmarking to individuals (improved knowledge and understanding), departments and institutions, subject or functional communities and the system as a whole. The following general observations identify a number of themes and issues that are important in the further development of benchmarking.

Maintaining the identity of a UK-wide HE system

The UK still regards itself as having a national HE system within which the overall quality of the education provided is of a high standard – regardless of the purpose or institutional context. While this concept was not problematic in a selective elitist HE system it has become much more problematic as the system has expanded and diversified. Increasing regionalism (e.g. the Scottish, Welsh, Northern Ireland dimensions) within higher education will also contribute to the loss of system-wide identity. The processes of benchmarking can become an important means of maintaining the UK-wide identity of the system and promoting understanding across national boundaries.

Collaboration versus competition

HEIs within the UK and other national systems are faced with demands from government and funding agencies both to reduce their dependence on public funding by becoming more competitive and to make more cost-effective use of available resources through increased collaboration. But the market imperative to gain competitive advantage is counterbalanced by the respect for collaboration as a means of improving both the quality and the reputation of the public service as a whole. Benchmarking answers both these needs: while it is frequently conducted with a view to increasing institutional competitiveness, the technique, in its fullest sense, involves a strong degree of collaboration. Several contributors to this volume remarked on the degree of openness, trust and honesty that attended benchmarking exercises in which they were involved as participants, or facilitators (Chapters 4, 5, 6, 11, 12 and 15).

The difficulty of promoting benchmarking as an aid to improvement when the outcomes of such activities might be used to drive down public funding or produce league tables

It is difficult to promote trust in a methodology when an important motivation for state-inspired benchmarking is to target funding, reduce or redistribute resources, or produce league tables that affect the reputation, market position and profitability of an institution. This issue is generic to all HE systems that are attempting to use benchmarking in this way. It needs to be resolved in a positive way if benchmarking is to continue to flourish.

The difficulty of applying notions of 'best' practice in many educational contexts

Academic practice in HE prefers to recognize that there are many different models of good practice that will vary according to context, rather than simplistic notions of 'best' practice. Benchmarking in much of HE needs to view best practice in terms of 'fitness for purpose' (CHEMS) or 'realistic management aspirations' (HEFCE).

The application of benchmarking to the solution of common problems

Benchmarking is particularly effective in identifying common issues and problems and the range of responses and practical solutions to such problems. It is therefore likely to appeal to academic communities if it is promoted as a vehicle for identifying smart (quick, cheap, effective) solutions to common problems as a means of self-improvement.

Weaknesses in the information bases and MIS to support benchmarking

A common difficulty, particularly during the early stages of benchmarking, is the realization that departmental and institutional management information systems are not designed to provide the type of information sought in many benchmarking exercises. The expansion of benchmarking methods will therefore be dependent on the willingness of institutions to develop information systems to support the enterprise.

Do the benefits outweigh the costs?

The quality of information and the learning that accrues from a benchmarking process is proportional to the effort invested. Individual participants may invest considerable amounts of time (an exercise in the industrial/commercial sector might require five people to each invest 100–200 hours of time over 3–8 months; Price 1994. In the authors, experience typical investments in benchmarking in UK HE typically involve 5–20 days per person). This level of commitment, particularly if it is to be sustained over a period of time, can deter would-be participants. This is also one of the main reasons for attrition in benchmarking exercises. While in cost-focused benchmarking it is easy to identify the direct benefits (savings), it is much more difficult to calculate the benefits in exercises that relate to educational or service processes and standards.

Group dynamics

The success of collaborative benchmarking exercises is largely dependent on creating a mutually supportive environment in which participants can trust one another. Face-to-face meetings and reporting strategies that protect the anonymity of individual institutions help develop this foundation of trust. The level of ownership of the benchmarking process (and mutual trust) is dependent on a systematic and sustained engagement in the process by group members. The collaborative enterprise derives from deciding what to do, doing it and sharing information and ideas, and learning individually and collectively from the experience. Given the need to create this sense of ownership quickly, it is not surprising that existing networks and consortia are often used as the basis for benchmarking. However, even within relatively small benchmarking groups responses to data-gathering instruments and feedback reports are variable and it is sometimes difficult for all individuals to attend all the meetings. This reduced commitment diminishes the overall effectiveness of the process and the potential for learning. While benchmarking exercises can be undertaken with only two members, the capacity for learning is increased with a larger, carefully selected group.

Difficulty of identifying partners

A related issue signalled in some of the case studies is the difficulty of identifying partners. This is compounded by the tension between wanting to seek partners who are in the institutional peer group, e.g. research-led universities, while acknowledging that good and innovative practice might lie elsewhere. A number of examples to illustrate the advantages of forming benchmarking groups are provided in Chapters 5, 12, 13 and 15.

Benchmarking for strategic purposes

While some functional areas can be benchmarked without reference to the overall institutional mission, several contributors emphasized the need to conduct benchmarking in the context of larger strategic change. Benchmarking has been successfully used to help determine strategic plans encompassing academic support, estates work and academic practice (Chapters 11 and 12) and growing confidence by practitioners in the use of benchmarking techniques deepens the strategic impact of their work (Chapter 11). Within academic practice also, processes are rarely self-contained and a benchmarking exercise focused, for example, on modularization or curriculum delivery can be part of the institution's broad strategic objectives or have far-reaching effects on its strategic development plans (Chapters 4 and 8).

Need for top management involvement

Senior management has a vital role to play both in demonstrating that the effort invested by staff is valued (Chapters 12 and 13) and in ensuring that the information and learning derived from the process is used (Chapters 4, 8 and 15). Involvement of senior managers in the benchmarking process can help to ensure that a topic is evaluated in the light of an institution's overall strategy and that learning is not 'captured' by one interest group (Chapters 9 and 13).

The appropriate balance of qualitative and quantitative aspects

Benchmarking in the management/administration sphere has tended to start out with a focus on quantitative measurement of 'performance' and some initiatives (examples in Chapters 9 and 14) still confine themselves to this approach. The dangers and limitations of evaluating performance solely or primarily by metrics (e.g. Chapters 9, 11, 12 and 14) is becoming increasingly apparent. A growing body of opinion, among both university practitioners and consultants, holds that performance can only be improved if benchmarking includes also a focus on quality of processes. On this understanding, 'good practice' is not necessarily equated with the cheapest and fastest way of doing things; user perceptions of the service and client satisfaction are important factors too (examples in Chapters 9, 11, 12, 14 and 15).

Conversely, when it comes to benchmarking academic practice, perform-ance has been evaluated mainly in terms of 'softer' qualitative judgements. Attempts have been made to use quantitative indicators within departmental reviews (Chapter 3) and to measure subject-specific and key skill standards as well as aspects of the student learning experience (Chapters 3, 6, 7 and 8) but this has not proved entirely problem-free and further work is needed to develop quantitative measures that academics believe are reliable.

The general absence of generic process benchmarking

To date, for reasons unknown, relatively little use has been made in higher education of generic process benchmarking; a few examples are given in Chapter 12.

The difficulties and potential rewards of transnational benchmarking

There are difficulties in developing performance measures and notions of best practice which can be applied across national HE systems since national contexts are so varied (Chapters 14, 15 and Appendix B). But the potential rewards of demonstrating excellence and, where appropriate, com-parability through transnational institutional alliances (Chapter 15 and Appendix B), international subject and professional networks (Chapter 14) and, potentially, national HE systems, are great.

The lesson for UK HE

These messages of tension and conflict, conceptual and practical difficulty and unfulfilled opportunities are to be expected in a time of rapid develop-ment and experimentation following the introduction of a new approach. They provide an indication of challenges that future benchmarking activ-ities will need to overcome and the benefits to those who are successful in exploiting the methodology. The twin drivers of public accountability and the need to improve competitiveness are promoting benchmarking for very different purposes. In our view, the full benefits from benchmarking in higher education will only be realized when a balance can be struck between the information demands that underpin the 'evaluative state' and evaluative processes that support the development needs of institutions and promote innovation and self-determined improvement. Achieving this balance should be the goal of every self-regulating system. Only then will benchmarking truly be a process for higher education.

Appendix A: An Approach to Quantitative Benchmarking

Norman Jackson

Description of a process used by a Nottingham-based firm of consultants to analyse, through quantitative benchmarking informed by more qualitative evaluation, the business processes that underpin educational processes. The information was kindly provided through interview with Mr Ben Johnson-Hill. Further enquiries about the application of the method should be directed to Ben Johnson-Hill Associates Ltd, 7 Gregory Boulevard, Nottingham, NG7 6LD.

Introduction

The primary goal of managerial practice in higher education is to maximize the opportunities for learning and provide the best possible quality of education at the most reasonable cost. Higher education is very much a fusion of business and educational processes and operations. But while the former are subject to the same laws of efficiency and profitability that govern commercial enterprises, the latter are motivated by value and belief systems that place the quality of the students' educational experience and achievement at the heart of the enterprise. Achieving the optimal balance between best possible quality and most reasonable costs is the goal of all HE managers but, given the enormous and continuous change in higher education and increasing public expectations, attaining this goal is not a simple matter. University and college managers and administrators employ an extensive array of quality evaluation and value for money review strategies (Jackson 1997b; Chapters 2 and 14, this volume) to help them achieve this objective.

Achieving this balance is the goal of an approach to benchmarking that has been developed by Ben Johnson-Hill Associates Ltd. The method is based on the objective (quantitative) and subjective (qualitative) evaluation and comparative analysis of over 700 performance measures. It was originally developed in the 1980s for the textiles industry but was adapted in the early 1990s for the educational environment. To date the methodology has been applied over 400 times for over 270 different clients including 240 FE institutions and 29 HE institutions (approximately 50 per cent universities and 50 per cent colleges of HE).

The method has been used to fulfil a variety of institutional purposes including:

- the objective assessment of the use of resources across all areas
- to inform managerial decisions and determine/confirm where action should be taken
- to help management and the governing body understand the institution better as a business
- to measure progress from one year to the next
- to provide objective data to justify strategic change
- as a predictive tool – e.g. to provide comparable data to help institutions model the consequences of fundamental change – collaboration, federation, merger, expansion of student numbers, or changes in the nature of the provision
- to provide supporting evidence for external inspection/audit or quality review
- to underpin the business excellence model of continuous improvement.

Above all, the approach seeks to provide an objective basis to inform and justify managerial decisions, particularly those that require substantial change and the redistribution of effort and resources.

Approach

Each benchmarking exercise involves a consultant working with a single institution. All projects are subject to a confidentiality agreement to ensure that the diagnostic reports are only used in the institution and the information is not disclosed to a third party or reproduced in league tables.

The primary investment is the construction of a quantitative database involving about 700 measurements for the last financial year. The data cover all areas of income, all elements of teaching performance, commercial enterprises and cost, all support, overhead and service functions and all use of space. The data bank can also be configured to provide comparative data for academic schools or departments. Each measurement compares an input of resource against an output, or vice versa, for example, the numbers of teaching staff FTE (full-time equivalents) per weighted student FTE; registry costs per student FTE; the various premises costs per m² of floor space; student resident costs per student night.

The data bank is continually developed as more universities and colleges of HE participate in the process. Data collection is normally completed over a four-week period and the use of standard software ensures that the task is completed efficiently. The database contains measurements for all the institutions that have participated in the benchmarking process. Customized reports contain information on the institution's data and the results for a group of other institutions for comparison. This comparator group could include for example:

- the average data for a cluster of other institutions with which an institution wished to compare itself
- the average data of institutions with a similar educational mission or of a similar type.

The comparator would never involve information for a single named competitor. Table A1 provides an illustrative example of a summary report of core costs per student FTE. This table would be one of 40 tables included in an institutional report. The first column provides a breakdown of costs against each item listed and a ratio based on cost/student FTE is given in the second column. Columns 3 and 4 provide a set of comparative data to enable the university to compare its costs per student FTE in relation to:

- data for other universities
- a typical large HE institution (similar in size to the university being studied).

The final column provides a set of values that provide a target for improvement of performance (reduced costs per student FTE).

Experience has shown that the values for each cost/performance measure will typically vary by a factor of four: in some areas rising to a factor of ten. For example, at the level of academic departments it can be predicted that there will be significant differences in income-generating capacity, marketing and consultancy activity, and in staff utilization. Simple ratios like student:staff hours and taught hours per teaching room can provide important insights into fundamentally different patterns of teaching and learning. While this might be perfectly justified on pedagogic criteria and the rationale be very difficult for an institutional manager to challenge, when such data are compared with similar departments in peer institutions it can provide leverage to challenge the assumptions and traditions on which practice is based.

Given the above, it can be predicted with a degree of certainty that every institutional data set will be unique. The full analysis of the institution's results identifies and quantifies all significant out-of-line costs. In a typical institution, this might highlight 25 areas of high cost or low performance (in the total matrix of 700 cost/performance measurements). Typically the sum of the excesses will exceed 10 per cent of total budget. Each area of *out-of-line cost and performance* provides a prompt for discussion with management. The consultants' role is to help management to determine and identify where action can be taken (and where not) and hence how the use of resources can be improved. This discussion brings into play a more qualitative approach in which the factual information relating to performance is considered in the light of the many contextual factors that influence overall performance. Experience has shown that this debate often challenges assumptions and management's current forward strategy.

Table A.1 A typical report for an HE institution showing the breakdown of core costs per student FTE

Item	Your value	Your ratio	Other universities	Large HE inst.	Suggested target
TOTAL COSTS AND COSTS PER STD FTE	23776472	3845	3552	3178	3252
Teaching depts expenditure:					
– Direct teacher salaries £	8884712	1437	1305	1301	1222
– Teaching support salaries £	943442	153	129	64	95
– Teaching admin. salaries £	1777696	287	254	250	253
– Teaching non-staff costs £	1116174	180	141	194	190
Subtotal £	12722024	2057	1829	1809	1760
Research expenditure:					
– Research salaries £	619340	100	207	68	114
– Research other costs £	426372	69	73	36	50
Subtotal £	1045712	169	280	104	164
Support expenditure:					
Library/LRC					
– Library LRC salaries £	655170	106	101	72	83
– Library LRC other costs £	325975	53	70	55	58
Subtotal £	981144	159	177	127	141
Student services					
– Student services salaries £	445514	72	86	56	68
– Student services other costs £	134876	22	42	42	46
Subtotal £	580390	94	128	98	114
Registry/Standards					
– Registry salaries £	472178	76	102	83	96
– Registry other costs £	95739	15	21	45	28
Subtotal £	567917	92	124	128	125
Training/Quality enhancement					
– Training/QE salaries £	41651	7	15	9	9
– Training QE other costs £	338023	55	45	33	33
Subtotal £	379674	61	60	43	41

Table A.1 (cont'd)

Item	Your value	Your ratio	Other universities	Large HE inst.	Suggested target
AVA/Printing					
– AVA/Print salaries £	87613	14	36	19	29
– AVA/Print other costs £	411534	67	54	62	59
Subtotal £	499147	81	89	81	88
Computer services					
– Central IT salaries £	616507	100	90	63	62
– Central IT other costs £	765669	124	56	78	72
Subtotal £	1382176	223	146	140	135
Marketing/PR					
– Marketing/PR salaries £	215785	35	44	18	25
– Marketing/PR other costs £	592467	96	66	48	47
Subtotal £	808252	131	110	66	72
Central admin. expenditure:					
– Central admin. salaries £	731653	118	171	166	165
– Central admin. other costs £	1080413	175	143	147	140
Subtotal	1812066	293	314	312	305
Premises expenditure:					
– Premises salaries £	567507	92	109	96	108
– Premises other costs £	2401729	388	291	201	254
Subtotal	2969236	480	400	297	362
Services expenditure:					
Catering costs £ (net)	168934	27	-10	2	-4
Cleaning costs £	289871	47	46	58	45
Student residences £ (net)	-524088	-85	-142	-85	-97
Creche/Nursery costs £	94021	15	2	0	1

Commentary

Compared to the FE sector, where over half the FEFC colleges have been involved in this process, participation of universities and colleges has been relatively modest (i.e. only 29 of over 180 HEIs have participated in this type of benchmarking to date). There are perceived to be two main reasons for this. First, the drive to reduce costs through state funding mechanisms has been much stronger in the FE sector and FE colleges have been forced to look at cost-focused benchmarking in order to survive! It is however becoming increasingly clear, as state per capita funding decreases and unit costs are driven down in HE, that more systematic and analytical approaches to the diagnosis of business operations and performance are required if universities are to prosper.

One trend that is common to both the FE and HE sectors is the increasing expectation that institutions will be engaging in ever more sophisticated methods of self-assessment. The type of information created through the benchmarking process provides a comprehensive data set on which to make informed self-assessments. Thus subjective judgements of educational effectiveness are more secure for being founded on an objective database.

Second, it is perhaps more difficult for universities with strongly devolved management structures to engage in this type of benchmarking exercise as a corporate activity. Many universities, particularly the older civics, are collections of departments and schools with a large degree of independence and autonomy that does not sit easily with processes that seek to make transparent the relative performance of individual departments. Quantitative benchmarking is more likely to be accepted by departments if the objective is to compare performance with similar departments in peer institutions rather than with other departments in the same university. Coupled to this there is also the possibility that the focus on business rather than educational processes makes it more difficult for senior institutional managers to 'sell' the method to the academic community. While it is true that the benchmarking process begins with the business processes there are many connections between business and educational processes. For example, the use of space, the use of learning resources like information technology and library resources to support teaching and learning, the use of teacher time and the use of support staff. The way in which these resources are deployed influences the quality of educational provision, the students' learning experience and the standards of student attainment. That there is a link between business performance and educational quality and student attainment can be inferred from the results of benchmarking in the FE sector where there is a good correlation between the colleges with the lowest FTE student costs and the highest FEFC quality ratings, the inference being that the best managed colleges are those that have achieved the goal of balancing highest quality with most reasonable cost.

Appendix B: Universitas 21

Dugald Mackie

Description of the background and initial development work relating to
Universitas 21: a new venture in transnational benchmarking.

Introduction

Universitas 21 is a global alliance of universities established in 1997 at an
inaugural meeting held under the auspices of the University of Melbourne.
As the underlying idea is of 'a small, tight-knit association of kindred institutions', the membership of the alliance is currently limited to the 12 founder
members[1] to which have been added universities in China (Beijing, Fudan
and the University of Hong Kong) and the United States (University of
Michigan). Further additions are expected which will add to the geographic
spread of the alliance; it is unlikely, though, to exceed a total membership
at any one time of 25 institutions.

It should be stressed from the outset that the primary concern of
Universitas 21 is not benchmarking. While benchmarking as a form of
collaborative activity may help to give some substance to the alliance as a
tangible entity, it is primarily a by-product of the existence of the alliance,
not a reason for it. In that context the reasons for creating the alliance
merit some further attention, not least because the likely benchmarking
activity will take a form shaped by those reasons.

Universitas 21 was formed in 1997, by which time the explosion in global
telecommunication which was so marked in the 1990s was well under way.
Improvements in performance and reductions in the price of personal com-
puters, sophisticated and user-friendly network software (web browsers, for
example), fibre-optic cables and satellites, coupled with the increasing preval-
ence of mobile/cellular telephones have led to a previously unimaginable
widening of personal and national horizons across the world. It has become
commonplace to be able to watch a constantly updated video clip of the
Manhattan skyline from a PC in Perth in Australia virtually in real-time, or
to be able to find out which classes are scheduled for that day in Duke
University, North Carolina, while sitting at a desk in Glasgow.

By their nature as institutions devoted to advanced learning and research, universities are at the forefront of these advances in global telecommunications. Worldwide websites are by now ubiquitous with that web-based approach used for external browsers now also forming the basis of rapid growth in internal communications – the internet and the intranet. The immense power and potential of the internet as a medium for information delivery has led to the development of 'virtual' universities, either by universities themselves or by education ministries anxious to widen participation in higher education[2] or by companies operating in a globally competitive marketplace who are dependent on the skills of their staff being constantly updated.[3]

A more worrying prospect for existing and well-established universities is the possibility of the producers of the software (Microsoft or Netscape for instance) linking with a communications company with an internet-provider subsidiary (a rapidly changing scene but, at the time of writing, Scottish Telecom and Demon) to deliver material produced by a large multimedia company such as Time-Warner, using the intellectual capacity – or even simply the name – of a university such as Harvard or Cambridge. The result would be a degree from Harvard, which, despite being delivered through a 'virtual' university would be only too real in nature.

The result of surveying such a prospect has been a move towards the creation of global alliances among universities of which one of the first has been Universitas 21. In the same way that the other great global revolution of cheap long-distance air travel has seen alliances of airlines circling the globe,[4] Universitas 21 circles the globe in that it has members in Europe, Asia, Australasia and North America. Those members are not simply a random collection of institutions but are universities that share a number of characteristics. To quote the mission statement, '. . . Universities of world-class standing, which deliver high quality education to undergraduate and graduate students, which undertake leading-edge research, and where all activities are supported by high quality infrastructure'. In order to give substance to any claims made by its members to be part of a real, working alliance, Universitas 21 members agreed at their 1998 meeting to work together in relatively small groups in order to promote the following joint actions:

- developing a 'Universitas 21 profile', i.e. a succinct, analytical summary of the defining characteristics of member institutions as comprehensive, research-intensive universities
- establishing rigorous international processes for benchmarking in key strategic areas of academic management, research and teaching and learning
- creating a series of Universitas 21 fellowships to be awarded to outstanding and innovative university teachers and administrators
- developing the capabilities of members to exploit new teaching and learning technologies, modalities and delivery systems

- promoting student mobility among members with a particular focus on developing combined international student and work placement opportunities
- developing international courses and curriculum materials and seeking means of broadening the basis of professional recognition among countries
- establishing a database of information to facilitate collaboration, inter-flexibility and the development of comparative management information systems on an international basis.

It was acknowledged at the time that this programme was ambitious and that it would take a number of years to achieve the objectives of each of its strands. It was also acknowledged that there might be failure along the way and that, use of global communication notwithstanding, practical barriers to collaboration might well prove insurmountable in certain areas.

Approach to benchmarking

Universitas 21 is at an early stage in developing benchmarking as a strategy to achieve the objectives outlined above. Benchmarking itself is, of course, a broad term that encapsulates a variety of approaches and actions (see other contributions to this volume). Nonetheless, there is a fair measure of agreement that benchmarking is fundamentally about learning from best practice rather than simply comparing key performance measures across like institutions or organizations. Indeed, in a global context, the latter exercise may well be meaningless for universities as national differences between, for example, where research is undertaken or how students are funded render inter-country comparisons as little more than a possibly interesting but ultimately futile academic, as opposed to practical, exercise. It would certainly be possible for Universitas 21 to ask each of its members to provide its own competitive analysis of where it stood in relation to its competitor institutions. A collation of where members came in such league tables might well give rise to some pause for thought and would certainly give rise to arguments but would it add any value to Universitas 21 as an organization?

Universitas 21 has decided on an approach that seeks to establish the key characteristics of a 'member' in relation to the stated mission of the organization, i.e. a 'Universitas 21 profile'. In view of the global span of the alliance, any attempt to make this profile complex and/or highly detailed immediately confronts the problems of comparing dissimilar national systems of higher education. While seemingly linked with the common word 'university' and with like missions of providing teaching and learning and undertaking research, the ability to compare the research performance of a university in, say, Canada with a university in New Zealand or China falls foul of the different ways in which basic research is undertaken and funded in each of the countries. Another example of the difficulty in making comparisons is that universities in China appear to work in a regime where bureaucratized state control is linked with a zeal for entrepreneurialism that would bring cheer to the heart of Baroness Thatcher but which is very different to the notionally autonomous but financially controlled system in the UK. The task confronting those members[5] charged with designing a profile has therefore been to devise a simple template which is readily accessible and understood across higher education systems in different countries, geographic regions and cultures, and is defensible on the basis of currently available data.

Some difficulties of transnational benchmarking

The difficulties outlined above in seeking to compare what on the surface might all look like apples but where some rapidly turn out to be pears mean that the profile can only focus on a relatively small number of factors. These factors are, however, designed to give substance to the defining characteristics of any or all of Universitas 21 members as comprehensive, providing high-quality education to undergraduate and graduate students, undertaking leading-edge research and operating within a high-quality infrastructure. An example of the difficulties involved in arriving at a common performance measure comes from the attempts to define 'high quality' through measuring the proportion of first-year undergraduate students enrolled from the 10 per cent higher achieving school leavers. The data collection involved in such a seemingly simple task is straightforward if you are in Australia but is not straightforward in the United Kingdom or Canada. It could in any case be argued that 'such a performance measure provides no information about the quality of education provided or the outputs'.[6] The group has therefore decided not to proceed with this particular measure but rather to look at institutional commitment to internal quality assurance processes for teaching (externally referenced or measured where appropriate) and at the success of graduates in gaining employment.

Leaving the profiling exercise aside, Universitas 21 is at an early stage in terms of benchmarking *per se*. It would be foolish to pretend that the simple act of establishing itself as a global alliance of universities somehow will take Universitas 21 straight to 'genuine best practice benchmarking'. There are difficulties of longitude and the fact that ten o'clock in Glasgow means the morning whereas it is night in Melbourne. There are differences in the relationship of universities to the state and to the structure of the state itself. There are cultural rivalries, not to mention inter-institutional rivalries within countries. There are the simple problems, as illustrated in the profiling exercise, of arriving at common definitions as well as devising performance measures that will mean the same in Beijing as in Ottawa. Nonetheless, the prize for overcoming these pitfalls and hurdles and for working together on the resolution of problems is potentially so great for each of the members and for the alliance as a whole that the investment of time and resources now will in the longer run provide a handsome pay-off. Benchmarking and, in particular, the encouragement and development of best practice will play a major role in working toward such a pay-off, not least in the material benefits which experience in other sectors has shown to be possible. It will also provide substance to the aim of Universitas 21 in establishing itself as a global brand name for excellence in universities. Where it leads, others will no doubt follow.

Notes

1. The founding members of Universitas 21 include the following universities: Australia: Melbourne, New South Wales and Queensland; Canada: British Columbia, McGill and Toronto; New Zealand: Auckland; Singapore: National University of Singapore; United Kingdom: Birmingham, Edinburgh, Glasgow and Nottingham.
2. See, for example, the Open University of Catalonia, established in 1994 – see http://www.uoc.es
3. In the UK, the most notable example is the British Aerospace Virtual University.
4. Most recent is the example of 'one world' which links American Airlines, British Airways, Canadian Airlines, Iberia Airlines and Qantas in various ways from code-sharing through to mutual shareholdings.
5. The Universitas 21 secretariat working with the Universities of Glasgow and Melbourne and McGill University and with Price Waterhouse Coopers.
6. Commentary provided privately by Price Waterhouse Coopers to the Universitas 21 Project Group.

References

AGR (Association of Graduate Recruiters) (1995) *Skills for Graduates in the 21st Century*. Warwick: AGR.

AIEF (Australian International Education Foundation) (1998) *International Office Benchmarking Survey Report*. Melbourne: AIEF.

Akhlaghi, F. and Tranfield, D. (1995) 'Performance measures: relating facilities to business indicators'. *Facilities*, 13 (3), 6–14.

Alderman, G. (1997) 'League tables merit improvement'. *Times Higher Education Supplement*, 19 September.

Alstete, W.J. (1995) *Benchmarking in Higher Education: Adapting Best Practices to Improve Quality*. ASHE-ERIC, Higher Education Report No. 5. Washington, DC: George Washington University.

Anon (1992) *Assessment of Departmental Academic Performance: Notes of Guidance*. Southampton: University of Southampton.

Appleby, A. (1999) 'Benchmarking theory: a framework for the business world as a context for its application in higher education' in H. Smith, M. Armstrong and S. Brown (eds) *Benchmarking and Threshold Standards*. London: Kogan Page.

ASHE (Academic Standards in Higher Education) (1993) *Academic Standards in Higher Education: Biochemistry*. Report of the Academic Standards Panel. Canberra: Australian Vice-Chancellors' Committee.

Ashenden, D. and Milligan, S. (1998) *Australian Universities: Courses and Campuses in 1999*. Subiaco, Western Australia: Ashenden Milligan Pty Ltd.

AVCC (Australian Vice-Chancellors' Committee) (1987) *Report of the AVCC Subcommittee on Academic Standards*. Canberra: Australian Vice-Chancellors' Committee.

Baldridge, M. (1992) *1992 Award Criteria: Malcolm Baldridge National Quality Award*. Milwaukee, WI: American Society for Quality Control.

Barnett, R. (1992) *Improving Higher Education: Total Quality Care*. Buckingham: SRHE and Open University Press.

Barnett, R. (1994) *The Limits of Competence: Knowledge, Higher Education and Society*. Buckingham: SRHE and Open University Press.

Barnett, R. (1997) *Higher Education: A Critical Business*. Buckingham: SRHE and Open University Press.

Barton, J. and Blagden, J. (1998) *Academic Library Effectiveness: A Comparative Approach*. British Library Research and Innovation Report. London: British Library.

Beecher, T. (1989) *Academic Tribes and Territories*. Buckingham: Open University Press.

Bell, A. (1995) 'User satisfaction surveys: experience at Leicester'. *New Review of Academic Librarianship*, 1, 175–8.

Bell, J. (1999) 'Benchmarking in law' in H. Smith, M. Armstrong and S. Brown (eds) *Benchmarking and Threshold Standards*. London: Kogan Page.

Bendall, T., Boulter, L. and Kelly, J. (1993) *Benchmarking for Competitive Advantage*. London: Financial Times/Pitman Publishing.

Billing, D. (ed.) (1979) *Indicators of Performance: Papers Presented at the Fifteenth Annual Conference of the Society for Research into Higher Education*. Guildford: SRHE.

Blagden, J. and Harrington, J. (1990) *How Good Is Your Library? A Review of Approaches to the Evaluation of Library and Information Services*. London: Association for Information Management (Aslib).

Boud, D.J., Keogh, R. and Walker, D. (1985) *Reflection – Turning Experience into Learning*. London: Kogan Page.

Boyle, A.P. and Paul, C.R.C. (1998) 'Benchmarking subject learning outcomes: earth science case study' in N. Jackson (ed.) *Pilot Studies in Benchmarking Assessment Practice*. Gloucester: Quality Assurance Agency.

Bridges, P., Bourdillon, B., Collymore, D. *et al.* (1999) 'Discipline-related marking behaviour using percentages: a potential cause of inequity in assessment.' *Assessment and Evaluation in Higher Education*, 24 (3).

Brockman, J. (ed.) (1997) *Quality Management and Benchmarking in the Information Sector: Results of Recent Research*. London: Bowker-Saur.

Brophy, P. and Coulling, K. (1996) *Quality Management for Information and Library Managers*. Aldershot: Aslib Gower.

BTEC (Business and Technology Education Council) (1992) *Common Skills and Core Themes: General Guidelines*. London: BTEC.

Burge, S., Jackson, N.J. and Tannock, J. (1996) *Specification for a Quality Management Framework at Departmental Level*. Occasional Paper No. 9. London: Engineering Professors' Council.

Burge, S.E. and Tannock, J.D.T. (1992) *Quality Assurance in Higher Education*. Occasional Paper No. 4. London: Engineering Professors' Council.

Camp, R.C. (1989) *Benchmarking: The Search for Industry Best Practices that Lead to Superior Performance*. Milwaukee, WI: American Society for Quality Control Press.

Camp, R.C. (1995) *Business Process Benchmarking: Finding and Implementing Best Practices*. Milwaukee, WI: Quality Press.

Cave, M., Hanney, S., Henkel, M. *et al.* (1997) *The Use of Performance Indicators in Higher Education: The Challenge of the Quality Movement*. London: Jessica Kingsley.

CBI (Confederation of British Industry) (1989) *Towards a Skills Revolution*. London: CBI.

CBS (Copenhagen Business School) (1995) CBS Methodology Development Project: Benchmarking Report on the Undergraduate Studies of the CHEMS-Partners. Unpublished report, CBS.

Chapman, K. (1994) 'Variability of degree results in geography in United Kingdom Universities, 1973–1990: preliminary results and policy implications'. *Studies in Higher Education*, 19, 89–102.

Cheetham, D.L. (1993) 'The Potential of Benchmarking for Higher Education Libraries'. Paper given at the Training Together 3 Meeting held at Manchester Metropolitan University, 22 April 1993. Also in *SCONUL Newsletter*, 62, 67–73.

Chemistry SBG (Subject Benchmarking Group) (1998) *General Guidelines for the Academic Review of Bachelors Honours Degree Programmes in Chemistry*. Consultation document, September 1998. Gloucester: Quality Assurance Agency.

CIPFA (Chartered Institute of Public Finance and Accountancy) (1995) *Treasury Management in Higher Education: A Guide*. London: CIPFA.

CNAA (Council for National Academic Awards) (1990) *Performance Indicators and Quality Assurance*. Discussion Paper No. 4. London: CNAA.

Codling, S. (1992) *Best Practice Benchmarking: The Management Guide*. Dunstable: Industrial Newsletters.

CUBO (Conference of University Business Officers) (1997) Unpublished material supplied to CHEMS by Derek J. Philips, Director, Domestic Services, University of Exeter.

Cuenin, S. (1986) 'International Study of the Development of Performance Indicators in Higher Education'. Paper presented to OECD, IMHE Project Special Topic Workshop.

Cullen, R. (1998) 'Does performance measurement improve organisational effectiveness? A post-modern analysis' in *Proceedings of the 2nd Northumbria International Conference on Performance Measurement in Libraries and Information Services*. Newcastle: Department of Information and Library Management, University of Northumbria at Newcastle.

CVCP (Committee of Vice-Chancellors and Principals) (1995) *Higher Education Management Statistics: A Future Strategy*. London: CVCP.

CVCP (Committee of Vice-Chancellors and Principals) (1996) *Final Report Executive Summary, Joint Planning Group for Quality Assurance in Higher Education*. London: CVCP.

CVCP (Committee of Vice-Chancellors and Principals) (1998) *Skills Development in Higher Education*. London: CVCP.

CVCP (Committee of Vice-Chancellors and Principals) and UFC (Universities Funding Council) (1992) *University Management Statistics and Performance Indicators in the UK*. 6th edn. London: CVCP/UFC.

CVCP (Committee of Vice-Chancellors and Principals) and UGC (University Grants Committee) (1987) *University Management Statistics and Performance Indicators*. London: CVCP/UGC.

Davis, D. (1996) *The Real World of Performance Indicators*. London: CHEMS.

DEET (Department of Employment, Education and Training) (1994) *Diversity and Performance of Australian Universities*. Canberra: DEET.

DEET (Department of Employment, Education and Training) (1996) *Diversity in Australian Higher Education Institutions*. Canberra: DEET.

DES (Department of Education and Science) (1985) *The Development of Higher Education into the 1990s*, Cmnd 9524. London: HMSO.

DES (Department of Education and Science) (1987) *Higher Education: Meeting the Challenge*, Cmnd 114. London: HMSO.

DES (Department of Education and Science) (1989) *Education Reform Act 1988*. London: HMSO.

DES (Department of Education and Science) (1991a) *Higher Education: A New Framework*, Cm. 1541. London: HMSO.

DES (Department of Education and Science) (1991b) *Performance Indicators in Higher Education: A Report by HMI*. Stanmore: DES.

DETR (Department of the Environment, Transport and the Regions) (1998) *Modern Local Government in Touch with the People* (White Paper). London: HMSO.

DETYA (Department of Education, Training and Youth Affairs) (1998) *The Characteristics and Performance of Higher Education Institutions* [online only]. Available at: http://www.deetya.gov.au/highered/otherpub/characteristics.pdf

DfE (Department for Education) (1992) *Further and Higher Education Act.* London: HMSO.

DfE (Department for Education) and Welsh Office (1993) *Environmental Responsibility: An Agenda for Further and Higher Education.* Committee Report (Chair: Professor Peter Toyne). London: HMSO.

DfEE (Department for Education and Employment) (1994) *Higher Education Developments: The Skills Link 2.* Employment Department Group. Sheffield: DfEE.

DfEE (Department for Education and Employment) (1998) *The Learning Age: A Renaissance for a New Britain.* Sheffield: DfEE.

Dill, D. (1998) 'Evaluating the "evaluative state": implications for research in higher education'. *European Journal of Education,* 33 (3), 361–77.

Dochy, J.R.C., Segers, M.S.R. and Wijnen, W.H.F.W. (1990) *Management Information and Performance Indicators in Higher Education: An International Issue.* Assen/ Maastricht: Van Gorcum.

Duffy, F. (1997) *The New Office.* London: Conran Octopus.

EDG (Employment Department Group) (1990) *The Skills Decade.* Sheffield: EDG.

Edwards, G. (1997) Independent Evaluation of the Implementation of the EPC9 Specification in Participating Departments. Unpublished report to the Engineering Professors Council.

eLib (Electronic Libraries Programme) (1998) [online]. Available at: http://www.ukoln.ac.uk/services/elib/projects/

Elliot Major, L. (1999) 'Securing a future'. *Guardian,* 12 January.

Elton, L. (1998) 'Are UK degree standards going up, down or sideways?' *Studies in Higher Education,* 23 (1), 35–42.

EPC (Engineering Professors' Council) (1998) *Developing an Integrated Quality Management Framework at Departmental Level: Summary Report.* London: Engineering Professors' Council.

European Foundation for Quality Management (EFQM) (1999) [online]. Available at: http://www.efqm.org

Farquhar, R. (1998) 'Higher education benchmarking in Canada and the United States of America' in A. Schofield (ed.) *Benchmarking in Higher Education: An International Review.* London: CHEMS and Paris: UNESCO.

FEFC (Further Education Funding Council) (1997) *Effective Facilities Management: A Good Practice Guide.* London: FEFC.

Ferdinande, H. and Petit, A. (1997) *Inquiries into European Higher Education in Physics.* Proceedings of the first EUPEN General Forum. Ghent: Universiteit Gent.

Fisher, D.C. (1995) *Baldrige on Campus: The Assessment Workbook for Higher Education.* New York: Quality Resources.

Fitzgerald, M. (1995) 'Towards a new learning environment: developing the educational strategy of TVU'. *TVU Bulletin Supplement,* 1 (23).

Fleming, D.N.V. and Storr, J. (1999) 'The Impact of Lecture Theatre Design on Learning Experience'. *Facilities,* 17 (7/8), 231–6.

Garrod, P. and Kinnell, M. (1997) *Towards Library Excellence: Best Practice Benchmarking in the Library and Information Sector.* East Grinstead: Bowker-Saur.

Goddard, A. (1999) 'Your day of judgement'. *Times Higher Education Supplement,* 12 February.

Grayson, C.J. (1998) 'Benchmarking in higher education' in J.W. Meyerson (ed.) *New Thinking on Higher Education.* Bolton, MA.: Anker Publishing Company.

Green, D. with Brannigan, C., Mazelan, P. and Giles, L. (1994) 'Measuring student satisfaction: a method of improving the quality of the student's experience?'

in S. Haselgrove (ed.) *The Student Experience.* Buckingham: SRHE and Open University Press.

Gregory, K. (1991) 'Assessing departmental academic performance: a model for a UK university'. *Higher Education Review,* XXIII.

Hart, E. (1995) 'The role of focus groups with other performance measurement methods' in *Proceedings of the 1st Northumbria International Conference on Performance Measurement in Libraries and Information Services.* Newcastle: Department of Information and Library Management, University of Northumbria at Newcastle.

Harvey, L., Burrows, A. and Green, D. (1992) *Criteria of Quality.* Quality in Higher Education Project. Birmingham: University of Central England at Birmingham.

HEFCE (Higher Education Funding Council for England) (1993a) *Audit Code of Practice.* Circular 29/93. Bristol: HEFCE.

HEFCE (Higher Education Funding Council for England) (1993b) *Value for Money.* Consultation Paper CP 8/93. Bristol: HEFCE.

HEFCE (Higher Education Funding Council for England) (1993c) *Joint Funding Councils' Libraries Review Group: Report.* Bristol: HEFCE.

HEFCE (Higher Education Funding Council for England) (1995a) *Profiles of Higher Education Institutions.* Bristol: HEFCE.

HEFCE (Higher Education Funding Council for England) (1995b) *The Effective Academic Library: A Framework for Evaluating the Performance of UK Academic Libraries.* Bristol: HEFCE.

HEFCE (Higher Education Funding Council for England) (1996a) *Quality Assessment Division: Assessors' Handbook,* M6/96. Bristol: HEFCE.

HEFCE (Higher Education Funding Council for England) (1996b) *Treasury Management: Value for Money National Report.* Bristol: HEFCE.

HEFCE (Higher Education Funding Council for England) (1996c) *Treasury Management in the Higher Education Sector: Management Review Guide.* Bristol: HEFCE.

HEFCE (Higher Education Funding Council for England) (1996d) *Energy Management in the Higher Education Sector: National Report.* Bristol: HEFCE.

HEFCE (Higher Education Funding Council for England) (1996e) *Value for Money Initiative: Consultation on Future Projects.* Consultation Paper CP 4/96. Bristol: HEFCE.

HEFCE (Higher Education Funding Council for England) (1997a) *The Impact of the 1992 RAE on HE Institutions in England,* M6/97. Bristol: HEFCE.

HEFCE (Higher Education Funding Council for England) (1997b) *Research Assessment: Consultation,* RAE 2/97. Bristol: HEFCE.

HEFCE (Higher Education Funding Council for England) (1997c) *Profiles of Higher Education Institutions.* 2nd edn. Bristol: HEFCE.

HEFCE (Higher Education Funding Council for England) (1997d) *International Comparison of the Cost of Teaching in Higher Education.* HEFCE Research Series. Bristol: HEFCE.

HEFCE (Higher Education Funding Council for England) (1997e) *Procurement Benchmarking for Higher Education.* Bristol: HEFCE.

HEFCE (Higher Education Funding Council for England) (1998a) *Research Assessment Exercise Confirmed for 2001.* Council Briefing No. 17, May. Bristol: HEFCE.

HEFCE (Higher Education Funding Council for England) (1998b) *Research Assessment Exercise 2001: Key Decisions and Issues for Further Consultation.* Bristol: HEFCE.

HEFCE (Higher Education Funding Council for England) (1998c) *Analysis of Estate Returns 1997.* Report 98/04. Bristol: HEFCE.

HEFCE (Higher Education Funding Council for England) (1998d) *Learning and Teaching: Strategy and Funding Proposals.* Circular Letter 36/98. Bristol: HEFCE.

HEFCE (Higher Education Funding Council for England) (1998e) *Building Repairs and Maintenance Study in the Higher Education Sector: National Report.* Bristol: HEFCE.

HEFCE (Higher Education Funding Council for England) (1998f) *Building Repairs and Maintenance Study in the Higher Education Sector: Management Review Guide.* Bristol: HEFCE.

HEFCE (Higher Education Funding Council for England) (1998g) *Information Systems and Technology Management Value for Money Study: National Report.* Bristol: HEFCE.

HEFCE (Higher Education Funding Council for England) (1998h) *Information Systems and Technology Management Value for Money Study: Management Review Guide.* Bristol: HEFCE.

HEFCE (Higher Education Funding Council for England) (1998i) *Environmental Audit: Report.* Bristol: HEFCE.

HEFCE (Higher Education Funding Council for England) (1998j) *Environmental Audit: Workbook.* Bristol: HEFCE.

HEFCE (Higher Education Funding Council for England) (1998k) Building Repairs and Maintenance: Issues Arising from the One-day Workshops, UKVFM 98/17. [online.] Available at: http://www.hefce.ac.uk/GoodPrac/vfm/default.htm

HEFCE (Higher Education Funding Council for England) (1998l) Energy Management VfM Study Review, UKVFM 98/13, Annex. Unpublished paper, HEFCE.

HEFCE (Higher Education Funding Council for England) (1999a) *Estates Management Statistics Project.* Report 99/18. Bristol: HEFCE.

HEFCE (Higher Education Funding Council for England) (1999b) *Estates Management Statistics Project – HEFCE 99/8,* Circular Letter 9/99. Bristol: HEFCE.

Henkel, M. (1991) *Government, Evaluation and Change.* London: Jessica Kingsley.

HEQC (Higher Education Quality Council) (1994) *Choosing to Change: Extending Access, Choice and Mobility in Higher Education.* London: HEQC.

HEQC (Higher Education Quality Council) (1995a) Higher Education Quality Profiles. Unpublished paper, HEQC.

HEQC (Higher Education Quality Council) (1995b) *Graduate Standards Programme: Interim Report.* London: HEQC.

HEQC (Higher Education Quality Council) (1995c) *Notes for the Guidance of Auditors.* London: HEQC.

HEQC (Higher Education Quality Council) (1996a) *Indicators of Programme Quality.* London: HEQC.

HEQC (Higher Education Quality Council) (1996b) *Quality, Standards and Professional Accreditation: A Mapping Exercise.* London: HEQC.

HEQC (Higher Education Quality Council) (1996c) *Guidelines on Quality Assurance.* London: HEQC.

HEQC (Higher Education Quality Council) (1996d) *Inter-institutional Variability of Degree Results: An Analysis in Selected Subjects.* London: HEQC.

HEQC (Higher Education Quality Council) (1996e) *'What are Graduates?'* Consultation Document. London: HEQC.

HEQC (Higher Education Quality Council) (1996f) *Modular Higher Education in the UK: In Focus.* London: HEQC.

HEQC (Higher Education Quality Council) (1997a) *Graduate Standards Programme Final Report,* 2 Vols. London: HEQC.

HEQC (Higher Education Quality Council) (1997b) *Assessment in Higher Education and the Role of Graduateness.* London: HEQC.

HEQC (Higher Education Quality Council) (1997c) *Managing Flexible Curricula in Higher Education: The Architecture of Modularity.* London: HEQC.

HEQC (Higher Education Quality Council) (1997d) *Regulatory Frameworks for Assuring Academic Standards in Credit-based Modular Higher Education.* London: HEQC.

HESA (Higher Education Statistics Agency) (1997) *HE Finance Plus,* CD-ROM. Cheltenham: HESA.

HESA (Higher Education Statistics Agency) (1998) *Students in Higher Education Institutions 1996/97.* Cheltenham: HESA.

History SBG (Subject Benchmarking Group) (1998) *History Subject Benchmarking Group Draft Statement.* Gloucester: Quality Assurance Agency.

Hodgkinson, L. (1996) *Changing the Higher Education Curriculum: Towards a Systematic Approach to Skills Development.* Open University Press and Department for Education and Employment. Buckingham: OU Press.

Hounsell, D., McCulloch, M. and Scott, M. (1996) *The ASSHE Inventory: Changing Assessment Practices in Scottish Higher Education.* Edinburgh: Centre for Teaching, Learning and Assessment, University of Edinburgh.

HUDG (1997) Interim Report of a Working Party of the History at the Universities Defence Group, unpublished report to the Quality Assurance Agency.

Hyland, T. (1998) 'Skill skam'. *Guardian,* 14 July.

Hyland, T. and Johnson, S. (1998) 'Of cabbages and key skills: exploding the mythology of core transferable skills in post-school education'. *Journal of Further and Higher Education,* 22 (2), 163–72.

Indepen Consultants (1995) *Review of Module Registration 1994/95.* Thames Valley University internal report, January. Partially reproduced in *TVU Bulletin Supplement,* 1 (16), 3 February.

IoP (Institute of Physics) (1998) *The Physics Degree. Core of Physics and Graduate Skills Base.* Draft specification, May. Institute of Physics.

Jackson, N.J. (1997a) 'Academic regulation in UK Higher Education. Part I – the concept of collaborative self-regulation'. *Quality Assurance in Education,* 5, 120–35.

Jackson, N.J. (1997b) 'Role of self-evaluation in the self-regulating UK higher education system' in N. Jackson (ed.) *Approaches to Self-evaluation and Self-regulation in UK Higher Education.* London: HEQC.

Jackson, N.J. (1998a) 'Introduction to benchmarking assessment practice' in N. Jackson (ed.) *Pilot Studies in Benchmarking Assessment Practice in UK Higher Education.* Gloucester: Quality Assurance Agency.

Jackson, N.J. (1998b) 'Benchmarking assessment practice in UK HE: a commentary' in N. Jackson (ed.) *Pilot Studies in Benchmarking Assessment Practice in UK Higher Education.* Gloucester: Quality Assurance Agency.

Jackson, N.J. (1998c) 'Pilot benchmarking study of assessment practice in seven engineering departments' in N. Jackson (ed.) *Pilot Studies in Benchmarking Assessment Practice.* Gloucester: Quality Assurance Agency.

Jackson, N.J. (1998d) 'Understanding standards-based quality assurance Part I – rationale and conceptual basis'. *Quality Assurance in Education,* 6, 132–40.

Jackson, N.J. (1998e) 'Understanding standards-based quality assurance Part II – nuts and bolts of the Dearing policy framework'. *Quality Assurance in Education,* 6, 220–31.

Jackson, N.J. (1998f) 'The potential role of credit in supporting a system of threshold standards in HE' in M. Armstrong, P. Clarkson, and M. Noble (eds) *Modularity and Credit Frameworks: The NUCCAT Survey and 1998 Conference Report.* Northern Universities Consortium for Credit Accumulation and Transfer (NUCCAT).

Jackson, N.J. (1998g) 'Academic regulation in UK Higher Education. Part III – the idea of "partnership in trust"'. *Quality Assurance in Education,* 6, 5–18.

Jackson, N.J. (1999) 'Programme specifications and their role in creating a more explicit environment for demonstrating and recording achievement'. *Journal of Further and Higher Education,* 23 (2), 197–210.

Jackson, N.J., Burge, S.J. and Tannock, J.D.T. (1996) 'Developing a departmental quality management framework' in K. Gregory and R. Aylett (eds) *Departmental Review in Higher Education: Proceedings of a Conference.* London: Goldsmiths' College, University of London.

Jackson, N.J., Burge, S.J. and Tannock, J.D.T. (1997) 'Review, evaluation and development of departmental quality management systems: case study of six engineering departments' in N. Jackson (ed.) *Managing Quality and Standards in UK Higher Education.* London: HEQC.

Jarratt (1985) *Report of the Steering Committee for Efficiency Studies in Universities.* London: CVCP.

Jenkins, A. (1997) *Course-based Profiling – Case Studies from Oxford Brookes.* Oxford: Oxford Brookes University.

Jenkins, A., Scurry, D. and Turner, D. (1994) 'Using profiling to integrate skill development in a large modular course' in A. Jenkins and L. Walker (eds) *Developing Student Capability through Modular Courses.* London: Kogan Page.

Johnes, J. and Taylor, J. (1990) *Performance Indicators in Higher Education.* Buckingham: SRHE and Open University Press.

Johnson, T. (1998) *The 1997 Course Experience Questionnaire.* Parkville, Melbourne: Graduate Careers Council of Australia.

Jordan, A. and Withnall, M. (1997) *The Core Attributes of Biological Sciences Graduates.* London: Institute of Biology/The Biochemical Society.

JPIWG (Joint Performance Indicators Working Group) (1994) Explanatory and Statistical Material to Accompany Consultative Report. Bristol: HEFCE (mimeo).

Karlöff, B. and Ostblom, S. (1993) *Benchmarking: A Signpost to Excellence in Quality and Productivity.* London: John Wiley.

Kells, H.R. (1990) (ed.) *The Development of Performance Indicators for Higher Education: A Compendium for Eleven Countries.* Paris: OECD/IMHE.

Kells, H.R. (1992) *Self-regulation in Higher Education: A Multi-national Perspective on Collaborative Systems of Quality Assurance and Control.* Higher Education Policy Series 15. London and Philadelphia: Jessica Kingsley.

Kells, H.R. (1995) *Self-study Processes: A Guide to Self-evaluation in Higher Education.* Phoenix, AZ: Oryx Press.

Kettl, D. (1997) 'The global revolution in public management: driving themes, missing links'. *Journal of Public Policy Analysis and Management,* 16, 446–62.

Law SBG (Subject Benchmarking Group) (1998) *Benchmark Standards for Law Degrees in England, Wales and Northern Ireland: Working Draft for Pilots.* Gloucester: Quality Assurance Agency.

Liebfried, K. and McNair, C. (1994) *Benchmarking: A Tool for Continuous Improvement.* London: Harper Collins and Coopers and Lybrand.

Linke, R. (1991) (chair) *Performance Indicators in Higher Education.* Report of a trial evaluation study commissioned by the Commonwealth Department of Employment, Education and Training. Canberra: Australian Government Publishing Service.

Lonbay, J. (1994) 'Governmental and professional power and influence in legal education in Europe' in T. Becher (ed.) *Governments and Professional Education.* Buckingham: SRHE and Open University Press.

Loveday, M. (1993) 'Measuring up to the model'. *Managing Service Quality*, Special Issue on Benchmarking, 41–4.

Lund, H. (1998a) 'Benchmarking in UK higher education' in A. Schofield (ed.) *Benchmarking in Higher Education: An International Review.* London: CHEMS and Paris: UNESCO.

Lund, H. (1998b) *Joining Hands: A Survey of Non-academic Collaboration between Commonwealth Universities.* London: CHEMS.

Lyons, F. and Bement, M. (1996) 'Graduateness and learning outcomes by levels of study: a guide for learners, tutors and workplace mentors' in N. Jackson (ed.) *Modular Higher Education in the UK: In Focus.* London: HEQC.

Maassen, P.A.M. (1997) 'Quality in European higher education: recent trends and their historical roots'. *European Journal of Education*, 32 (2), 111–27.

Machung, A. (1998) 'Playing the rankings game'. *Change*, July/August, 13–16.

McKinnon Walker/IDP (1998a) Project to Develop and Trial Benchmarking Criteria: Summary of Meeting on 26 October 1998. Unpublished paper, McKinnon Walker Consultants/IDP Education Australia.

McKinnon Walker/IDP (1998b) Project to Develop and Trial Benchmarking Criteria: Progress Report, December. Unpublished paper, McKinnon Walker Consultants/IDP Education Australia.

Margham, J.P. (1998) 'Benchmarking of regulatory frameworks in northern universities' in N. Jackson (ed.) *Pilot Studies in Benchmarking Assessment Practice.* Gloucester: Quality Assurance Agency.

Margham, J.P. and Jackson, S. (1999) 'Benchmarking across subjects in an institution' in H. Smith, M. Armstrong and S. Brown (eds) *Benchmarking and Threshold Standards.* London: Kogan Page.

Massaro, V. (1998) 'Benchmarking in Australian higher education' in A. Schofield (ed.) *Benchmarking in Higher Education: An International Review.* London: CHEMS and Paris: UNESCO.

Matzdorf, F., Price, I. and Akhlaghi, F. (1997) *Facilities Future for Higher Education?* Sheffield FMGC Higher Education Forum report [online]. Available at: http://www.shu.ac.uk/schools/urs/fmgc/pubsz.htm

Melton, R. (1997) *Objectives, Competencies and Learning Outcomes: Developing Instructional Materials in Open and Distance Learning.* London and Stirling (USA): Kogan Page.

Mintzberg, H. (1994) *The Rise and Fall of Strategic Planning.* Hemel Hempstead: Prentice-Hall.

Moon, J. (1996) 'Generic levels descriptors: their place in the standards debate' in N. Jackson (ed.) *Modular Higher Education in the UK: In Focus.* London: HEQC.

Morgan, G. (1986) *Images of Organisation.* London: Sage.

Morrison, H.G., Magennis, S.P. and Carey, L.J. (1995) 'Performance indicators and league tables: a call for standards'. *Higher Education Quarterly*, 49 (2), 128–45.

Murphy, R. *et al.* (1998) *Staff Development Pack.* Sheffield: DfEE.

NACUBO (National Association of College and University Business Officers) (1998) [online]. Available at: http://www.nacubo.org/website/benchmarking/program.html

NAO (National Audit Office) (1992) *University Purchasing in England*, HC635. London: NAO.

NAO (National Audit Office) (1996) *The Management of Space in Higher Education Institutions in Wales*, HC458. London: NAO.

NCC (National Curriculum Council) (1990) *Core Skills 16–19.* London: NCC.

NCIHE (National Committee of Inquiry into Higher Education) (1997) *Higher Education in the Learning Society.* Report of the National Committee of Inquiry into Higher Education (Dearing Committee), 2 Vols. Norwich: HMSO.

NUCCAT (Northern Universities Consortium for Credit Accumulation and Transfer) (1998) *Modularity and Credit Frameworks: The NUCCAT Survey and 1998 Conference Report.* NUCCAT.

Oakland, J.S. (1993) *Total Quality Management: The Route to Improving Performance.* 2nd edn. Oxford: Butterworth Heinemann.

Oates, T. (1991) *Developing and Piloting the NCVQ Core Skills Units.* R&D report No. 16. London: National Council for Vocational Qualifications.

Pascale, R.T. (1991) *Managing on the Edge.* New York: Simon and Schuster.

PCFC (Polytechnics and Colleges Funding Council) (1990) *Performance Indicators: Report of a Committee Chaired by Mr Alfred Morris.* Bristol: PCFC.

PCFC (Polytechnics and Colleges Funding Council) and CNAA (Council for National Academic Awards) (1990) *The Measurement of Value Added in Higher Education.* Bristol: PCFC.

Pollitt, C. (1993) *Managerialism and Public Services: Cuts of Cultural Change.* 2nd edn. Oxford: Blackwell.

Porter, M.E. (1980) *Competitive Strategy: Techniques for Analyzing Industries and Competitors.* New York: The Free Press.

Price, I. (1994) *A Plain Person's Guide to Benchmarking.* Special Report of the Unit for Facilities Management Research. Sheffield: Sheffield Hallam University.

Price, I. and Akhlaghi, F. (1999) 'New patterns in facilities management: industry best practice and new organisational theory'. *Facilities,* 17 (5/6), 159–66.

Price, I. and Kennie, T.R.M. (1997) 'Punctured Strategic Equilibrium and Some Leadership Challenges for University 2000' in *Proceedings of the Second International Conference on the Dynamics of Strategy, April 1997.* Guildford: Survey European Management School.

Price, I. and Matzdorf, F. (1998) Space Utilisation Benchmarking – The Qualitative Side. Unpublished report. FMGC Higher Education Forum, Sheffield Hallam University.

Price, I. and Shaw, R. (1996) 'Parrots, patterns and performance – the learning organisation meme: emergence of a new management replicator' in T.L. Campbell (ed.) *Proceedings of the Third Conference of the European Consortium for the Learning Organisation.* Copenhagen: ECLO.

Price, I. and Shaw, R. (1998) *Shifting the Patterns: Breaching the Memetic Codes of Corporate Performance.* Chalford: Management Books 2000.

QAA (Quality Assurance Agency) (1998a) 'An agenda for quality'. *Higher Quality,* 3 (Consultation Issue). Gloucester: QAAHE.

QAA (Quality Assurance Agency) (1998b) 'The way ahead'. *Higher Quality,* 4. Gloucester: QAAHE.

QAA (Quality Assurance Agency) (1998c) *Graduate Standards Programme Report on Subject Association Pilot Projects: 1997.* Gloucester: QAAHE.

QAA (Quality Assurance Agency) (1998d) *Guidelines for Preparing Programme Specifications.* Gloucester: QAAHE.

QAA (Quality Assurance Agency) (1998e) *Pilot Studies in Benchmarking Assessment Practice.* Gloucester: QAAHE.

QAA (Quality Assurance Agency) (1999) *Draft Statements – Benchmark Standards for Chemistry, History and Law.* Gloucester: QAAHE. [Also online.] Available at http://www.qaa.ac.uk/public.htm

Ramsden, P. (1991) 'A performance indicator of teaching quality in higher education: the Course Experience Questionnaire'. *Studies in Higher Education*, 16, 129–50.

Rees, D.G. (1997) 'The current state of facilities management in the UK National Health Service: an overview of management structures'. *Facilities*, 15 (3/4), 62–5.

Rees, D.G. (1998) 'Management structures of facilities management in the National Health Service in England: a review of trends 1995–1997'. *Facilities*, 16 (9/10), 254–61.

Resnick, L.B., Nolan, K.J. and Resnick, D.P. (1995) 'Benchmarking education standards'. *Educational Evaluation and Policy Analysis*, 17 (4), 438–61.

Reynolds (1986) *Academic Standards in Universities*. London: CVCP.

Royal Society of Chemistry (1995) *Chemistry in the UK – Will it Survive? Conclusions of the Royal Society of Chemistry Workshops*. London: Royal Society of Chemistry.

SCFC (Scottish Centrally Funded Colleges) (1992) *Performance Indicators*. Final Report of the Working Party of the SCFC Committee of Principals. Edinburgh: SCFC.

Schaffer, R.H. and Thompson, H.A. (1992) 'Successful change programmes begin with results'. *Harvard Business Review*, (Jan/Feb), 80–9.

Schofield, A. (ed.) (1998) *Benchmarking in Higher Education: An International Review*. London: CHEMS and Paris: UNESCO.

Schön, D. (1973) *Beyond the Stable State*. New York: Norton Library.

Schön, D. (1987) *Educating the Reflective Practitioner: Towards a New Design for Teaching and Learning in the Professions*. San Francisco: Jossey-Bass.

Schreiterer, U. (1998) 'Benchmarking in higher education in Europe' in A. Schofield (ed.) *Benchmarking in Higher Education: An International Review*. London: CHEMS and Paris: UNESCO.

Schwartz, P. (1992) *The Art of the Long View. Scenario Planning – Protecting your Company against an Uncertain Future*. London: Century Business.

SCONUL (Standing Committee of National University Libraries) (Annual) *Annual Library Statistics*. London: SCONUL.

Scott-Morgan, P. (1994) *The Unwritten Rules of the Game*. New York: McGraw Hill.

Seymour, D. *et al.* (1996) *High Performing Colleges: The Malcolm Baldrige National Quality Award as a Framework for Improving Higher Education*, 2 Vols. Maryville, MO: Prescott Publishing.

Seymour, E. and Hewitt, N.M. (1997) *Talking about Leaving: Why Undergraduates Leave the Sciences*. Oxford: Westview Press.

Shaw, M. and Stoney, M.C. (1995) 'Assuring quality and standards in a large modular scheme'. *Innovation and Learning in Education: The International Journal for the Reflective Practitioner*, 1(2), 24–31.

Shaw, M. and Stoney, C. (1996) 'Evaluating the use of a level framework' in N. Jackson (ed.) *Modular Higher Education in the UK: In Focus*. London: HEQC.

Shove, E. (1993) *The Black Holes of Space Economics*. Discussion Paper, University of Sunderland.

Silver, H. (1990) *A Higher Education. The Council for National Academic Awards and British Higher Education 1964–89*. London and Washington, DC: The Farmer Press.

Sizer, J. (1979) 'Indicators in times of financial stringency, contraction and changing needs' in D. Billing (ed.) *Indicators of Performance: Papers Presented at the Fifteenth Annual Conference of the Society for Research into Higher Education*. Guildford: SRHE.

Smithers, A. and Robinson, P. (1995) *Post-18 Education: Growth, Change, Prospect*. London: Council for Industry and Higher Education (CIHE).

Spendolini, M.J. (1992) *The Benchmarking Book.* New York: American Management Association.

Tannock, J.D.T. and Burge, S.E. (1994) *A Practical Approach to Implementing Quality Management in Higher Education.* Occasional Paper No. 7. London: Engineering Professors' Council.

Tannock, J.D.T., Jackson, N.J. and Burge, S.J. (1999) *The Quality and Standards Workbook: A Resource for Departments in Higher Education.* London: Engineering Professors' Council.

Tenner, A.R. and DeToro, I.J. (1992) *Total Quality Management: Three Steps to Continuous Improvement.* Reading, MA: Addison-Wesley.

Thompson, A. (1979) 'Higher education systems at national level' in D. Billing (ed.) *Indicators of Performance: Papers Presented at the Fifteenth Annual Conference of the Society for Research into Higher Education.* Guildford: SRHE.

Town, J.S. (1996) 'Benchmarking as an approach to quality' in B. Knowles (ed.) *BUOPOLIS 1: Routes to Quality. Proceedings of the conference held at Bournemouth University, 29–31 August 1995.* Bournemouth: Bournemouth University Library and Information Services.

Town, J.S. (1998a) 'Benchmarking Processes in Academic Libraries', paper presented to the LISU Seminar on Academic Library Statistics and Benchmarking at Loughborough University, June.

Town, J.S. (ed.) (1998b) *The Future Library: A Concept Paper.* Shrivenham: RMCS Information Services.

Treloar, D.W.G. (1997) The Course Experience Questionnaire. Unpublished paper, University of Western Australia (mimeo).

TVU (Thames Valley University) (1996) Modularization: A Survey. Unpublished report, Thames Valley University.

UCAS (Universities and Colleges Admissions Service) (1998a) *A Statistical Bulletin of Subject Trends, 1996 Entry.* Cheltenham: UCAS.

UCAS (Universities and Colleges Admissions Service) (1998b) *Annual Report, 1997 Entry.* Cheltenham: UCAS.

UCAS (Universities and Colleges Admissions Service) (1999a) *Annual Report 1997–1998.* Cheltenham: UCAS.

UCAS (Universities and Colleges Admissions Service) (1999b) *Statistical Summary, 1998 Entry.* Cheltenham: UCAS.

UCAS (Universities and Colleges Admissions Service) (1999c) *Annual Statistical Tables, 1998 Entry.* Cheltenham: UCAS.

UFC (Universities Funding Council) (1989) *Research Selectivity Exercise 1989. The Outcome.* Circular Letter 27/89. London: UFC.

UGC (University Grants Committee) (1986) *Planning for the Late 1980s: Recurrent Grant 1986/87.* Circular Letter 4/86. London: UGC.

UGC (University Grants Committee) (1988) *Research Selectivity Exercise 1989.* Circular Letter 45/88. London: UGC.

UMIST (University of Manchester Institute of Science and Technology) (1998) 'UMIST's stock rises'. *UMIST Times,* 25 May.

University of Essex (1997) *Management Information. Volume 3: Comparative Statistics.* Colchester: University of Essex.

University of Hull (1998) 'Times table does it again for Hull'. *University of Hull Bulletin,* June.

University of Leicester (1998) 'League tables'. *University of Leicester Newsletter,* June/July.

Vroeijenstijn, A.T., Waumans, B.L.A. and Wijmans, J. (1992) *International Programme Review: Electrical Engineering*. Utrecht: Vereniging van Samenwerkende Nederlandse Universiteiten (Association of Universities in the Netherlands).

Wagner, L. (1998) 'What is the Point of University League Tables?' Speech given to CVCP Conference on The Use and Abuse of University League Tables, and reproduced in *CVCP News*, July.

Watson, D. (1989) *Managing the Modular Course: Perspectives from Oxford Brookes University*. Buckingham: SRHE and Open University Press.

Watson, G.H. (1993) *Strategic Benchmarking: How to Rate your Company's Performance against the World's Best*. New York, NY: Wiley.

Wolf, A. (1995) *Competence-based Assessment*. Buckingham: Open University Press.

Woolf, H. and Turner, D. (1997) 'Honours classifications: the need for transparency'. *The New Academic*, Autumn, 10–12.

Wright, J.R.G. (1997) Correspondence from James R.G. Wright, Chairman of the HEMS Group to the Commonwealth Higher Education Management Service (CHEMS).

Yorke, D.M. (1991) *Performance Indicators: Observations on their Use in the Assurance of Course Quality*. CNAA Project Report 30. London: CNAA.

Yorke, M. (1995) 'Taking the odds-on chance: using performance indicators in managing for the improvement of quality in higher education'. *Tertiary Education and Management*, 1 (1), 49–57.

Yorke, M. (1996) *Indicators of Programme Quality*. London: HEQC.

Yorke, M. (1997a) 'The elusive quarry: total quality in higher education'. *Tertiary Education and Management*, 3 (2), 145–56.

Yorke, M. (1997b) 'A good league table guide?' *Quality Assurance in Education*, 5 (2), 61–72.

Yorke, M. (1998a) 'Performance indicators relating to student development: can they be trusted?' *Quality in Higher Education*, 4 (1), 45–61.

Yorke, M. (1998b) 'Transforming Learning and Teaching in Subject Disciplines: What can be Learned from Student Non-completion?' Paper presented at the HERDSA Conference, Auckland, New Zealand, July.

Yorke, M. (1998c) 'The *Times*' "league table" of universities, 1997: a statistical appraisal'. *Quality Assurance in Education*, 6 (1), 58–60.

Yorke, M. with Bell, R. *et al.* (1997) 'Undergraduate non-completion in England, report no. 1' in *Undergraduate Non-completion in Higher Education in England*. Bristol: HEFCE.

Yorke, M., Bourdillon, B. *et al.* (1998) 'Benchmarking academic standards: a pilot investigation by the Student Assessment and Classification Working Group' in N. Jackson (ed.) *Pilot Studies in Benchmarking Assessment Practice*. Gloucester: Quality Assurance Agency.

Yorke, M., Cooper, A. *et al.* (1996) 'Module mark distributions in eight subject areas and some issues they raise' in N. Jackson (ed.) *Modular Higher Education in the UK: In Focus*. London: HEQC.

Zairi, M. (1992) *Competitive Benchmarking: An Executive Guide*. Letchworth: Technical Communications Publishing.

Index

quality assurance, 5, 15–16, 24, 31, 54,
56, 71, 114, 235
Joint Planning Group for, 23
Dearing Committee's
recommendations for, 23–4
see also HEQC, QAA
quality audits, 19
quality framework, 29
quality management, 31, 36, 56, 57,
58, 65, 152, 154, 155
in engineering, 54
see also TQM

Ramsden, P., 70, 71
Rank Xerox, 4, 5, 139, 141
Rees, D.G., 141, 146
regulation
of academic practice, 29–30
of assessment, 38
see also benchmarking for regulation,
self-regulation in HE
research assessment, 21–2, 183
research management, 177
Reynolds Committee, 15
RMCS (Royal Military College of
Science), 120–1, 152, 153, 154,
156, 157, 158, 159, 164
Royal Society of Arts, 107
Royal Society of Chemistry, 21
Rushforth, J., 165, 166, 167, 169,
170, 173, 175, 176, 177, 178,
179

SCFC (Scottish Centrally Funded
Colleges), 17–18
Schofield, A., 4, 7, 8, 184
Schön, D., 106, 145
Schreiterer, U., 191, 192, 193
SCONUL (Standing Committee of
National and University
Libraries), 22, 121–2, 151, 152,
159, 164
advisory committee on performance
indicators (ACPI), 152, 159
benchmarking manual, 159, 164
benchmarking pilot projects, 151,
152, 159, 164
self-assessment/evaluation/audit, 3, 4,
5, 19, 25, 40, 55–6, 57, 58–9,
61, 120, 160, 169, 173, 185, 195,

197, 201, 203, 207, 208, 215,
217, 218–19, 220, 231
self-regulation in higher education, 5,
54, 102, 225
semesterization, 42, 45, 47
Seymour, D., 12, 185, 197
SHEFC (Scottish Higher Education
Funding Council), 18–19,
124–7, 166
Sheffield Hallam University, 122, 140
see also FMGC
Silver, H., 17, 32
single regeneration budget
partnerships (SRBs), 140
skills/attributes, 63, 87–8, 93, 94, 187
key/generic, 36, 39, 104, 105–6,
107, 108, 109, 110, 111, 113–14
key skill national standards, 35, 104,
113–14, 216, 225
subject specific, 36, 39, 63
transferable, 49, 85
South Africa, 198
space charging/utilization, 147–9
Spendolini, M.J., 6, 141
SRHE (Society for Research into
Higher Education), 15
staff development/training, 8, 63, 101,
114, 155, 159, 164, 173
standardized academic testing (SATs),
40
student acceptances, 130, 131, 133,
135
student applicants/applications, 129,
130, 131, 132, 134, 135, 136,
138
from ethnic minorities, 132, 134,
135, 136
from mature students, 132
from partly-skilled/unskilled social
classes, 132
Student Assessment and Classification
Working Group (SACWG), 38,
75–7
student experience, 69–73, 78, 81, 83,
231
student feedback/satisfaction surveys,
43, 67, 68, 70–3, 78, 193
Course Experience Questionnaire
(Australia), 70, 71
University of Central England, 71–2